Kim Adelman has crafted a practical, down-to-earth, soup-to-nuts manual on getting the most out of the short-film experience — from succinct tips on all phases of production, to making the most out of the film-festival experience, and beyond. A must-read for any filmmaker who values thorough advice delivered with energy, humor, and a sincere affection for the medium.
Christian Gaines
Director of Festivals, Withoutabox – a division of *IMDb.com*

Making It Big in Shorts is a great resource for aspiring filmmakers! It provides valuable information about New Media, Web 2.0 and how to market your film in the digital age!
David Lehre
Director, *myspace: the movie*

Kim Adelman walks you through the minefield that is making short films, exploring all aspects of production and the new arenas in which to show and distribute short films. A perfect book for anyone with a YouTube account.
Matthew Terry, screenwriter/teacher/filmmaker
www.hollywoodlitsales.com

This book is required reading for all aspiring filmmakers, whether making their first short or their fiftieth. Written in a breezy, conversational style, this book is jam-packed with invaluable information and insider tips.
Shane Smith, programmer, Sundance Film Festival

A great guidebook to the world of short films. Outside of showing them to your friends at parties, Adelman's book is written from the point of view of an experienced short-film producer who knows her way around. Anything you might need to know to get the resources to produce your film can be found here, as well as useful information from someone who has done it all before.
Jesse Trussell
Director of the Young Filmmakers' Program at the Austin Film Festival

Making It Big in Shorts is an essential guide for anybody who wants to make short films, which is great, because I love the short-film format. It's the best!
Bill Plympton
Animator: *Hair High; Mutant Alien; I Married a Strange Person*
www.plymptoons.com

Kim Adelman knows shorts: she ran the short-film program at Fox Movie Channel, produced 19 short films, and a series of DVD-shorts collections for Warner Home Video. Her latest venture offers numerous helpful tips for aspiring short filmmakers — from developing story ideas to budgeting to postproduction to marketing and selling the finished product.
Filmmaker Magazine, The Super 8

Kim is the undisputed queen of the short-film world. No one has a better resume, better relationships, and more passion for this particular art form than does she, and her willingness to share this knowledge, especially the hard-won lessons, is inspiring. I particularly relate to her production modus operandi: "Everything For Free!" This one piece of advice — and the examples she gives on how to apply it — will save filmmakers money, heartache, and family/ friend relationships. And, inspire better movies.
Mark Stolaroff
Producer/Founder, No Budget Film School
www.nobudgetfilmschool.com

I have been exhibiting and distributing short films since 1996, but Kim's book taught me many new and relevant aspects to short-film exhibition and distribution.
Joel S. Bachar, Microcinema International

I wish this incredible resource had been around when I got my Masters in Production at USC! Packed with tons of practical information, Adelman has created a real bible on how to maximize the time and money you will spend on your short to achieve results. She covers all aspects: from brainstorming your idea to using your finished film to open doors. Adelman peppers the book with candid stories from filmmakers on the front lines, providing a well-rounded, honest assessment of the shorts world. Her advice, based on her vast experience, is pure gold. This should be required reading at film schools, and for anyone about to make a short film. Consider this the best investment you can make on your way to a groundbreaking short!
Stephanie Young Rosen
Chair, Alliance of Women Directors

I enthusiastically recommend reading Kim Adelman's book *Making It Big in Shorts* to my colleagues and students before starting to write a script. It's a great resource for what makes a successful short film. Kim breaks down the process in a logical, organized way to help you understand not only how to get your film made and seen, but also how to decide if your film is worth making in the first place.

Todd Davis, film professor and filmmaker
In the Tradition of My Family
(2006 New York Film Festival)

Making a short film is an art form pursued by many, but perfected by few. And, with the rise of online-viewing platforms, there are more places than ever to get showcased. Kim Adelman's book is a stellar, all-in-one guide on how to get your short made and how to get it seen.

Tari Akpodiete, filmmaker/journalist
www.digipendence.com

This killer book is a must-read for any filmmaker currently working or looking to launch a career with shorts. Solid, important, and easy-to-digest instruction clearly explains what it takes to make a successful short film, find an audience, and profit from the experience.

Mark Steven Bosko
Author, *The Complete Independent Movie Marketing Handbook*

Encouragement oozes from the pages of *Making It Big in Shorts* by Kim Adelman. She thoroughly examines the pros and cons (my favorite part) of various aspects of making short films. You find yourself thinking, "I bet I could write a groundbreaking script, call in favors to gather actors and crew, borrow a camera and keep it moving, and direct my own movie, this weekend."

Mary J. Schirmer, screenwriter/writing instructor/film critic

Who knew there was so much to say about shorts?! Kim Adelman's new *Making It Big in Shorts* is just that — a virtual encyclopedia on the subject, chock full of practical, real-world advice that will appeal to filmmakers of all types and genres. This mini-course in every aspect of the topic is sure to make filmmakers devoted to shorts stand tall for years to come.

Morrie Warshawski
Author, *Shaking the Money Tree: How to Get Grants and Donations for Film and Television*

Kim Adelman has not only taught me the nuts and bolts of short filmmaking, more importantly, she gave me a strong sense of empowerment. Her words "You are the studio" kept ringing in my ear while I was in the middle of shooting the short that set off my career.

Lexi Alexander, filmmaker
Johnny Flynton (2002 Academy Award nominee, live action short)
Punisher: War Zone and *Hooligans*

From concept to budgets, from legal rights to getting the most out of the festival circuit, Kim Adelman covers absolutely everything you will need to know when it comes to making a "short," and she does it in such an entertaining and insightful way. But the best-kept secret about *Making It Big in Shorts* is that so much of what she covers can be applied to making it in television, cable, and theatrical features, as well!

Kathie Fong Yoneda
Paramount Pictures story analyst/development specialist
Author, *The Script-Selling Game*

This book is a must-have for short filmmakers in the age of YouTube, Vimeo, and FunnyorDie .com. It not only guides you through the practical and creative processes of making a short film, it gives you hands-on advice for producing and distributing that short in the brave new world of cyberspace. And, frankly — if you're a filmmaker today and you don't have interest in distributing your short in cyberspace, you shouldn't have much interest in shorts. Period.

Chad Gervich
TV writer/producer (*Reality Binge, Foody Call, Speeders*) who has worked in development and production at the Littlefield Company, Paramount Television, NBC Studios, CBS Productions, and 20th Century Fox. He also is the author of the best-selling book *Small Screen, Big Picture: A Writer's Guide to the TV Business.*

MAKING IT BIG IN SHORTS

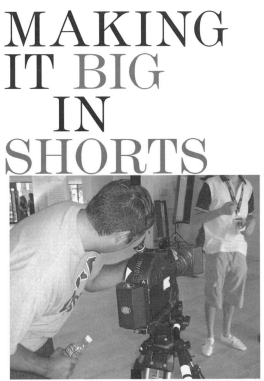

THE ULTIMATE FILMMAKER'S GUIDE TO SHORT FILMS
2ND EDITION

KIM ADELMAN

MICHAEL WIESE PRODUCTIONS

Published by Michael Wiese Productions
3940 Laurel Canyon Blvd. – Suite 1111
Studio City, CA 91604
(818) 379-8799, (818) 986-3408 (FAX).
mw@mwp.com
www.mwp.com

Cover design by MWP
Interior design by William Morosi
Copyedited by Arthur Insana
Printed by McNaughton & Gunn

Manufactured in the United States of America
Copyright 2009

Library of Congress Cataloging-in-Publication Data
Adelman, Kim
 Making it big in shorts : the ultimate filmmaker's guide to short
films / Kim Adelman. -- 2nd ed.
     p. cm.
 ISBN 978-1-932907-58-2
1. Short films--History and criticism. I. Title.

PN1995.9.P7A35 2009
791.4302'3--dc22

                                              2008052041

Printed on Recycled Stock

Mixed Sources
Product group from well-managed
forests and other controlled sources
www.fsc.org Cert no. SW-COC-002283
© 1996 Forest Stewardship Council
FSC

CONTENTS

PART III: MARKETING YOUR FILM

INTRODUCTION TO THE SECOND EDITION

YouTube didn't exist when the first edition of this book was published. MySpace and Facebook were so brand new that no one thought of them as essential tools for filmmakers. And film festivals still preferred that you submitted your work on VHS. Ah, what a difference a few years make! Now it's impossible to think of a book for short filmmakers that doesn't mention iTunes!

Frankly, there has never been a more exciting time to be making short films. Now you can show your work to a worldwide audience across myriad platforms. A decade ago when I first started going to film festivals with the shorts I produced for Fox, I'd hear the other short filmmakers complain that the only way they could get exposure for their films was either festival screenings or television. Back then, the biggest concern for most short filmmakers was scraping up enough money to cut their negatives and strike prints for festival screenings. Nowadays it's a rare short filmmaker who even attempts to shoot on film, let alone strike a print. It's a digital age. The reality is more people will see your shorts on their computers or iPhones than in movie theaters.

The other reality is more people are making films than ever before. Every year the number of shorts submitted to the Sundance Film Festival leaps exponentially, while the amount of films the festival can actually play remains relatively paltry. In 2008, the stats were 5,632 entries (up 10% from the year before) with only 83 picked as official selections. Meanwhile, YouTube reports that 10 hours of video are uploaded to its site every minute of every day.

Where do you fit into this picture? Are you planning on being one of the 5,632 Sundance hopefuls? Or are you generating five minutes of those 10 hours of YouTube uploads? If you're either — or both — this book is for you.

I originally decided to write this guide back in 2004 because so much of the good information about how to be a successful short filmmaker is passed on by veteran filmmakers to newcomers. When I first started produc-  ing shorts, two directors who had great success with their films gave me invaluable guidance. During the course of producing 19 short films that played over 150 film festivals world- wide and won over 30 awards, I learned a lot about the short-film world. I picked up even more insight as I recorded hours of director commentary for the 14 DVD collections of short films that I produced for Warner Bros. Home Video. And I've gleaned even more insider knowledge since I started covering short films for *indieWIRE*, a gig that has allowed me to speak to filmmakers whose works screen at festivals, online, and on television.

Since writing the first edition of this book, I've continued teaching my UCLA Extension class "Making and Marketing the Short Film" — but I now do it online so aspiring filmmakers from around the world can partake. Consequently, my online students have shared with me the reality of filmmaking in such remarkable locations as Qatar. Leading short-film workshops across Canada and New Zealand also increased my international perspective. There also were emails sent to me from such far-flung places as Helsinki — from readers of the original guide who had questions relating to their particular situations. So while all of my personal producing experience has taken place in Hollywood, this new edition benefits from my broadened horizons.

You'll find questions emailed to me from readers of the first edition of this book sprinkled throughout this new version. Because of increasingly accessible and affordable filmmaking tools, more and more aspiring auteurs are working outside the structured environment of film school and don't know whom to turn to for practical advice.

As you have probably discovered, there are many books written about the various aspects of movie making, but most are geared toward feature-length work. Although the basics of filmmaking are the same, there is a world of difference between making and marketing a 10-minute-long piece versus a two-hour opus. The few books that do focus on shorts often don't address the primary concern of directors who have invested time, money, and dreams into their projects: how do you "make it big" with a short film?

In putting together this second edition, I asked even more experienced directors, festival insiders, and industry experts to share their hard-won wisdom. Everything we know about the artistic and business sides of short-form filmmaking is in this book. We'll tell you the unvarnished truth (including when to lie). After powering through *Making It Big in Shorts: The Ultimate Filmmaker's Guide to Short Films — 2nd Edition*, you, too, will know how to successfully make, exhibit, and sell a film of limited length in today's marketplace. And you'll learn how to parlay that little film into a big career.

Making It Big in Shorts: The Ultimate Filmmaker's Guide to Short Films is divided into three parts. The first section, Welcome to the Short-Film World, will help you make an educated decision about what kind of film you should make. In these first eight chapters, I'll cover what defines a short film, what defines a *good* short film, the seven secrets of successful short filmmakers, how to work YouTube to your advantage, why short films can and should be made in two days, and how to raise production funds. Each chapter ends with a recap of five important points to keep in mind as you embark on your filmmaking adventure.

The next section, Making Your Film, is a hands-on, step-by-step guide from story development through postproduction, with extensive advice from the trenches. You'll learn how to avoid the two things that ruin most shorts (bad acting and bad sound) and the two things that can cripple your film when you're ready to market it (Guild agreements and festival-only music licenses).

The final section, Marketing Your Film, focuses on what to do with your finished film, with inside information about how to get into the best festivals, how to develop a fan base, how to deal with the press, how to make money off your film in the domestic and international marketplace, how to win an Oscar®, how to get your short on iTunes and cell phones, and how to make a real career for yourself. As you'll discover, there are a lot of essential "how to's" in this guide!

By the way, if you're interested in watching any short films referenced in this book, do a Google video search. I'd be very surprised if you can't find the majority of them on iTunes, YouTube, or any of the burgeoning video-hosting sites.

"Kim not only taught me the nuts and bolts of short filmmaking, more importantly she gave me a strong sense of empowerment," proclaims Lexi Alexander, a student who took my UCLA class and then went on to direct the Oscar-nominated live-action short, *Johnny Flynton.* "Her words 'You are the studio' kept ringing in my ear while I was in the middle of shooting the short that set off my career."

Although much has changed from the first edition, the goal of *Making It Big in Shorts: The Ultimate Filmmaker's Guide to Short Films – 2nd Edition* remains the same: to empower each and every one of you to go out and make an amazing film that will set off your career. Are you ready? Let's get started!

PART I:

WELCOME TO THE SHORT-FILM WORLD

CHAPTER 1

SO YOU WANT TO MAKE A SHORT

THE ONLY PERSON WHO CAN STOP YOU FROM MAKING A SHORT FILM IS YOU.

Celebrating his twelfth Academy Award nomination (for his performance in *About Schmidt*), Jack Nicholson confessed a shocking secret desire in an *Interview* magazine profile. Jack Nicholson — of *Easy Rider, One Flew Over the Cuckoo's Nest*, and *The Shining* fame — wished he could come up with an idea for a great short film. Even Jack Nicholson is not immune to the lure of short filmmaking! Of course, in Nicholson's case, it isn't surprising. Sure, he's a big old movie star. But he's also a graduate of the Roger Corman school of low-budget filmmaking, a long-time reader of O. Henry stories, and a fan of the student films that play on the Independent Film Channel (IFC).

What's stopping Mr. Nicholson from making a short? Certainly it isn't money. Although that's the major stumbling block for most wannabes, all Jack would have to do is put his courtside Lakers seats on eBay and he'd have instant funding for a pretty swanky little film. And it isn't because he doesn't have any ideas. Jack's been around long enough to know that ideas come to you all the time. No, Nicholson won't be making a short anytime soon because he has too much respect for the format. Acknowledging that making a good short is something to be proud of, Jack is going to stay out of the pool rather than recklessly jumping in, feet first, to see what kind of splash he might make.

COME ON, IT'S EASY

In this digital era, making a short is absurdly easy. First, you need to come up with an idea. Easy. Next, you have to round up the necessary people, places, and things to turn your idea into a reality. Also easy. Then, instead of having to pull strings to borrow a film camera, beg for free film stock, plead for discounted processing, and pray for gratis telecine (like we used to do in the old days), all you have to do is get your hands on a digital video camera. With an editing system on your home computer, postproduction is also a breeze.

The most crucial ingredient is this: a burning passion to make a film. "One of the most common excuses for not making a short is claiming you don't have the right toys," filmmaker Robbie Consing said. "I once thought 'I can't do this unless I buy the right camera, unless I have a computer with iMovie.' Well, I bought those things, and I haven't done a short since!"

Luckily, you're not like Robbie. You're motivated. You're going to make a film. Now here's the bad news: It's so easy to make a short film in this new era that everyone's doing it. The hard part is not getting an idea, assembling the toys, or getting passionately motivated. The hard part, as Jack Nicholson wisely pointed out, is making a short you can be proud of. Almost every filmmaker adds an apologetic commentary when showing his or her work: "The sound isn't quite right here," or "I wish I had moved the camera more in this sequence," or "I know she's no Meryl Streep, but my sister isn't half bad in this scene, don't you think?"

Forget about minor disappointments. Think big picture. Just making a short is a big accomplishment. You've crossed the treacherous bridge that many never traverse: On one side are those who want to be filmmakers but haven't yet made anything, on the other side are those who have made shorts and therefore are filmmakers.

An aspiring filmmaker named Adrian emailed me: "I have a question regarding contests for short-film scripts. Do you feel they are worthwhile or should a filmmaker concentrate on making the film and getting it into festivals?" Making the film should always be your priority. But why not have the best of both worlds? Write something new for the contest while putting the majority of your time and effort into getting your original script made. I'm actually a big fan of contests (as long as the entry fees aren't prohibitive), because you never know what might result from participating in them. Short filmmakers should always take advantage of every opportunity for success. But the most important thing is not to write a million different scripts that never get made. You want to hire some actors to say those lines you typed and record that for posterity.

"Just do it. Just pick up a camera and start shooting something," is the advice *Titanic* director James Cameron gives aspiring filmmakers in an online interview. "Don't wait to be asked because nobody is going to ask you, and don't wait for the perfect conditions because they'll never be perfect. You just have to take the plunge and just start shooting something, even if it's bad. You can always hide it, but you will have learned something, you know."

What's amazing is that there is no one to stop you from making a film. You don't need an official piece of paper such as a license or a diploma. You don't need a "greenlight" from the head of a major motion picture studio. You don't even need to be related to Francis Ford Coppola — although that never hurts! You just need to get a hold of a camera, point it at something and shoot, give your film a title, and you've done it. In fact, the very first motion picture by the Lumière Brothers in 1895 was essentially that. To mark the centennial anniversary of that achievement, 40 acclaimed feature filmmakers such as Wim Wenders, David

Lynch, Spike Lee, and Peter Greenaway took a turn at running 52 seconds of film through the original hand-cranked Lumière camera. You can check out the results on the DVD *Lumière & Company* (Fox Lorber Home Video, 1997). Truth be told, most of the pieces made by these modern masters aren't ground-shakingly amazing — once again proving that making a good short is a lot harder than you'd think!

EVERYONE IS WELCOME TO GIVE IT A TRY

Are you very old? Very young? Female? Asian? Disabled? Gay? Great! While Hollywood may practice ageism, sexism, or racism when it comes to hiring filmmakers to helm studio pictures, there's nothing stopping anyone from directing a short. The resulting diversity is one of the reasons why the most exciting ideas and groundbreaking work happen in short films. In fact, it even works to your advantage if you are not a heterosexual white male because there are countless film festivals around the world which champion films by women, Asians, gays, etc.

So who makes short films? Everyone!

■ BIG NAME DIRECTORS

We're not talking about the short films made by directors back when they were nobodies enrolled in film school, like Spike Lee's 1983 NYU film, *Joe's Bed-Stuy Barbershop: We Cut Heads*, or George Lucas's 1967 USC piece, *Electric Labyrinth: THX 1138 4EB*. Or even Sofia Coppola's pre-*The Virgin Suicides* effort, the IFC-funded *Lick the Star*.

We're talking about already-established directors tackling the short format, such as the distinguished gentlemen who attempted the Lumière anniversary project. Or A-listers like the Coen Brothers, Alexander Payne, and Wes Craven contributing short pieces to the *Paris, Je T'aime* feature film. Brett Ratner, Allen Hughes, and Mira Nair did the same for the American version, *New York, I Love You*. And if you've never seen the BMW shorts starring Clive Owen that John Woo, Ang Lee, Tony Scott, and Guy Ritchie made, you can catch 'em on YouTube. Meanwhile, Wes Anderson made a splash by giving his *Hotel Chevalier* short away for free on iTunes. And Joss

Whedon of *Buffy the Vampire Slayer* self-funded a pricy 40-minute musical called *Dr. Horrible's Sing-Along Blog*, which he created as a three-part Internet short.

If you are in this league, the rest of us salute you for bringing attention to the short format. Thanks for reminding the world that shorts are an art form worthy of your time and effort. You might, however, not enjoy the experience of making a short film. Many feature film directors discover that it's easier to do a good job on a big studio picture because you have the money, resources, and screen time to make it work. With a short, screen time is so limited that to construct a satisfying story requires a completely different filmmaking skill. Comparisons to writing a short story versus a novel (or running a 100-yard dash versus a marathon) apply.

■ MOVIE STARS

Hot off his success in *No Country for Old Men*, Josh Brolin stepped behind the camera to direct his young daughter in a 16-minute HD drama called *X*. "To me, the whole reason you do a short is to understand your strengths and weaknesses. It's about the storytelling," Brolin told a *Variety* reporter at the HollyShorts Film Festival.

"I love making short films, and I love watching them," actor Matthew Modine told me when I interviewed him shortly after his latest short *I Think, I Thought* played the 2008 Tribeca Film Festival. "With this new technology of HD filmmaking and the rather affordable Panasonic HVX 200, my friend and producing partner Adam McClelland and I decided we would experiment and see how few elements we could make a film with."

We should all commend any stars who are willing to go out on a limb and make shorts when they could just as easily spend their precious spare time cheering on the Lakers. Right, Jack?

■ INDUSTRY PROFESSIONALS

Everyone wants to direct, but it's hard to break free from the industry perception of you. When choreographer Adam Shankman decided to make the transition, studio executives must have scoffed, "He's just a dancer. How do we know he can direct?" Shankman proved it in 1998 by creating a slick 20-minute short called *Cosmo's Tale*. Now he's directing big studio pictures starring Jennifer Lopez (*The Wedding Planner*), Steve Martin (*Bringing Down the House*), and Adam Sandler (*Bedtime Stories*).

If you're a working professional, you have the advantage of invaluable connections and favors you can call in. Don't save them up for later. If you want to make the transition, now's the time to capitalize on all the good will you've built up over the years. Remember, your colleagues want you to succeed so that you can hire them when you're directing Adam Sandler features. They want to help you join the big leagues. Let them.

■ REGULAR PEOPLE WITH NO INDUSTRY CONNECTIONS

The actual number of established directors, actors, or industry professionals making shorts is very small. The majority of people picking up cameras are regular, everyday people with the burning passion to make films. Don't think just because you live in Nebraska and don't know anyone in Hollywood that you can't make a successful short film. If you review the list of filmmakers who get their shorts into the Sundance Film Festival, you'll be amazed by how many of them you've never heard of. Because they're just regular people with no Hollywood connections. People just like you. Certainly YouTube has made the entire exhibition process much more democratic, where anyone anywhere can film something and share it with the world within minutes. Why not join the ranks?

■ STUDENTS

Of course, students still make up a large percentage of the short-filmmaking population. University of Southern California (USC) School of Cinema-Television graduate David Birdsell points out, "It's tough to break into filmmaking, to just decide 'I'm going to be a professional filmmaker!' If you go to film school, you immediately are in this little community of aspiring filmmakers. You have access to your fellow students and the equipment. You're also learning from each other and helping each other on projects. So it's not as lonely and daunting a prospect." In this digital era, it's usually the students who are still shooting on film, because of school requirements.

LET'S TALK ABOUT FILM SCHOOL

You would think the perfect way to become a filmmaker is to go to film school. After all, doctors have to go to med school and lawyers to law school before they can practice. Shouldn't the

same apply to filmmakers? In the old days, going to film school made a lot of sense because you had to get your hands on expensive and not very accessible filmmaking equipment to make movies. In this new era, anyone with a computer and a credit card can be a filmmaker. Why waste your money on tuition when you can better spend it buying an entire camera package and editing system on eBay? Before dismissing the idea of film school, let's give it the trusty pros and cons evaluation.

PROS OF GOING TO FILM SCHOOL

• Film school teaches you the basics of filmmaking.

• You learn from experts. Although street smarts, natural ability, and the school of hard knocks have their good points, how much better is it to study at the feet of the masters? In the real world, mentors and gurus are harder to come by.

• You make mistakes in a no-risk environment. By the time your "official" film school project is unspooled in front of industry executives at a special screening organized and paid for by your school, you will have made countless unwatchable films that no one but your teachers and fellow students have seen. You don't have to be self-conscious about showing your peers these disasters because you know they're making equally bad monstrosities.

• You don't have to struggle to meet and hire crewmembers or actors. They're right there at school with you.

• If you go to a prestigious film school, you'll have a solid entry point into Hollywood. Most of the major film schools around the country arrange annual Los Angeles premieres of their students' work, which Hollywood insiders take seriously. Industry bigwigs might not personally attend, but they'll send their assistants or request screeners. No one wants to miss out on the next Spielberg. Additionally, alumni are notoriously benevolent to new graduates. If you cold-call former students and mention your connection, you'll get some meetings.

CONS OF GOING TO FILM SCHOOL

• You have to pay money for the privilege of learning. Why pay an institution when you can learn on your own? Take a page from the Kevin Smith playbook. He quit school and used his tuition money to make the feature film *Clerks*. It worked out pretty well for him, didn't it?

- You can't do whatever you want in terms of filmmaking. It's a structured environment. If you're a rebel or a maverick, such restrictions will chafe.

- Although all you really want to do is direct, you'll have to take a variety of classes that have nothing to do with directing. What a waste of time!

- Some film schools own your work. Who owns George Lucas's student films? USC.

- Even if you wanted to go to film school, you aren't necessarily guaranteed admission to the best schools. If you get stuck studying film in Nowheresville, will your degree mean anything to people in Hollywood? Probably not.

WHAT SHORT FILMMAKERS SAY ABOUT GOING TO FILM SCHOOL

"In film school, you get a chance to dabble with filmmaking, which you can do on your own, too, but film school is the place to do it," suggests USC grad David Birdsell. "Doing a bunch of shorts very quickly, you get the hang of filmmaking and an inkling of your own sensibility and your own approach to filmmaking, which isn't necessarily a given. You don't just know automatically, 'Oh, I make this kind of film!' You try a few things while there's nothing at stake. You just dabble. Hopefully you know what you're doing by the end of that. Just like writing. You have to write some stuff to get a sense of your own voice."

Animator Eileen O'Meara is a perfect example of someone who found her filmmaking voice in school. "I did undergrad in Fine Art," O'Meara says. "Did a lot of photography, thought I was starting to repeat myself, and wanted to add the dimension of time. So I went to USC film school. When I was there doing live action, I took a side course of animation and realized that was the medium that fit my personality the most."

David Birdsell adds, "No one can teach you how to make a good film, but film school can teach you a lot of things that go into good film. Classes on screenwriting and cinematography are useful. But you can't really learn filmmaking without doing it. And film school provides an opportunity to do it on a small scale without a lot at stake. Other than tuition. Which, in my case at USC, was high."

Can't afford USC? Your local college probably offers more reasonably priced film-oriented classes you can take. The two filmmakers who made one of the first Internet sensations, *405*, went to California State University, Long Beach (majoring in film production) and the University of Kansas (studying industrial design!).

ALTERNATIVES TO FILM SCHOOL

Not sold on film school? There are other avenues you might want to explore.

■ ART SCHOOL

Especially for animators. "At art school, what was so great was that everybody was so supportive and not competitive with each other," raves Eileen O'Meara. "It was, 'How are you expressing yourself? How can we do it better? Let me help you. Borrow my paint brush.' I loved it."

■ FILM CLASSES AT A REGULAR UNIVERSITY

Signing up for a one-off class allows you to take advantage of institutional learning without making the full film-school commitment.

■ ASKING A FILM STUDENT TO PRODUCE YOUR SHORT

You can benefit from some of the student's privileges (discounts) without having to pay for school yourself.

■ VOLUNTEERING TO WORK ON STUDENT PRODUCTIONS.

Students are always glad for an extra hand, and you're making friends and contacts. And learning from their mistakes.

THE MAJOR STUMBLING BLOCK TO MAKING SHORT FILMS

If it's so easy to make a film and anyone can do it, why aren't millions of shorts being made every year? The answer is lack of motivation — and money. Moviemaking at all levels — from the most guerilla indie shoots to the most bloated Hollywood blockbusters — requires funding. Although you will learn as you make your way through this book that the short filmmaker's mantra must be "Everything for Free!", the inescapable fact remains that it does cost money to make and market a successful short film.

The good news is it doesn't take as much money as it takes to make and market a feature. The old budgetary figure people used to throw around is $1,000 a minute, to make a short film. So if you wanted to make a five-minute short film, you have to come up with $5,000. In the digital era, anything goes. The thing to keep in mind is that you can easily spend thousands of dollars on a short, but unless you sell it to European television channels that pay well, you probably won't get your money back.

We'll talk more about how to fund your short in Chapter 8. But the reality is that how much money you need to make a short depends on (a) the nature of your project, (b) how much you can get for free, and (c) how much you are willing to spend. If you can get away with it, don't spend anything. Beg, borrow, and steal. Cash in every favor owed. Barter services. Do anything you can do to make your film. After all, you want to be a short filmmaker, don't you?

RECAP

- Everyone makes shorts — famous directors, movie stars, industry professionals, students, and regular folk from all over the world.

- No one can stop you from becoming a filmmaker. All you need is motivation and money.

- Pick up a camera and shoot something. Title the piece. You are now a filmmaker.

- Making a short is something to be proud of. Just ask Jack Nicholson.

- The hard part is making a good short.

CHAPTER 2

VENI, VIDI, VICI: SURVEYING THE FIELD

MANY STRANGE AND WONDER-
FUL THINGS CAN HAPPEN IN A
VERY SHORT TIME.

Too many filmmakers cling to the outdated idea that to be successful they have to make a short that could be mistaken for a feature film. In their minds, that means 30 minutes (or longer), with Hollywood-quality production value. Certainly, amazing work has been done in the 30- to 50-minute range. But it's wrong to assume that a "good" film has to be a mini-feature. Not only are half-hour pieces financially daunting, they aren't necessarily the best use of the format. Before you begin thinking about making your own masterpiece, do yourself a favor and check out what other filmmakers have done with the genre. You'll discover that with a little innovation and a lot of creativity, one can make a film that will blow everyone away, and it doesn't have to be more than a few minutes long.

WHAT DEFINES A SHORT?

Because shorts can incorporate so many different kinds of filmmaking (narrative, experimental, live action, animation, documentary, mixed media, etc.), the best way to define a short is by running time. The Academy of Motion Picture Arts & Sciences classifies a short film as "an original motion picture that has a running time of not more than 40 minutes, including all credits." The 2009 Sundance Film Festival application spells out a running time of 69 minutes or less for narrative pieces and 49 minutes or less for short documentaries. And the Screen Actors Guild defines a short to be a maximum of 35 minutes.

Practically speaking, however, anything over 30 minutes is on the long side. Those films are sometimes jokingly called "mediums." For festivals, online exhibition, and potential theatrical distribution, shorter is definitely better.

SHORTS SHOULD BE SHORT, SHOULDN'T THEY?

A filmmaker named Peter emailed me, concerned that the running length of his film was holding him back: "Here's the thing: our film is 40-minutes long. We actually had a version that was 44 minutes and cropped it down a bit because we fell out of consideration for a number of festivals if we were above the 40-minute length. But the thing is, being just under that 40-minute mark doesn't seem to help much. We've done OK so far, festival-wise, but not great; certainly not as well as I've done with previous shorts, and I think this is far and away the best film I've done. I was at a festival with the film, and I ran into an old programmer friend of mine, who went to one of our screenings. He rushed up to me afterwards and said:

'Peter... two things. First, this is one of the best shorts I've ever seen. Ever. I'm nuts about this film. Second, you've made a virtually un-programmable film here (he was referring to the run time of the film). You're going to be crushed by that all over the place in the festival circuit.' I sensed he was right (and it did, in fact, kind of crush me). It's a beautiful film, a moody caper film, shot in Manhattan, that turns into an unlikely romance; we shot on 35, had an ample budget (not that that necessarily translates into anything, but everyone who sees it agrees that, among other things, it looks and feels gorgeous), and it revolves around an amazing performance from a young actress who, all on the crew agreed, is going to be a star. So given all that, my question is: do you agree with my programmer friend's assessment of our chances? (I noticed that 12-15 minutes seemed to be the most common length of films on the top-ten list in your recent piece in *indieWIRE*). Also, if this were your film, how would you market or position it? I think we can actually, at 44 minutes, qualify as a feature in some festivals."

I replied that longer shorts are just extremely hard on the exhibition side. Even 30-minutes long is tough to program at festivals and on TV. However, there are two important venues that love long shorts. One is the Academy. Long shorts seem to do better than short shorts when it comes to getting nominations. And if you manage to get a nomination, then the same festivals that would never program a 40-minute short will make an exception for your film. The second is apparently iTunes. I was on a panel at a festival with an executive from Shorts International (which has a deal to exhibit shorts on iTunes), and she said longer shorts do well on that platform. My last suggestion to anyone in a similar situation would be if you really want festival play, then butcher your film. If you can carve out some 10-minute piece that can stand on its own, make that what you send on the festival circuit. Then use your longer short as a calling card for your directing talent.

Ask any festival programmer, sales agent, or acquisition executive, and they will tell you that most shorts are too long. Thomas Ethan Harris, who programmed the Los Angeles Film Festival and the Palm Springs International Festival of Short Films and now is a professional film consultant, remarks, "When a short goes over 15 minutes, you watch the film thinking, 'This could be shorter. What could be edited out?'"

Amy Talkington, who has written and directed five short films, an Internet series, and the feature film *The Night of the White Pants*, admits, "My first film was 18-minutes long. It was an example of a feature story trying to fit in a short film. My fifth short was nine minutes, and that feels like a good length. Stories can be told in 15 minutes or less — and should be. Just being practical, the festival environment really doesn't allow for films over 15, at least not very much."

"Think about it," director George Langworthy chimes in. "If you're a festival programmer and you have a film that's 30-minutes long, you can play three to six other shorts in the time taken up by this long one. So the longer film often gets knocked out. Personally, I think a half-hour short is awesome. But it's difficult to play festivals. If you make a one-minute long film and it's good, chances are very good that it's going to play everywhere — because programmers always have an extra minute! However, you can't really do much in a minute. I'd say the great shorts are generally around 12 to 15 minutes."

Knowing that shorter is better for festivals, some filmmakers resort to shaving off credit time when reporting their lengths. For example, when asked the running time of his film *White Face*, Brian McDonald replied, "It's 12 minutes. With the credits, it's a little over 14 minutes." Mat Fuller also played that game with his student film *Deveria*. "I started telling my movie length minus the credits just to get it in festivals," Fuller confesses. "I said 20, but it's really 22."

Shorter is also better for television sales. "I get a lot of filmmakers who assume they should make a 22-minute film because of the half-hour television slot," declares distributor David Russell, whose Palm Springs-based company, Big Film Shorts, has been in business since 1996. "But nobody's buying independently produced short films to fill half-hour slots. Shorts are used as fillers and interstitials in most cases. To make your film thinking that's the perfect length to sell to TV, that's just wrong. With those novella lengths, you're not going to get theatrical exhibition or be played on television as filler. However, with Video-on-Demand, DVD collections, and now iTunes, there is some room for longer lengths in the marketplace."

Megan O'Neill, a former short-film distributor and now VP/ Content Acquisitions and Development at *Atom.com*, adds, "Longer is always tougher. The longer you make your short, the higher the bar you've set for yourself. It has to be phenomenal, like Peter Sollett's *Five Feet High and Rising*, which is 29 minutes but won all sorts of awards. It has to be such a great short that people will go out of their way to program it. A festival or a television programmer, an online or a DVD acquisition executive, somebody is going to have to say, 'This film is so good that we need to give it to our audience, no matter what!' In the last 15 years, I can probably name on two hands how many longer films that have had that kind of success. Once you go over 30 minutes, it's almost impossible. Longer is definitely a harder sell. You better get an Academy Award nomination. You better be a festival darling. Otherwise, 15 minutes and under is always better for sales."

SEE FOR YOURSELF

To check out what filmmakers are doing right now, go to film festivals, short-film showcases, the iTunes short-film section, YouTube, and the many websites that host short films.

As far as festivals go, you'll discover that festivals do play films of all lengths. But you'll also note that the longer films are ghettoized in short-film programs. It's the 15-minutes-or-less films that get to play with the big boys in prime time, opening for the premieres and in front of the competition films.

Many things will happen as you begin to view a wide variety of films. You'll see many terrible shorts, which will serve to inspire you in an "I can do much better than that!" kind of way. You'll also see some amazing pieces that will inspire you to want to make something equally as great. On the downside, you might get depressed when you realize that there are filmmakers out there who have access to more money and better resources than you do. How can you expect to compete? Easy answer: By making something unique. Remember, everyone sees top-of-the-line filmmaking every day in feature films and on television. No one expects your little short to be in that league. What viewers want to see is the unexpectedly wonderful and weird stuff that they can only see in shorts. Everyone's looking for moments of YouTube genius. "What I like best about short films is the world that they take me to," remarks Sundance Film Festival programmer Trevor Groth. "People take chances with shorts that they can't do with features. You'll see stuff that you couldn't imagine, that you never thought you'd see on film, and there it is!"

What festival programmers hate seeing is clichéd scenes. Kim Yutani, who programs for both Outfest and Sundance, says her bête noire is a film that starts with an alarm clock ringing and a hand reaching out to shut it off. Think about it, even you've seen this shot a million times before. The world doesn't need it captured on film again!

EIGHT MILLION STORIES IN THE NAKED CITY

If you watch a lot of films, you might discover that your great idea for a short has already been done. Take, for example, *The Lunch Date*. Filmmaker Adam Davidson was still a student at Columbia in the late 1980s when he made this 11-minute piece, shot in black and white at Grand Central Station. The story focuses on an elderly suburban woman who comes into the city to shop and misses her train back. With extra time on her hands but very little cash, she orders a salad from one of the food establishments in the train terminal. She sets her shopping bags and salad down at a table, then realizes she's forgotten to get a fork. When she returns to her table, there is a homeless man sitting there, eating her salad. She doesn't know what to do! She's hungry, has no money to buy another salad, and doesn't want to be intimidated by the homeless man. So she picks up her fork and begins eating the salad as well. The homeless man gives her a look, but continues to eat her salad. There's a nice moment when he gets up and returns with a free pack of crackers, which he shares with her. But they never speak.

Her train is announced, and the woman gets up to leave. She's halfway down the track when she realizes she forgot her shopping bags back at the food stand. She rushes back, to discover her uneaten salad on the table with her shopping bags. She laughs as she realizes she mistook the homeless man's salad for her own. *The Lunch Date* is a wonderful, pitch perfect film which was awarded the student Academy Award, the Palme D'Or at Cannes, and the 1990 Oscar for best live-action short.

Every so often there's another version of a *Lunch Date*-like encounter showing up on the festival circuit. Once it was a stuffy British businessman at a London train station thinking another business man had stolen his packet of potato chips, only to discover his had fallen to the ground. Another was a guy on a subway accusing another man of stealing his watch, only to discover later he left his watch at home. It's a situation that works in many variations.

An Occurrence at Owl Creek Bridge is another story told and retold. The 1962 original, directed by Robert Enrico and based on an Ambrose Bierce story, begins with a Civil War-era soldier being hanged. At the moment the rope is about to snap his neck, the rope breaks and the man escapes. He runs home, where his wife is waiting to greet him — only to be jerked out of that fantasy when the hanging really does take place. In the Fox Movie Channel short I produced, *Hope Street*, writer/director Alex Metcalf set the story in modern day Los Angeles during a car jacking. Another short used a mountain-climbing accident as the trigger. You can probably come up with your own version right now. It's not wrong to do your own twist on this classic tale, which clearly works well in the short format. You should just be aware that it's been done before.

A FRESH TAKE IS ESSENTIAL

"Forget about any kind of love story," counsels short-film distributor Fred Joubaud of Premium Films. "We've seen so many love stories that unless it's a very original one...."

Even if a genre is over mined or played out, an original take will garner notice. For example, sharing the *Shaun of the Dead* zeitgeist, shorts about zombies have been all the rage in recent years. Personally, I'm a huge fan of Spencer Susser's Australian zombie-infested teen romance *I Love Sarah Jane* and Vince Marcello's musical *Zombie Prom*, which can best be described as *Grease* with a zombie in the John Travolta role. "I picked up a short called *Zombie-American* by Nick Poppy," shares Joubaud. "Technically, it's about a zombie, how it's difficult for a zombie to live. The director made this short film on the weekend with a friend of his, Ed Helms from Comedy Central's *The Daily Show with Jon Stewart*. Just because it was funny, original, and well done, I sold it to many TV stations."

TEN MUST-SEE SHORT FILMS

To spur your creativity and make you realize how much can be accomplished in a very short time, here's a listing of 10 shorts that I'd highly recommend any aspiring filmmaker view — arranged from shortest to longest. In some cases, these films launched the filmmaker's subsequently spectacular career. In others, they're examples of influential cinematic work made by creative geniuses. In all cases, they're films that captured viewers' attention when they first debuted and have continued to attract eyeballs ever since. Let's hope you all make films that people still want to watch five years, 10 years, 50 years from now.

1

THE LANDLORD

Filmmaker: Adam McKay

Year: 2007

Running time: 2 minutes

Both Adam McKay and Will Ferrell have day jobs as Hollywood heavyweights. Perhaps you've heard of McKay's previous directorial efforts, *Talladega Nights: The Ballad of Ricky Bobby* and *Anchorman: The Legend of Ron Burgundy*. But having already-established feature careers didn't stop the duo from joining the short-film online revolution and founding the website *FunnyorDie* as a home for comedy shorts on the Web. The jewel in the *FunnyorDie.com* crown is a two-minute piece starring McKay's toddler daughter Pearl (who also happens to be Jeremy Piven's niece) as Ferrell's foul-mouthed, beer-toting landlady.

Although the specifics are very Hollywood, the production is actually very true to organic no-budget filmmaking. Location: director's home. Actors: his best friend and his daughter. Shoot: one day (45 minutes, in fact). The film was an immediate pop cultural phenomenon, getting more than seven million views in 24 hours and earning massive mainstream press attention. In less than a year, it became the third most watched online video ever, with 45 million hits. "On the Web you do ideas you can't use anywhere else," McKay told *Wired Magazine* in 2007. "Like, a baby landlord would never work as a movie. We were excited by getting this chance to goof around with those kinds of ideas." Unfortunately, McKay and Ferrell couldn't shake their old school Hollywood mentality and rushed into production with an ill-conceived sequel. It flopped.

2

SPIRIT OF CHRISTMAS

Filmmakers: Trey Parker and Matt Stone

Year: 1995

Running time: 5 minutes

When I do workshops, I ask the participants how they would

define the most successful short film of all time, encouraging them to dream as big as possible. They often start out with the obvious (Oscars, movie adaptations, Hollywood careers, *Time* magazine covers, etc.), and then even grow more ambitious. I remember one woman at a Filmmaker's Alliance seminar yelled out, "They erect statues in honor of my film." It always amazes me no matter how outrageous they think their suggestions are, one short film has actually managed to achieve every thing they list, including having statues made (if you consider cardboard standees in movie lobbies or stuffed toys as the equivalent thereof). That short film is inarguably the most financially and culturally successful short film ever made, *Spirit of Christmas,* the five-minute piece of crude animation that launched the *South Park* empire.

When television executive Brian Graden gave Trey Parker and Matt Stone two thousand dollars to make a video Christmas card, little did he know a pop cultural phenomenon would spring from their crudely animated story of four foul-mouthed kids who have to pick sides when Santa and Jesus have a showdown at the local mall. Although the filmmakers didn't plan it, the short was a de facto pilot for the series, establishing everything from the South Park location to the "killed Kenny" catch phrase. Here's to hoping that your short will be as creatively outrageous and outrageously profitable as *Spirit of Christmas*! After all, the world needs more statues erected in honor of short films.

3
MORE

Filmmaker: Mark Osborne
Year: 1999
Running time: 6 minutes
The perfect no-dialogue short is a six-minute claymation masterpiece about an elderly corporate drone working on a secret project that could bring bliss to the world. The

animated film, which the director made while teaching stop-motion at CalArts, won the 1999 Sundance Film Festival and was nominated for an Academy Award. It's also the first stop-motion animated short originally filmed in the 70mm (IMAX) format. Filmmaker Mark Osborne explains, "Oddly, when I initially made *More*, it was just an attempt to make a spec music video. It turned into something much bigger, of course. But it was inspired by the music, the New Order song, and it represents the type of music video that I love and would want to do. It cost about $120,000 total to make. People think that's expensive for a short, but if you look at it as an IMAX film that was done independently, if it weren't for all the donated services, we would have spent half a million on it."

The film's sales agent, Carol Crowe of Los Angeles-based Apollo Cinema, adds, "There's been such a huge continued interest in this film. I think even Mark Osborne would tell you he's surprised it keeps going. Why is it so popular? I think the subject matter is timely with everything going on with corporate America today. It has no dialogue, but it has a strong message. It's also a beautiful film. And the music is incredible, too." *More* is one of the short films YouTube used to launch their 2008 Screening Room showcase. Osborne credits the short for helping him get his feature-helming gig, *Kung Fu Panda*.

4

PEEL

Filmmaker: Jane Campion
Year: 1982
Running Time: 9 minutes

Peel is arguably the most perfect narrative short ever made under 10 minutes. Although many people are fans of Jane Campion's *Passionless Moments*, the greatness of her first film (a Palme d'Or winner) cannot be denied. Set during a family outing, the film is about a little boy throwing orange peels out the car window and the driver who wants him to stop.

"It is so profound," raves fan George Langworthy. "It brings to the floor some of the most profound issues about family, parenthood, childhood, love, and stubbornness. It goes into this very sublime moment toward the climax. It's filled with suspense, and it's funny! It's an amazing film." Basically, the essential production elements on this film were three actors, a car, and an orange. Even 25 years later, *Peel* is still being revived and shown in theaters around the world.

5
PELUCA
Filmmaker: Jared Hess
Year: 2002
Running time: 9 minutes
Before there was the feature *Napoleon Dynamite*, there was a black and white student film that Jared Hess made at Brigham Young University. *Peluca* is one of the best recent examples of a short used to convince financers to cough up cash for an extremely low-budget ($400,000) feature adaptation. The short's original press kit offers the following production notes: "*Peluca* was shot in Hess' native town of Preston, Idaho in two days and made for under $500. Due to limited funds the film was shot on grainy 16mm b&w negative. The actors who played Pedro, Giel, and Randy are Preston High School juniors with little interest in acting. Their performances naturally portrayed rural Idaho teenage life. Locations, such as La Tienda, were secured the day of shooting due to the town's kick back attitude.
Running Time: 9 minutes
Camera: Arri SRII
Lenses: 5.9mm, 12mm, 50mm
Film: Kodak 7222 16mm B&W"

6
SPIDER
Filmmaker: Nash Edgerton
Year: 2007
Running time: 9 minutes

If audiences have been trained to expect a twist ending for a short, *Spider* overloads with twist upon twist upon twist. As the title suggests, the plot depends on a toy spider that a guy (played by the director) gives to his girl. As the tagline from the film promises, "It's all fun and games until someone loses an eye." Edgerton explained in a 2008 interview with *AMCtv.com* where he got the idea: "I used to have a rubber spider when I was a kid that I would hide in a different place in the kitchen for my mum to find. Then my brother and I had a run-in with a large spider once while he was driving. Usually if I have an idea, it just keeps recurring in my head and I've got to make it. *Spider* was one of those things that I couldn't stop thinking about."

Spider is a rare example of a film that originally debuted online and yet still has afterlife. "*Spider*'s such a good film that it transcends," says Sundance Film Festival shorts programmer Shane Smith, explaining why the festival played Edgerton's film even though it was on the Internet. Fred Joubaud of Premium Films further explains, "The thing is *Spider* was produced by QOOB, a TV channel in Italy. QOOB has played it on the Internet. People downloaded it and then uploaded it on YouTube." Nevertheless, Joubaud was able to sell it to a television network in Spain, explaining, "The people who are going to watch shorts on a TV program are not those kind of people who are going to be on the Internet looking for the film."

7

HARDWARE WARS

Filmmaker: Ernie Fosselius

Year: 1977

Running time: 13 minutes

If you want to make a short film that people will clamor to see (and it's not about sex!), make a *Star Wars* parody. Thanks to George Lucas's tolerance, there's a whole slew of *Star Wars*-inspired shorts. In fact, there's a popular annual online contest devoted to

Star Wars Fan Films. As you might expect, the first entree into the genre took place shortly after the original *Star Wars* was released. Ernie Fosselius wrote and directed an intentionally super cheesy and very funny flick that has a devoted following to this day.

How to explain *Hardware Wars'* continued popularity? "Filmmakers enjoy the joke (and see the potential for their own work) of making something look 'big' with cheesy effects, sets, and costumes," surmises producer Michael Wiese. "They are inspired by the insight that they can parody their favorite films, characters, and TV shows. I even heard during a film festival panel a career strategy proposal that 'you can get rich and famous by making a parody of *Star Wars!*' For me, I like that we made something for nothing and it worked."

The magic of *Star Wars* parody worked again in 1999 when Joe Nussbaum retold *Shakespeare in Love,* substituting USC film school student George Lucas as the hero struggling for inspiration. Unlike its predecessor, *George Lucas in Love* is not a cheap film. High production value, a strong story, good acting, and a rich score make it heads and shoulders above the average *Star Wars* parody. In fact, when *George Lucas in Love* was first released on home video, it sold more copies on Amazon than Lucas's most recent *Star Wars* installment.

8
TANGHI ARGENTINI
Filmmaker: Guido Thys
Year: 2006
Running Time: 13 minutes
This office-based comedy in which the mild-mannered hero asks a male co-worker to help him learn to dance in preparation for a blind date is the kind of delightful modern fairytale, boasting an excellently structured storyline and a glossy 35mm production value, that delights audiences, festival jurors, and the Academy of Motion Picture Arts & Sciences. To tell more of the plot would only ruin the film's twists and turns. Nominated for an Academy Award, the Belgium *Tanghi Argentini* lost to France's *Le Mozart*

des Pickpockets, a 31-minute comedy by Philippe Pollet-Vilard about a pair of inept thieves who join forces with a child prodigy. Whereas both are typical of the type of shorts the Academy has been honoring in recent years, Guido Thys's film racked up a ton of awards while it played the festival circuit during the year previous to the Oscars. Both Thys and producer Anja Daelemans credited the film's success to the script by Geert Verbanck, although the fact that the actors spent three months learning how to dance also helped.

9
UN CHIEN ANDALOU
Filmmaker: Luis Buñuel (with Salvador Dali)
Year: 1928
Running time: 17 minutes
This extremely weird silent film was shot in two weeks with money supplied by the filmmaker's mother. The highly experimental piece was a collaboration between Luis Buñuel and Salvador Dali, two relatively unknown artists who wanted to make something that would shock audiences — and call a little attention to themselves. Decades later we're still disturbed by the imagery, including the infamous razor blade to the eyeball. When *Entertainment Weekly* ran a 2003 cover story ranking the Top 50 Cult Movies of all time, *Un Chien Andalou* came in at 22, between *Pee-Wee's Big Adventure* and *Akira*.

10
LA JETÉE
Filmmaker: Chris Marker
Year: 1962
Running time: 29 minutes
Another oldie but goodie that will blow your mind. Made in 1962 by photographer/filmmaker Chris Marker, this French film feels more complete than the 1996 Brad Pitt/Bruce Willis feature-length adaptation, *12 Monkeys*. What's amazing about this very experimental yet mesmerizing time travel tale is that the entire

film consists of still photographic images (with one short section of moving pictures). A filmmaker couldn't pull that off for 90 minutes, but for half an hour it gives viewers a movie-watching experience they'll never forget.

You own a digital still camera, you have the computer software — go out and make your own *La Jetée*-inspired piece. But make it 15 minutes or less!

RECAP

- Shorts can be any length — but 15 minutes or less is ideal.

- Longer films are harder to get into festivals and on television. Why invest all that time and money if no one will want to show it?

- If your "original idea" has been done before, make sure you have a good twist — and that yours is better than your predecessors'.

- Shorts are the perfect venue for trying out different filmmaking or storytelling techniques. Clichés = bad, experimentation = good!

- Make a short that people will still want to watch decades after you made it. That's the true definition of a successful short.

CHAPTER 3

THINK LIKE A SHORT FILMMAKER

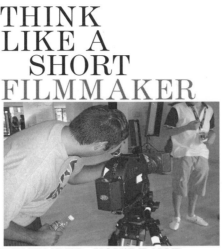

REMEMBER, YOU'RE NOT MAKING A FEATURE!

Feature filmmakers have to play by the rules. They are creating very expensive works of art that have potentially great commercial value. Short filmmakers aren't. Therefore, we don't have to play by any rules. This is why short filmmaking is artistically more fulfilling than feature filmmaking.

Too many people approach short filmmaking with a feature mentality. Those are the people who blow $75,000 on a 30-minute film that no one wants to see. Meanwhile, scrappy DV filmmaker Brian McDonald spends $1,000 on a 14-minute mockumentary called *White Face*, which wins the Audience Award at Slamdance, sells to HBO, gets picked up by a diversity training company, and ultimately nets him $100,000. Which path do you want to follow?

If you want to make a short film for practically no money, you don't have to sacrifice production value. You just need think differently.

31

YOU ARE NOT MAKING A FEATURE — YOU ARE MAKING A SHORT!

Always remind yourself that you're not making *Gone with the Wind*. No one expects your little film to be the next great cinematic masterpiece that will change the face of filmmaking forever. It's just a short film. So relax and have fun.

"It's the truest form of filmmaking that exists," declares Carol Crowe, President of Los Angeles-based short-film distribution company Apollo Cinema. "You don't need big names, big wows, or special effects. You just need, truly, a good story. In fact, a good short is like a short story, it can stick in your memory and last."

Don't obsess about making *pretty* pictures that can match the multi-million-dollar extravaganzas you see at the local multiplex. Obsess about making *moving* pictures.

Moving — meaning there is motion on screen. Too many shorts are static: stationary camera, actors planted in one spot, and very little action taking place. You're not directing a play — or a soap opera!

Moving — meaning the film is well paced. Unlike feature filmmakers, you don't have enough screen time to show mundane activities like walking somewhere, knocking on the door, waiting for it to be answered, then crossing over the threshold. After sitting through dozens of shorts while his own played the festival circuit, director Noah Edelson noticed how many began with someone walking somewhere. It got to the point where Edelson wanted to yell at the ambling characters, "It's a short film! You should be there already!"

Moving — meaning your film affects the viewers — makes them jump, laugh, cry, or close their eyes in fear. "The audience isn't expecting the same sort of formula as a feature film," explains filmmaker David Birdsell. "They're willing to go in a completely unknown direction. At the same time, you made a short film, and you had limited resources, right? It doesn't matter to the audience what your resources were. They just want to be entertained or enlightened or whatever."

Short-film viewers will forgive a variety of filmmaking flaws as long as they're enjoying the flick. "Audiences really get a kick out of seeing shorts that take chances that a lot of the features can't," points out Trevor Groth, programmer of the Sundance Film Festival. "Over the many years that I've been doing this, the short programs at Sundance have been the highest attended of any of the sections of the festival."

"I've always felt that anyone who is truly interested in independent film should pay attention to shorts," notes Sundance founder Robert Redford in the 2008 festival catalogue. "They are often an indication of what's coming down the creative pike."

Redford means not only are the filmmakers the voice of the future, but they're on the frontline when it comes to addressing issues and exploring experimental filmmaking techniques. Long before Hollywood portrayed the events that happened on September 11, 2001, short filmmakers were making a variety of animation, live action, and documentary films on the subject. Short filmmakers were also the first to depict the war in Iraq.

As for experimenting technically, shorts have always broken new ground. Because unlike feature filmmaking, there are no rules in short filmmaking. Anything and everything can happen in a short. "I had fun doing a piece where I made silicone molds of feet, hands, and a head," shares animator Eileen O'Meara. "Then I poured colored candle wax into the molds. I took the detailed and brightly colored body parts, melted them frame by frame with a blowtorch, and shot it backwards. The result was a sort of creation myth piece where humans form from a pool of wax. When I started the project, I realized I had to figure out how to make realistic wax body parts. I found the guy that made statues for the Hollywood Wax Museum. He had trained at Madame Tussauds and generously showed me the technique from beginning to end. It was great. The good thing about making a short is that if you do everything yourself and you fund it through your day job, you're not going to have an executive breathing down your neck telling you what to do. You get to make your own film and have complete control over it. The only problem is if it's not any good, you can't blame anyone else."

Allow yourself to run amok creatively. Go outside your comfort zone. Learn how to do amazing new things. Push the envelope. Don't play it safe. Come up with outrageous story ideas. Encourage your actors to take chances. Try some wacky tricks in post. Have fun with your titles and credits. Why not? After all, you're not making *Gone with the Wind*.

"Most people, they do a few shorts, then for the rest of their lives they concentrate on feature-length films," sighs *Coven* director Mark Borchardt. "Features are a whole new universe — a whole new spectrum of money, a whole new spectrum of recognition. So these filmmakers kiss the short format goodbye. Whereas I'm interested in accommodating my personal ideology. If an idea calls for the length of a short film, I'll pursue that. But I think, for a lot of people, as soon as they make it, the idea of short film is over, is out."

Spanish short-film director Nacho Vigalondo is determined to bring his short-film-maverick mindset with him always. He reported back in 2006, "I like to think I'll be making short films all my life, but my next project is a feature film, to be shot this summer. It's going to be a low-budget (even compared with Spanish budgets) sci-fi film. The surprising thing is that Scott Free, the company of Ridley and Tony, are going to be executive producers of this film. It's going to be called *Cronocrímenes (Timecrimes)*, will have erotic elements, a very twisted plot, and the bad guy will be a pink mummy."

Filmmaker Karl Hirsch firmly believes you should not give up on shorts, even after you've graduated to features. "The best thing about short films is that they're fun to make, they're fun to watch, and it's a great inexpensive way to express yourself and to exercise the craft without going crazy and spending millions of dollars," exclaims Hirsch. "I've made a couple of features, and I have made several short films, none of which have cost over a thousand dollars. I've achieved more professionally, creatively, and emotionally from making those short films than I did doing features. Of course, I'm trying to make more features. But in the interim, it's a lot of fun to go on a set, shoot for a day with some actors — and have a blast."

Becoming a filmmaker isn't always fun in the sun. There's a big learning curve when you cross that bridge from wannabe film-maker to actual filmmaker. Quite often we wish could take Noah Edelson's advice and "be there already." The thing to remember is it doesn't have to be so hard. With the right mindset, it can be a blast. Let's aim for that!

WHY SHORTS ARE MORE FUN TO MAKE THAN FEATURES

■ SHORTS REQUIRE LESS TIME INVESTMENT THAN FEATURES.

Features shoot for weeks on end. You can make an entire short film in a weekend. In fact, weekends are the best time to shoot because that's when people and equipment are available. Don't procrastinate. Make a date to start shooting, and then start shooting! Features wait forever to get a greenlight. You go now.

■ SHORTS REQUIRE LESS CREW THAN FEATURES.

"Keep it simple," advises Matthew Modine, who has more expe-rience with both feature and short-film sets than most. "I'm always surprised when I see short films that have 'movie' cred-its on them — so many people involved! You should try to take responsibility for as many of the aspects as you can if you're the filmmaker. Whether that's the writing and the locations, set design, costumes — just try to do it all yourself. Because in many different subtle ways, it sets the tone of the piece — the more that you can become involved with those kind of decisions. Especially if you're aspiring to become a feature filmmaker, it will give you an appreciation of the difficulty of doing costumes, set design, props, and things like that — and for the people who specialize in those things on a feature film. It will give you more appreciation of all of those people's jobs because you will have done it."

Short filmmaker David Birdsell also appreciates the smaller crew. "The DV short I made was probably the most fun I've had making a film because it didn't involve all the logistical hassles of dealing with a crew. It was more immediate. You have an idea, you tell three or four people, and you do it. You can watch it right away. It's easier to do things on the spur of the moment. You have a lot more flexibility with a smaller crew, less equipment."

■ NO STARS NECESSARY.

In feature filmmaking, if you have any hope of getting your film picked up for distribution, you better have recognizable names in the cast. With shorts, there is a certain amount of fuel behind a short that has a star involved, but it isn't necessarily a guarantee of success. Stars, in fact, distract from the short and make it feel more like television or a feature. In addition, you'll get less credit as a director. People won't say you made a great film, they'll exclaim, "That Neil Patrick Harris short was great!" This is true also of star crewmembers. If you get Spielberg's director of photography [shorthand: DP], everyone will remark, "Of course that short is great, Spielberg's DP shot it!" However, don't let that stop you from going after names. Because they are gettable. And you will have an entirely different experience than you would if your best friend starred in it or shot it. Just remember it isn't necessary.

Megan O'Neill, VP/Content Acquisitions and Development at *Atom.com*, adds, "I try to say this on every panel because it's really true. I've produced a feature, and with features you have a lot of other pressures on you — actors who want trailers, distributors who want the film to have a poster that looks like every other poster ever made, etc. With a short, you don't have any of that. This is your baby. You can really be an auteur on this film. So don't get hung up on stars. Make the best film you can. That's what's important."

■ SHORT FILM PLOTS ARE LESS COMPLICATED TO
CONSTRUCT THAN FEATURES.

"When you make a short film, the world is yours," reminds
Coven director Mark Borchardt. "Any idea goes. You're not regi-
mented to any structure. When you make a feature film, you
lose a certain amount of freedom. A feature has a sense of pace
you must — you must! — be adherent to, and that can get sticky
and complicated in the crafting of the story. Whereas a short,
man, a short can ride on a singular idea without the fabric of
multiple plot twists, subplots, and secondary characters. It can
be a single, flaming, meteoric idea."

■ SHORT FILMMAKERS HAVE MANY MORE OPTIONS
WHEN IT COMES TO HOW TO SHOOT THEIR FILMS.

Want to shoot 70mm or on a toy camera? Both are completely
valid options for short filmmakers. Mark Osborne made his
animated film *More* on the biggest format available, and his
short has played in IMAX theaters in New York and London for
six months, opening for the blockbuster *Everest*.

While only the most independent feature films still shoot
16mm or Super-16, short filmmakers (especially those in film
school) still enjoy the smaller format. "A cool black-and-white
16mm short could really kick ass," points out film-enthusiast
George Langworthy. "Feature films can't be in black and white
(unless you're doing *Schindler's List* and you're Spielberg) — it's
one of the things shorts can do. It would look great, and you
would not go totally broke.
You could probably fit it onto
one credit card. In fact, 16
is pretty cheap these days
because all the equipment is
just sitting around. You can
get a camera for nothing."

Let's not forget the old and
trusty friend of generations

of short filmmakers: 8mm. There's a whole subculture complete with film festivals still devoted to that simple format. Why shoot Super-8 when video is so prevalent? George Langworthy points out, "It's really fun. That's absolutely the key word. Your effort involved is very little, and it's all about fun. Super-8 is affordable, accessible, cheap, fun, beautiful, works lovely in the short format. Super-8 filmmakers are doing it for the joy of filmmaking."

And what's the video equivalent of Super-8 (i.e., a camera of the past, which has become a beloved tool for short filmmakers)? Yes, it's pixelvision. The actual camera is called the PXL-2000, which sounds very impressive, but in reality it's a kid's camera that records video on standard audio cassettes to create pixelvision. Manufactured only in the late 1980s, the camera itself is no longer being sold but can easily be scored off eBay for a hundred dollars or so. The original PXL-2000 packaging proclaims that the camera "lets kids create their wildest dreams," and indeed many short filmmakers have found the format delightful. Similar to 8mm film fests, there are also festivals devoted to exhibiting pixelvision shorts.

"I love shooting film," sums up actor/director Matthew Modine. "If I was going to shoot a feature, I would absolutely want to shoot film and I'd shoot Kodak. But for shorts, the idea is to shoot HD and not have to develop film and get into the realm of having to transfer things to cut in an Avid or Final Cut Pro — it just doesn't make sense to shoot film." John Halecky, a short-film consultant and filmmaker himself, agrees, reporting that his latest production was shot with the Panasonic HVX 200 camera, so it doesn't even go to tape. "With a P2 card, you just pop it right into the computer," marvels Halecky. "It's that quick."

A filmmaker named Jeff emailed a question about which camera is best to use: "In college I made a couple shorts with my friends on my Hi-8, for fun more than anything. Well, I just graduated and recently came up with an idea for a short. I have a lot of confidence in my abilities as a writer, but my problem is I never knew much about the technical stuff. Recently, I spent some time with a famous British director and he mentioned that Panasonic has a really good DV camera out right now that he was high on. Unfortunately, I did not get the model number of the camera he was speaking of, but looking at their website I would assume that he meant the DVX100A. I was just curious if you had an insight on this product. Anything would help."

My answer to Jeff is already out-of-date, but what I generally reply to filmmakers fixated on which camera they should buy is that they shouldn't buy a camera at all. With such rapid technological advances, cameras are not a good investment. It's better to borrow last year's hot camera from a friend than spend your precious cash buying this year's latest and greatest model. The best camera for you is whatever works best aesthetically for your film and financially for your budget. It's not the camera that makes a good film — it's the filmmaker. So whatever you can get your hands on when you're ready to make a film, that's the camera you should use.

Life After Death director Jordan Horowitz sums up the format question for short filmmakers, "If you've got an idea that you know in your heart is solid, then do whatever it takes to get that made. All the countless discussions about film versus video really only amount to one thing: It doesn't matter. The reality is your budget will choose your tools for you. You can make a film with a Fisher Price camera, which people have done successfully, and if it's good, people will watch it."

RECAP

- No-budget short filmmakers have it much easier than their feature equivalents.

- The most cutting-edge and maverick filmmaking takes place in shorts.

- Shorts have a different pace than features.

- Unlike feature filmmakers, directors of short films have a wide variety of shooting formats to choose from.

- You can keep on making shorts even after you graduate to features.

CHAPTER 4

SEVEN SECRETS FOR SUCCESS

SET YOURSELF UP FOR
SUCCESS.

After conducting countless short-film seminars, I've refined my insights into how to approach short filmmaking into seven golden rules. Or rather, I used to call them golden rules — until I was reminded that there are no rules in short filmmaking. So consider these guiding principles, standard operating procedures, concepts, mantras, mottoes, whatever you want to call them. Knowing them will help you to retrain your brain to think like a short filmmaker and give you an unbeatable edge as you begin your filmmaking career. They will set you up for success.

1

YOU ARE THE STUDIO.

When you're directing a feature film for Paramount, Paramount is the studio, and you are a person employed by Paramount to make a work-for-hire. Who finances the film? Paramount. Who has final creative control? Paramount. Who is in charge of marketing the film? Who gets to design the poster? Who is responsible for distributing the film? Who makes decisions regarding home video? Who profits from the film? Who gets sued if something goes wrong? Paramount, Paramount, Paramount, Paramount, Paramount, Paramount.

When you make a short, you are not only the person responsible for directing the film, you are also the studio. The answer to all of the above questions is you, you, you, you, you, you. Never again in your career will you have such an opportunity to handle every single part of the filmmaking process. It's exciting, educating, and very time consuming.

So, you are the studio. What kind of studio are you? Do you make big-budget films or low-budget films? Do you do all your paperwork properly and play by the rules, or are you a down-and-dirty, guerilla-style production house? What are your capital assets? How much money do you want to spend on creating product? Do you expect to make any of this money back? What happens if someone does sue you, what will you do? These and many more questions must be answered.

You are the studio. As we go through the steps of production, know that each studio is unique. Make the decisions that work best for your studio. For example, for the shorts I produced for the Fox Movie Channel, I always paid for location permits. Didn't want to risk being shut down and felt it was worth the money. However, I know plenty of "studios" that risk it all the time. As a studio, I don't believe there are enough opportunities in terms of exhibition and distribution to produce a 30-minute-long film. You, as studio, might only want to produce longer films — especially if you want to win an Academy Award (the Academy loves the longer films).

Whenever I do short-film workshops, aspiring filmmakers always ask me "Should I" questions (e.g., "Should I put my short on the Internet?"), and my answer is always the same: "Only you know the correct decision for your particular studio." There's no wrong or right when you're the studio.

It's worth your while to really sit down and plan out a future for your studio. "If you're making shorts to get into features," counsels writer-director Amy Talkington, "make a film that is similar in tone and spirit to the feature you want to make. That is so incredibly important. I never stopped and said 'I want to do films about young people' — that's just what I did. I made several shorts about teenagers. So that's who I am. That's the kind of projects people bring to me. Because I'm making films about young people. And that's fine. But an intelligent person who is shaping her career might stop and think about it, and create a short similar in tone to her first feature script. That's a problem I've had with a feature script that I've recently gone out with. They say 'Yeah, we see she's a great filmmaker, and it's a great script, but she hasn't made a film that really reflects this tone.' And I just want to strangle them! Because, look, you can see that I've nailed four or five different tones, why wouldn't I be able to nail this one?! But that's what they say. They really need to see it. So, ideally, that's what you go for."

Bergen Williams is an actress who took my UCLA Extension class and decided she was going to be a studio that made 12 DV shorts in a year — as a learning experience. She went on eBay and bought a DV camera and Final Cut Pro. Knowing she was going to do a full year's worth of filming using Screen Actors Guild talent, she bought a year's worth of workers compensation insurance. Thus armed, she officially opened her studio and went into business. And how did it turn out? Her first film landed her a writing gig on a television series! She made one other short, but I don't think she continued to do one a month. You could say her studio went out of business.

Some studios are strictly YouTube endeavors. You're building up an entire play list of pieces you've created to share with the masses over the Web. Or maybe you're making webisodes or pieces for cell phones. Bigger studios are hungry for such content so this is definitely a strong avenue to pursue.

So, what kind of studio are you? The time to think about this is now — before we begin digging into the filmmaking process. This is your chance to do things the way you want. Your true character will be revealed. Don't want to do proper paperwork? Fine, you're the kind of studio that doesn't do paperwork. Don't want to clear your music? Fine, you're the kind of studio that is purely making art films and doesn't care about commercial exhibition. Don't want to feed your crew? Fine, you're the kind of studio no one wants to work for ever again.

Some people run their studios with an "I'm just a dumb short filmmaker, I don't know anything" mentality. Actually, I am a big proponent of this great excuse — it's true, you are just a dumb short filmmaker, you don't know anything, and sometimes it behooves you to take this easy out. Especially when you're getting busted for shooting without permits. But all the time? If your studio never interacts with professionals, then do whatever you want. It's when you ask others to take your studio seriously that you get in trouble. When you sign contracts, you're not just some dumb short filmmaker with $20 in the bank — you are a studio that can be held accountable. People are expecting your studio to act just as professionally as a real business.

Think of it this way. As much as you'd like to think you're just messing around, you are building a property. When Mike Judge drew two moron heavy metal kids for his short *Frog Baseball*, he did not think he was creating the Beavis and Butthead empire. Nor did Trey Parker and Matt Stone with *Spirit of Christmas*. Ditto Jared Hess with *Peluca*. Your little tiny film might result in something that can make your studio far richer than your grandest dreams. Take it seriously.

2

MAKE A FILM THAT PEOPLE WANT TO SEE.

YouTube filmmakers know this better than anyone else. If you make something people want to see, then you and your film rise to the top. It's all about capturing the eyeballs and making that viewer-count-number grow. You can easily get people you know to watch your film, but if they don't spread the word to others, your fan base will remain your own circle of friends.

Making a film that people want to promote to others is the key to success. How do you get into the Sundance Film Festival? Make a film that the programmers want to show their ticket-buying customers. How do you get a Hollywood deal? Make a short that agents are dying to hype to studio and television executives saying, "You gotta see this!" How do you get press? When I'm covering shorts for *indieWIRE*, I go to festivals showing hundreds of shorts — I can't review every one. So I ask people at the fest what they've seen and what they've liked. It's these "you should watch" recommendations that I highlight so that my readers will seek out those films.

If you consistently make short films that people will want to watch, you can make a living as a short filmmaker. Animators Bill Plympton and Don Hertzfeldt are perfect examples. Almost every year they each produce new animated shorts that become festival darlings. Each has been nominated for Oscars, Plympton twice for *Your Face* and *Guard Dog* and Hertzfeldt for *Rejected*, and both have won multiple festival prizes. They have screened in touring theatrical exhibitions that Hertzfeldt and Mike Judge organized called The Animation Show, which they merchandized as if it were a rock concert (T-shirts, posters, and DVDs for sale in the lobby). Plympton and Hertzfeldt actually make a living selling DVDs of their shorts to their fan base from their websites, *www.plymptoons.com* and *www.bitterfilms.com*, respectively. How can you emulate Plympton and Hertzfeldt? Be in the business of making shorts people want to see.

3
"EVERYTHING FOR FREE! EVERYONE WORKS FOR FREE!"

If you've got the money to make a short paying full rate for goods and services, go ahead and do so. Or stretch that amount out and make a feature. But most short filmmakers are operating on a dime. If you're a "we have no money" studio, your working motto must be "Everything for Free! Everyone Works for Free!" This is not something you keep secret — you tell everyone. Write it in big letters, shout it from rooftops, tattoo it on your forehead: You are a studio that operates under the mandate "Everything for Free! Everyone Works for Free!"

You'll be surprised how many people are willing to work for free if they understand that no one is getting paid. It's only when people feel like they are being taken advantage of (or undervalued compared to others) that problems arise.

Always recite your list of freebies when asking for something else free: "Everyone's working for free. Panavision is going to give us a free camera, Kodak is going to give us free film, won't you give us free processing?" The more people and organizations who have waived their fees, the more others feel like they should jump on the bandwagon.

Remain constantly vigilant to your "Everything for Free!" modus operandi. Robert Rodriguez is your patron saint when it comes to this way of thinking. For *El Mariachi*, he refused to buy a can of black spray paint so they could paint the cover of a guitar case to match the hero guitar case. He found a way to shoot around the mismatched cover rather than paying a buck for a can of paint! As our patron saint says, once you start spending money, it's hard to stop. It becomes a dollar here, a dollar there, all of a sudden your budget goes out of control. Just refuse to spend money.

"Get out of Los Angeles or New York," advises bi-coastal filmmaker Amy Talkington. "Go to communities where people are more excited about a little movie. I made my two first shorts in Long Island, and found a lot of people were interested in donating free things. In both cases, we needed a picture car. We went to parking lots near our shooting locations and put flyers under the windshield wipers saying 'Do you want to be in pictures?' And we got cars for free in both instances."

New York-based Madeleine Olnek took an opposite approach, shooting her entire student film in her local corner store. She got the store for free because she was a regular, although she did have to agree to let it stay open for business during shooting of *Hold Up*.

Be willing to ask for freebees for whatever you need. *That Strange Person* director Eileen O'Meara discovered a downside of this modus operandi. "Once you start to get everything for free, your film's credits become frightfully long," O'Meara sighs. One way to solve this problem is having two versions of your film. One is the "thanks version" which only exists on DVD and does indeed list all involved and their logos in large type. This version is given to everyone associated with the film. The other, "festival version" of your film, can have radically streamlined credits.

4

THINK ORGANICALLY.

If your studio is well financed, then you can be ambitious and plan on shooting anything anywhere. But if you're trying to stretch a buck, don't let your reach exceed your grasp. The best way to operate is to think organically. Organically means using people, places, and things that are naturally found near you, and coming up with stories that can use such elements.

The beauty of organic filmmaking is it results in a film that only you would make. Instead of adapting that Stephen King story you've always loved but will cost tens of thousands to do properly, take a walk around your neighborhood, look around your bedroom, investigate what's up in your grandparents' attic, check out that classic Chevy Nova your sister's no-good boyfriend is so proud of. These are unique things which only you have access to — for free. Other filmmakers are wasting weeks leaving notes on the windshields of Novas all over this country, begging for free access. You can get one anytime you want. What story can you tell using a Nova?

The universe has already lined up freebies for you if you would only open your eyes and look. Don't ask your volunteer art director to buy paints to alter a blank store window to read "Chicken For Sale" when a perfectly acceptable alternative might already be painted on the El Pollo restaurant two blocks from your house. You've got a home court advantage, use it!

5
IT'S JUST A MATTER OF GETTING THROUGH A NUMBER OF 'NO'S' UNTIL YOU HIT THAT ONE 'YES.'

As you've discovered, the trick to getting things for free is simply to ask for them. Sometimes you have to leave notes on 100 cars before an owner will call you back and say "yes." Sometimes the first person you approach will agree. When all this scrounging around gets you down, just remember there is a "yes" out there somewhere. What if you quit just five minutes before you come across it?

Why should people help you out? See rule number 6 below.

The same "yes" rule applies to festivals, as well. "I got seven rejection letters in a row," recalls *The Back Room* director Greg Ivan Smith. "And then in one weekend I got Outfest on Saturday, and Palm Springs on Sunday. Which were two of the big ones I really wanted to get into. Then that night, I was entering them into Withoutabox and noticed next to Rhode Island it said 'accepted'! Since then, I've gotten into four or five others."

6
YOU ARE A VERY TALENTED FILMMAKER WHO IS GOING TO GO FAR. PEOPLE ARE LUCKY TO BE WORKING WITH YOU.

This is the easiest principle of all to remember because you know it's true, but it doesn't hurt to remind yourself of it when you feel weird about begging. If Spielberg asked you to come work on his film for free, would you say "yes"? You're not Spielberg yet, but you might be. This is why people will say "yes" to you, too.

Remember, shorts are where the most exciting work is taking place. Most industry professionals wish they could work on projects they passionately believed in. Your passion and determination are very attractive to them. They want you to be a genius. They want you to achieve your dream. They want to be on your team. They want to be nice guys. Give them the opportunity to do so. Go ahead. Ask.

Number One Fan director Amy Talkington is great at asking. "I really wanted my first short to look great and have a dark, moody feel," Talkington says. "There's a director of photography whose work I had admired, Jim Denault. He had shot Michael Almereyda's films and many other features. [He's since done *Boys Don't Cry*.] I picked up the phone, dialed information — and he was listed! I called, he answered. I told him that I was a film student and had a script, that I knew he wasn't doing short films anymore, but would he take a look at it? He said, 'Sure, shove it under my door.' I did, he loved it, we met, he did the film for free. The lesson I learned is don't assume that someone doesn't want to do your project. If you have something that you're passionate about, and it's interesting, you'll be surprised what high levels of people are interested in coming along for the ride."

You will be a paying client for the rest of your career. Vendors want your business. Just remind yourself of this when you approach vendors. It is why you will get free film, free cameras, free lights, free dollies, free processing, free telecine, free titles, etc. Kodak wants to get you while you're young and impressionable. That's why they give student discounts. Panavision wants you to know no other camera but theirs. That's why they will lend an inexperienced cinematographer extremely expensive equipment.

Why should a rental house do you a favor? Because you will give them loyalty for the rest of your career. Or so they hope. It's a buyer's market, even if you're not really buying right now. So go into rental houses to investigate the equipment. Get free lessons. Ask to borrow that Hi-Def camera for the weekend so you can do some tests before committing to rent it for your four-week-long feature film shoot (lie). That's how free cameras are unofficially scored.

The same desire to be in business with short filmmakers as they grow into successful feature filmmakers also dominates the festival circuit. Having you as "alumni" is something they want to brag about. For example, the Los Angeles Short Fest claims, "We have a proud history, 30 of our festival shorts have received Oscar nominations, including nine winners." Even the Oscars aren't immune. Every year when they announce the winners of the Student Academy Awards, they remind everyone that "past Student Academy Award winners have gone on to receive 35 Oscar nominations and have won or shared six Academy Awards."

7
SHORTS ARE LEARNING EXPERIENCES FOR EVERYONE.

Festival programmers and short-film distributors will tell you that they watch thousands of painfully amateurish disasters every year. Not that this is a surprise to anyone, because shorts are generally made by first-time directors trying to learn their craft. The proliferation of inexpensive digital cameras and editing systems means more people are giving filmmaking their best shot. Let's just say not everyone who dreams of growing up to be Martin Scorsese turns out to be as talented as Martin Scorsese.

The important thing to remember is that the world doesn't need another Martin Scorsese. That slot is already filled, thank you. So give yourself a break if your little boxing piece isn't quite up to *Raging Bull* standards. However, if your film really is a disaster, you as the studio can make the decision to shelve it. No need to admit the real reason that film is no longer on your release schedule. Lie and tell people that the lab ruined your negative, or the editing system crashed. Mark the disaster down as a learning experience and move on. But don't be too hasty. Most filmmakers cringe in horror when they go back to see their first efforts. Even George Lucas, who still hasn't learned pacing, must think his student film is ungodly long (it is!). But that doesn't mean you and I aren't interested in seeing it. What if George put *Electric Labyrinth: THX 1138 4EB* in the vault and never let anyone see it?

Thankfully, Lucas knows (and we know) that shorts are a learning experience for everyone.

This rule, which applies to you as a filmmaker, also applies to everyone else involved in your project. If you're lucky and very connected, you might get Spielberg's DP to shoot your film. But more likely you'll get the camera assistant who pulls focus on Spielberg's second unit to be your DP. Everyone wants to move up the ranks, and one way to build up experience and credits is to work on shorts. Will this lowly camera operator make mistakes that a seasoned pro wouldn't? Yes. But before you kill him, remind yourself that shorts are a learning experience for everyone.

RECAP

- When you assume the role of a studio, you are responsible for everything. Do whatever you want, but take responsibility for your actions.

- Give people the privilege of helping you achieve your dream.

- Look around you for valuable things you can get for free.

- You can make a living as a short filmmaker if you can develop a solid fan base willing to buy your work.

- When things go wrong (and they will), avoid getting an ulcer by remembering that shorts are a learning experience for everyone.

CHAPTER 5

WHAT KIND OF SHORT SHOULD YOU MAKE?

MAKE THE KIND OF FILM
THAT YOU WANT TO MAKE,
CAN MAKE, AND SHOULD
MAKE.

Whet hen Dave Silver came up with the idea for his film *Gasline*, he didn't think, "Ah, this will win me the Jury Award at the Sundance Film Festival!" It just so happened that it did. But Silver's real motivation was his love of storytelling. He wanted to capture on film something he had remembered from growing up during the 1970s. The result was a 16-minute tale about a gas station during a fuel shortage.

"Stay true to the film you want to make," advises Trevor Groth, senior programmer at the Sundance Film Festival. "There aren't any boundaries or set rules that you have to follow. That's the beauty of a short. It's whatever you want to make it. Just stay true to your passion and tell the story you want to tell."

John Halecky, who worked for the pioneering short-film viewing website *IFILM.com* (now *Spiketv.com*), agrees. "At IFILM, we would always tell filmmakers 'don't alter your ideas because you think your film might not look as good on the Web, or you don't think a distributor will buy it, or it may not play well at festivals. If you do that, then you're not making the film you want to make. Just tell a good story. And make it something that people want to watch.'"

When I interviewed the Dean of Columbia University's film school for *indieWIRE* after a remarkable 10 out of the 71 official short-film selections of the 2007 Sundance Film Festival were made by his students, he said there was no magic formula other than "the nature of our program, which treats all aspects of film-making from the point of view of storytelling. That's been very successful for us."

AMAZE US

In most cases, short filmmakers have the kind of absolute creative freedom that feature directors dream of. Because you are your own studio, you control your own budget, get final cut, and have total say on marketing. Because the format itself has no rules regarding length, structure, or content, anything goes. "You'll see stuff you couldn't imagine," marvels Sundance's Groth.

Take the Jesus film, for example. While poor Martin Scorsese was practically crucified for making the controversial feature *The Last Temptation of Christ*, short filmmakers fearlessly produce much more outrageous Christ stories all the time. Who can forget *Spirit of Christmas*, in which Jesus wrestles Santa in front of an audience of profanity-spewing South Park boys? Perhaps because Jesus is such an established figure that filmmakers don't have to waste time creating his character, Christ shows up in a wide variety of short films. Just when I thought Jesus Christ had been used in every possible way, a student in my short-film class shocked me by showing his film in which Hitler is revealed to be Christ. As I told the director at the time, "I've seen a lot of shorts with Jesus, and I've seen a lot with Hitler, but this is the first I've seen them together." If you want to make a short about Jesus (or Hitler), go ahead. Just be original and unique.

AND THEN THERE WAS STAR WARS

John Halecky laughingly offers up a mock formula for guaranteed success — at least with male viewers on the Internet. "If you're making a short film that you really want to get a lot of eyes to, it better be about sex or *Star Wars*. If you make one that has sex *and Star Wars*, you've got a hit on your hands!"

On the *FunnyorDie* website, the title of the second most popular video ever is *Masturbation*, while the man-eating-porn *Pornocopia* is also a big draw. It's obvious why sex is popular, but why *Star Wars*? Probably because it's a film that continues to be a touchstone for generations of filmmakers. And like Jesus, everyone knows the characters, what they look like and represent. Just the title *Chad Vader: Day Shift Manager* has a certain "want-to-see" appeal.

So let's say you want to make a *Star Wars* homage film. If you're Kevin Rubio with access to extensive postproduction favors and a costumer who can pull together very realistic storm trooper uniforms on a penny, then you can achieve something like *Troops*, a "what if you do *Cops* with storm troopers?" noodle of an idea that became an 11-minute cult classic. If you're Joe Nussbaum with a production company willing to finance a fairly big-budget shoot and a friend who looks a lot like young George Lucas, you can pull off a slick *Shakespeare in Love* parody called *George Lucas in Love*. Of if you're Ernie Fosselius, a visionary genius who pioneered the *Star Wars* parody business with *Hardware Wars*, you could create perhaps one of the most enduring, beloved, and financially successful low-rent shorts of all time.

There are a million ways to do a riff on *Star Wars*. Do a search and you'll find the many that have already been made for the Fan Film contest. If you want to do one, first come up with an original twist, then evaluate whether you can bring your concept off. Do you have the skills, resources, and finances to do it right? If not, you can still give it your best shot and have fun doing it. But be aware that it's hard to parlay a *Star Wars* short into anything more because many superior filmmakers have already beaten you to the punch — do you really want to compete against *George Lucas in Love*, *Troops*, or *Hardware Wars* with inferior material?

If the piece you really want to do is something beyond your capabilities at this point in time, put it aside until you are ready. In the meantime, think of another piece that you can do and do well. Then attempt your grand masterpiece as your next project. If you still want to.

IDEAS CAN COME FROM ANYWHERE

Don't be afraid to talk to people about your short-film ideas. You never know what ideas might be spurred. For example, Hollywood actor Matthew Modine came up with his best short-film idea while promoting a big Hollywood film. "I was doing a pirate film in Malta, quite an expensive pirate movie. And I was doing some publicity with someone who had seen my two short films at the Sundance Film Festival, loved them, was encouraging me to continue to make films, and asked me if I had one that I was working on. Wanting to keep my hat in the arena (as they say), I started bullshitting about how I was going to make a film while I was on this film. The reporter said 'Oh really, what's it about?' I replied, 'Well, it's a story about a boy who gets kidnapped and taken aboard a pirate ship and he learns to accept things that are beyond his power.' The reporter said, 'Wow, that sounds fantastic.' When I hung up the phone, I thought, you know what, it does sound like a really fantastic film. I had a bunch of film with me, 16mm film, certainly enough to shoot a good 15- to 20-minute short film. So I wrote the screenplay and filmed it. And I think it's my favorite short film I've made."

Mark Borchardt recalls, "When I was growing up, I'd say to people, 'Hey, man, I want to make a film about this dude delivering newspapers.' And they'd laugh and say, 'You're not making a movie, you're making something about yourself.' Their idea of a movie was drug lords with machine guns and dark sunglasses.

That's what qualifies as subject matter for films. Which is bullshit. Obviously. Think for yourself. Give your own ideas birth. Time goes by so quickly that you really need to stop and think clearly about what you're doing. Don't let other people and situations dissuade you."

THINK AHEAD

The important thing to remember is the film you make does brand you. Shorts are a way of establishing your persona as a filmmaker. Filmmaker David Birdsell made a short featuring a pug; Hollywood studio executives offered him dog projects. If your ultimate goal is to be directing *My Friend Flicka* remakes for the Disney Channel, doing a *Star Wars* parody is probably not the best use of your resources.

So before you begin your filmmaking career, take an assessment of who you are and where you want to go. Once you know that (and that's big), look at what you actually can do.

First, list five feature films you wished you had made. What do they have in common? This should help define your personal style. If you wanted to make a film similar to those films, what would you need? If you like dramatic character pieces, you'll need a strong story, good dialogue, and talented actors. If you like war movies, your story might be inspired by a visit to the local army surplus store where you can score free props and wardrobe.

Let's say you have the perfect idea for a short — it's something unique and special, reflects your taste, and shows potential employers what you can you do. But realistically, you'll have to shoot for five days, feeding at least 20 people. Even if there were no other costs but $10 a meal for 20 people for five days, you need $1,000 to get through production. If you don't have a grand, you can either wait until you can raise that money, or you can come up with another idea that you can do well within your means.

A frustrated filmmaker named Nicole emailed me: "I am currently planning the productions for three very short videos set in homes. However, I have encountered problems with finding and securing a location. One of the short movies that I made in the past was shot at my mother's house. After experiencing trouble with people who were not involved in the production, I decided that in the future, I would not shoot at a friend or relative's house. I have posted classifieds on Craigslist as a last resort. However, I have been scolded by a close friend who is concerned about safety when shooting at a stranger's house. I am very frustrated because I have spent over three months trying to find a home to shoot in. My budget is $50, which will be used for videotape and snacks for the actors." Based on all the trauma Nichole already experienced involving houses, all signs clearly point to the fact that her "studio" shouldn't be making shorts based around houses. The question to ask is whether the stories can be reset in a different type of location, perhaps outdoors in a public spot? If not, I'd recommend scrapping the films and spending the $50 on another idea.

Don't get sold on one idea that you must, must, must make. There are millions of ideas out there. It's like shopping. You have to take a bunch of stuff into the dressing room, try them all on, and only buy what looks best on you. Perhaps you need to put something back on the rack and shop around just to make sure, then come back later to purchase it.

Take filmmaker Noah Edelson, for example. He's a funny guy who has a hundred funny ideas for short films. He's got one called *He Had a Hat*. It starts with an old lady walking down the beach with her grandson (please note that Noah is the one who complains that all shorts begin with someone walking somewhere — and here his film starts with someone walking!). All of a sudden a huge wave crashes to shore and drags the little boy out to sea. The old woman drops to her knees and prays. Her dialogue is something like "Dear God, I'll be eternally grateful if you bring my grandson back alive." Another huge wave hits, this time returning the little boy, who is sopping wet but miraculously alive. The old lady responds (to God), "He had a hat!"

Noah lives in Los Angeles, so the beach isn't a problem, nor are the actors. The problem? The huge wave. Unlike *Troops* director Kevin Rubio, Noah doesn't know special effects people who could do this for him for free. He could have made some cold calls to companies that specialize in CGI, getting through the "noes" until he found a "yes," but he decided to put this idea aside and do something that didn't require CGI. By the way, Noah still might do *He Had a Hat* one day, so don't steal the idea!

On the other hand, you may be at the stage of your filmmaking career where you need to take it up to the next level. "You reach a point in which you need to show your talent in the most expensive way," Spanish filmmaker Nacho Vigalondo told the Los Angeles Times when justifying why he shot his musical *7:35 in the Morning (7:35 de la Mañana)* in 35mm. The three-day shoot in a local bar cost the equivalent of $25,000 (U.S. dollars). It also netted him an Oscar nomination and launched him as a filmmaker in the United States. I think we'd all agree the investment paid off.

FOOLPROOF SHORT-FILM FORMULAS

If you're shopping around for a short film to make but don't have an already existing idea, you might be inspired by these tried and true formulas.

■ PARODY/HOMAGE

You can take almost any feature film and find a way to lampoon it. One notorious example was *Saving Ryan's Privates*. As you can probably surmise, it had a lot of penis jokes. A parody can do very well in Hollywood and very often land the filmmaker an agent ("funny is money," as they say). It's also an easy way to come up with an idea because you don't have to start from scratch. If you sit down and think for five minutes, you can probably come up with a parody that you can easily knock off for no money with a borrowed DV camera. Brainstorming parodies in my short-film class, filmmaker Jakob White came up with *My Big Fat Hillbilly Wedding*. Googling "YouTube parodies" I came across a blog with an embedded video identified *Obama-Clinton Star Wars YouTube Parody"* — of course I watched it. I also found a link from *Businessweek.com* to an ad agency parody of *A Few Good Men*. Why not shoot a quick parody, just for kicks? Put it up on YouTube, see what happens. Meanwhile, you'll be even more confident about tackling your "real film," having logged some experience behind the camera.

One caveat: parodies don't do well on the festival circuit. "A parody, however loving and funny it can be, is often something that capitalizes on the moment and that's all it has to offer," explains short-film consultant Thomas Ethan Harris. "In other words, there are very few *George Lucas in Loves*. That film is an all-out creative original approach to telling the backstory of how *Star Wars* came to exist. And it's a very good film, very good filmmaking. But most people are taking the conceits of *Memento* or whatever, and they're just riffing on them. I always feel a little empty inside when I watch a parody. And I wonder where the creativity went."

■ ADAPTED WORKS

Many short filmmakers want to adapt something that already exists, such as a classic short story. Parodies you can do without getting permission (although you do have to be careful about copyrighted or trademarked elements), but fashioning a legitimate adaptation of previously published material requires permission.

Let's say you want to adapt a Stephen King story. King's work is actually the easiest to adapt since he has a policy in place to grant filmmakers permission to adapt his works under his "Dollar Baby" policy. To go about contacting other authors properly, you need to contact their representatives. To do this, you look to see which company originally published the book or short story, then contact that publishing house's subsidiary rights department.

You'll most likely be forwarded on to the agent who represents the author for film and television sales. Contact that agent and explain that you would like to adapt the story as a short film.

Naturally, agents are in the business of generating revenue for their authors and taking a percentage of that revenue as their payment. As you might imagine, an agent, who has many clients and many money deals in various stages of negotiation, might not be thrilled to hear from you, a nobody filmmaker wanting to get the rights to adapt his client's story for free. Some agents will be extremely unhelpful. You'll have to win them over with your passion for the material. One way is to make it impossible to say "no" to you. If you can draw amazing storyboards, you might storyboard out your version of the film and mail it to the agent, who will, perhaps, feel obliged to send it on to the author rather than trashing it. You hope, then, that the author will be equally impressed.

What exactly are you asking for when you contact the writer's representative? You can ask for the ultimate — exclusive rights to adapt the original work in all formats, in perpetuity, through-out the universe — just like you would for a feature film. In reality, very few people will grant you such permission. Why should they?

Here are the two words you need to know because you will use them time and time again, as you approach rights holders: "gratis" — which is a fancy way of saying "free" — and "nonex-clusive." Nonexclusive means the original author can grant the story's film rights to you, to the next guy who asks, and anyone and everyone who comes along down the line. Therefore, the writer's not losing any money by giving it to you for free because he still maintains the rights to sell it to another filmmaker who might come along one day, with money. Of course, the only reason anyone will do this is if you promise you're not commer-cially exploiting the original work for financial gain. Because if there's money involved, people want to get paid. Instead, you're asking only for permission to make a piece of art that is a learn-ing experience and which will only be shown in festival settings. Many short filmmakers have been able to score nonexclusive fes-tival rights, gratis, from pretty big authors.

Before you start tracking down Stephen King's "Dollar Baby" agreement, think about whether you really should do an adaptation. Although the obvious advantage is that there's a built-in interest factor in a King adaptation (festivals will want to book it because they know audiences will be interested), you won't necessarily benefit. If people like the film, they'll ascribe all the good things to King. Additionally, if you do a great job with your adaptation, you'll get offers from television stations and DVD companies to license the film, but you'll be hamstrung by your agreement with King not to commercially exploit the film. Although you say you don't care about commercial exhibition now, you will once you're in massive credit card debt and people are dangling a few thousand in front of you.

Naturally, works that are in the public domain don't require permission. But you still have the problem that people will say, "Sure she did a good adaptation of *Occurrence at Owl Creek Bridge*, but can she come up with an original idea of her own?" Save adaptations for later. Find something you want to adapt into a feature, then when you get meetings with Hollywood executives based on your outstanding original short film and they ask you if you have something you want to do next, bring up the adaptation. Make the studio execs do the legwork of securing the rights for you. Have them pay you to do the adaptation. That's a much better plan of action.

■ CELEBRITY SHORT

The three biggest North American short-film festivals (based in Toronto, Los Angeles, and Palm Springs) all program approximately 300 shorts every year. And of that 300, there's always a special screening of celebrity shorts. Those are shorts that have well-known actors in major roles or are written, directed or produced by stars. In 2008, Palm Springs Shortfest proudly included in its press release that it had: Kate Hudson directing *Cutlass* starring Dakota Fanning, Virginia Madsen, Kurt Russell, and Chevy Chase; Kirsten Dunst directing *Welcome* starring Winona Ryder;

Matthew Modine directing and starring in *I Think I Thought;* Jessica Biel starring in and producing *Hole in the Paper Sky;* Dana Delany starring in *Flying Lessons;* David Arquette in *Nosebleed;* Rainn Wilson in *Missing Pieces;* Tony Shalhoub in *LA Actors;* Whoopi Goldberg narrating *The Descendant;* Sir Ian McKellen as a character in the animated *For the Love of God;* and Robert Redford providing narration for *The New Environmentalists.*

If you can get a celebrity to be in your short, your short now falls into the "celebrity" category and will get a lot of festival play and press — if it's good. Shane Smith, who is one of the short-film programmers at the Sundance Film Festival, assures us that there are a lot more bad celebrity shorts that don't get programmed.

On the Web, celebrity shorts are also big attention getters. Dan Beers' *FCU: Fact Checkers Unit* on *FunnyorDie.com* is a big hit not only because it's a funny film but because Bill Murray is in it.

If you have a connection to a celebrity, why not think of a story you can frame around him/her?

■ MOCKUMENTARY

Mockumentaries work particularly well in the short format and are fun to make. Director Brian McDonald had great success with *White Face*, which he shot for a grand and has earned him a hundred times its budget back. "It's weird, though, because it didn't help me the way I thought it would, as a sample of my writing and directing," McDonald admits. "Because the way the film is, I really worked hard to get very natural performances and to adhere to the documentary form. So people think the performances are improv — even though it's fully scripted, and the script won an award, and the movie is almost exactly like the script. People think, 'Well, the actors made it up, and Brian caught it on film.' So the film actually does better than I do! For example, I had a major star's production company call me after they saw the movie. They said, 'We just can't tell if you can direct from this film.' The problem is it's a mockumentary. Next time, I have to make a film that looks like a film."

■ WEEKEND PRODUCTION

There is a magic formula that many short filmmakers swear by — including me. I firmly believe making a weekend short is the best way to get the most bang for your buck. If you rent equipment on Friday, you only pay one rental day and you can keep everything until Monday morning. You can easily recruit crew and actors for the weekend because you're not impinging on their workweek. Ditto locations.

The most economical weekend shoot is one day, one location. The second is two days, one location. Lastly, one or two days, many locations. Knowing these boundaries, can you come up with a story you can do well?

If you like these constraints, you might go the extra yard and apply for the various 48-hour film contests. Many people find having to shoot and edit an entire film in two days can be creatively freeing. We'll talk more about this in Chapter 7.

■ LOCATION-INSPIRED STORY

Is there an intriguing location that you can get free access to? Can you create a story around it? David Birdsell found this odd street in downtown Los Angeles when he was scouting for his first short, *Blue City*. He was fascinated by the two palm trees in the middle of that industrial setting. When it came time to make a second short, *Phil Touches Flo*, he set his story on that street.

Nacho Vigalondo set his short *Choque* in a bumper car arcade. In the film, kids who rule the arcade menace a successful young businessman trying to impress his date. "The place itself is a real location under La Gran Vía (Madrid's Broadway, more or less)," reports Vigalondo. "I used to spend my loneliest moments there, playing with the plastic guns, surrounded by younger people. It's a very strange place with different rules than the surface, and I had this idea about a winner trying to win a game in a world where he's a loser."

■ PERSONALITY-INSPIRED SHOWCASE

Do you know someone who deserves to be in pictures? Not an already existing star, but someone who has such a strong persona that you think he or she can carry a film. Write something for him to star in. Or perhaps you're an actor creating a showcase for yourself. If that's the case, make sure you do yourself justice. Before he was a big movie star, Vin Diesel wrote, directed, and acted in a short he called *Multifacial*. The flick starts off with Vin telling a story about proposing to his girlfriend in a restaurant. The reveal is that he's actually auditioning for a part in a movie. The short becomes a series of auditions, none of which he gets because he's either too black, too white, too Italian, etc. *Multifacial* is not only a great showcase for Vin's range as an actor, it has something to say about identity and race. It was on the basis of that short that Spielberg cast Diesel in *Saving Private Ryan*.

Of course, the "personality" doesn't have to be an actor. Perhaps it's a neighbor. David Birdsell was so inspired by his friend's feisty little old lady neighbor that he cast her as the title character in his most recent short film, *Hairlady*.

Shorts centered around a strong personality tend to do well on line, especially if you can continue that character into a series of pieces. Loyal viewers are interested in following that personality's ongoing adventures and interacting with that character via postings, video tributes, etc. You may find that personality has a life outside of your short that you can further develop, turning that personality into a YouTube star.

■ A JOKE

As filmmaker Noah Edelson well knows, jokes with strong punch lines ("He had a hat!") work well as short films. The great thing about jokes is they have strong beginnings, middles, and ends.

For the online short-film class I teach, one assignment we always do is adapting "guy walks into a bar" jokes into short-film scripts. There are a million very cinematic variations on this theme. Matthew Modine describes his short *Cowboy* as "just a joke. I don't even know if you can call it a short film. It's just a cowboy goes into a bar – and that's it." If you know a joke, you can make a short film.

Urban myths also translate extremely well. Francine McDougall's *Pig!* is a prime example. *Pig!* begins with a snooty woman driving her Mercedes up a winding rural road. Coming down the road in the other direction is a motorscooter driven by a gross guy picking his nose. She yells out to the nosepicker, "Pig!" Cut to the sound of a crash. The motorscooter is flipped on its side as a big snorting pig wanders around in the middle of the road. That film did very well on the festival circuit and online.

■ SKILL-INSPIRED DEMO PIECE

Do you have a skill that you want to show off to get future work? Display your wares. Come up with a short that will also function as a demo. Perfect example: the guys who made one of the first Internet sensation films, *405,* about an airplane landing on the freeway, used computer programs such as LightWave 3D by Newtek, Digital Fusion by Eyeon Software, Adobe Photoshop, Adobe Premiere, and Illusion to make a heavily computer-generated short that rivals Michael Bay blockbusters. Needless to say, they got a lot of work off of that flick!

■ INTERNET OR CELL PHONE PIECES

While film festivals are great, only a few hundred people see your film at a festival. On the Web, your audience is in the millions. Think of the *lonelygirl15* pieces. Originally launched as a "real Web blog" but in reality crafted by professionals, the series has had more than 110 million combined viewers.

"Obviously, one of the most important things to remember if you want your film on the Internet, shorter is better," counsels *www.Atom.com*'s Megan O'Neill. "Comedies work very well. Also flash animation, and animation in general. Titles definitively matter online. We have a short by Amy Talkington called *Our Very First Sex Tape*, which has done tremendously well. When people see 'sex' in the title, they go right to that!"

Filmmaker Tara Veneruso has made shorts for both the Internet and cell phones. "Something that is going to be on a cell phone needs to be under two-minutes long," Veneruso explains. "It has to be something that someone can fast forward through, and it will have the same effect. Sound is extremely compressed, so minimal dialogue is good. Certain things work really well: parodies, comedies, but also experimental. In general, things you might imagine seeing on an old fashioned nickelodeon work well on new devices."

■ A SHORT THAT WANTS TO BE A FEATURE

Bottle Rocket began life as a short film. So did *Napoleon Dynamite* and *Half Nelson*. You can make a short that is either part of a larger project, or a short that can obviously be developed into a feature project.

Or you can make a short that is as ambitious in scope as a feature but is constrained by the short format. There are plusses and minuses to doing that. Columbia grad Amy Talkington recalls, "My first student film was 18-minutes long and it was sort of unresolved. It was an example of a feature story that was trying to be in a short film. A lot of feature producers were interest in talking to me about features because, while it wasn't the most successful short, it did display the ability to create a more complicated story and a more complicated character. It wasn't that successful of a short film, so it didn't make that leap for me, but it did get me some interest."

■ CONTEST FILM

There are so many contests popping up practically every day that if you want to make a film and you don't have a burning passion of what you want to make, why not make one specifically tailored for a contest. It could be a "make a film in a certain time period" type of contest (we'll talk more about that in Chapter 7). Or it could be a contest in which you are asked to make a specific type of film. For example, here's a contest that ran on Metacafe in June of 2008: "I Love NY Short Film Competition. Tell us what you love about New York State in a 60-second short film and you could win prizes, travel, and more!" Would entering such a contest be worth your while? Well, the prizes certainly could launch you as a filmmaker: The winning film got to be part of a commercial during the Macy's Thanksgiving Day Parade broadcast and appeared on IFC, jetBlue Airway's in-flight entertainment system, *nypost.com,* and at several NY film festivals.

The IFC Media Lab always seems to be running new contests (check out their website) and certainly *indieWIRE* is filled with notices of filmmaking contests. YouTube has a whole section on contests. Why not give it a shot? Who knows, you could end up winning enough cash to pay for your next film!

RECAP

- Stay true to your passion and tell the story you want to tell.

- Take advantage of the form's creative freedom to make something that is original and unique to you.

- It's better to mount a realistically scaled production that plays to your strengths rather than attempt a too-ambitious project that you can't do well.

- Don't make a film in a specific genre/style if that's not the direction you see yourself heading in the future.

- Your film will be judged against those that have come before it. Aim to make the best film you possibly can.

CHAPTER 6

TURNING YOUTUBE INTO METUBE

EXPLOIT YOUTUBE!

Every year I help program the American Cinematheque's Focus on Female Directors screening. To promote the screening in 2007, I cut a trailer that the Cinematheque posted on YouTube and then embedded the video on their official website and MySpace page. The following year we asked women filmmakers to make their own trailers and post on YouTube. All those trailers are still online, attracting viewers and promoting female directors. In fact, more people have seen the trailers than the actual screenings at the Cinematheque.

If you want to be a populist short filmmaker, i.e., making short films to reach the masses, the Web is the way to go. After all, as Peter Chernin, who oversees both MySpace and Fox Television likes to point out, "The homepage of MySpace has a bigger audience than *American Idol*, the number one television show."

While there is an ever-growing number of digital distribution platforms, there's no doubt about YouTube's popularity and power. Over 150,000 videos are uploaded to the site daily. It's the number one destination site for online video watching, accounting for 73% of visits to online video sites. As a comparison, in August of 2008, Hulu only had 2% of YouTube's traffic. On YouTube, 51% of users visit the site weekly, and 52% of the 18- to 34-year-old users share videos with others.

"Having produced over 25 short films and having watched hundreds, if not thousands," says producer Daniel Dubiecki, "I now find myself watching more shorts on YouTube. It is a very fair and democratic way of allowing people all over the globe to watch films, rate them, and have the opportunity to speak about their feelings."

Many people post their videos hoping to be discovered and make it big. The dream is to be like 18-year-old Bo Burnham, who began recording himself singing funny songs in his bedroom as a way to keep in touch with his college-bound older brother. Posting on YouTube, *Break.com*, MySpace, and *CollegeHumor.com*, his pieces racked up millions of hits and developed a hardcore group of followers way beyond the family members Burnham originally targeted. Hollywood took notice. Gersh talent agency and 3 Arts Management Company signed young Bo, who went on to showcase his comic and musical talents at the Just For Laughs Festival in Montreal. That live performance resulted in a four-album deal, a special with Comedy Central, and the attention of Judd Apatow, who hired Burnham to create and possibly star in a feature film.

But even David Lehre of *MySpace: The Movie* fame knows star-making online pieces are more the exception than the norm. Lehre is on record telling *The Washington Post*, "I'd say 99 percent of Internet [video] content is really, really bad. There's not like professional people doing strictly Internet video. It's mostly like kids lighting poop on fire. So I don't see the Internet being the place to go to harvest new talent. I see it being a pure entertainment forum where people turn their brains off and watch what's silly."

Whether you make your film originally for the Web or not, I truly believe most short films' final resting place will be on the Internet. That's not to say you have to put your entire short film up for free viewing right away. An excerpt or a trailer can do you just as much good. In fact, one of the biggest mistakes short film-makers make is posting their entire films online before they've exploited other markets. Before we go any farther, let's examine the benefits and consequences of online exhibition.

PROS OF PUTTING YOUR SHORT ONLINE

- You can reach a worldwide audience immediately. Your film is available to be seen by anyone in the world, 24 hours a day, 7 days a week, forever.

- You can receive direct, unfiltered feedback from viewers.

- Viewers can contact you. Who knows who might discover you online? And you can contact viewers, building a fan base for your other work.

- Your film can be linked to, and embedded in, other websites.

- You can potentially earn money via advertiser revenue sharing.

CONS OF PUTTING YOUR SHORT ONLINE

- Once your film goes online, you lose control of it. People can put it on other sites without your permission.

- You've invested a lot of time and money in your film. If you're not gaining anything financially from having it online, you're depreciating your investment.

- If people can watch your film for free online, they may not be willing to pay for it in other formats (i.e., via iTunes downloads, DVD purchases, etc).

- Festivals and television stations may not be willing to program your film if it's already exposed on the Web.

- The Academy of Motion Picture Arts & Sciences considers a short playing on the Internet as a "broadcast" and will consider your short ineligible for Oscar consideration unless you qualified it before it was broadcast (see Chapter 16 for more about the Academy rules).

WHAT TO PUT UP ON YOUTUBE

Time to think of yourself as a studio again. If you're Warner Bros. and you've just made *Dark Knight*, are you putting it directly on YouTube? No, but you're not avoiding YouTube either. You're putting your trailer up. You're putting interviews with the director and cast up. You probably even posted video diaries back during production. There's nothing to stop a short filmmaker from following the big studios' lead. However, as a studio making short films, you probably have a different agenda than the makers of *Dark Knight*. Your goal is not to push ticket buyers toward attending a theatrical release but to build interest in you and your talent.

If you're a personality-based filmmaker or you make comedies, YouTube is the perfect venue for launching your work. Luke Barats and Joe Bereta's *Mother's Day* captured 4.5 million viewers and got enough interest for NBC to commission the team to write and star in their own television pilot.

The beautiful thing about YouTube is everyone can truly make it MeTube. For example, I'm always encouraging my short-film students to enter filmmaking contests. Why not make a film for the contest, but then also upload it to YouTube? Even if you don't win the contest, you never know who might see it online and where that could lead you. South by Southwest Film Festival has an online contest called SXSWClick, and I've heard good things about Filmmaka. Building a catalogue of short pieces made for contests (or just for fun) and putting them up on YouTube never hurt anyone.

And let's not forget webisodes. If you're seriously interested in consistently making online pieces, you should consider creating a continuing series. Matt Bledsoe and Troy Hitch of the ad agency Big Fat Institute created the popular Internet series *You Suck at Photoshop* narrated by "Donnie Hoyle" (really voiced by co-director Hitch). Consisting of 10 episodes in the first season, the Web series notched over nine million page views and won Webby awards for "Best How-to" and "Best Comedy Series — People's Voice." It also became a cult sensation with many tribute videos being made by fans.

In fact, it seems like pieces anchored by strong personalities — a character that people are interested in interacting with and following his or her continued adventures — is the way to use YouTube to your advantage. Can you think of ways your main character might be able to be featured in a special piece you create strictly as a promotional piece on YouTube? For example, I remember seeing a student film that was quite funny called *My Roommate is a Ninja*. If *Ask a Ninja* didn't already exist, doing something like *Ask a Ninja* might be a great way to use the film's character in a series of promotional pieces to promote the actual short. Wouldn't it be gravy if the promotional pieces ended up making enough noise that you get noticed and great things started to happen for you?

HOW TO UPLOAD YOUR SHORT TO YOUTUBE

Uploading to YouTube is ridiculously easy. As the site spells out, YouTube can accept almost any video format for upload, but the following settings work best:

- Video Format: MPEG4 (Divx, Xvid)
- Resolution: 640x480 pixels
- Audio Format: MP3

- Frames per second: 30
- Maximum length: 10 minutes
- Maximum file size: 1 GB

YouTube accepts video files in the .AVI, .MOV, .WMV, and .MPG file formats. To upload, look on the upper-right-hand corner of any YouTube page for the "Upload" button. Upload time can range from minutes to hours. Of course, tech specs are always changing. Check the YouTube site to get the most up-to-date information.

Uploading is only part of the game. The other elements that you need to pay great attention to:

■ NAMING YOUR UPLOAD

Just like any other product hoping to attract consumers, the name of your film is vitally important in terms of attracting potential consumers. You need to be succinct and accurate, yet alluring. And as we already know, if you have "Sex" or "Star Wars" in your title, you're golden.

■ DESCRIBING YOUR VIDEO, CREATING TAGS AND IDENTIFYING THE CATEGORY

Make sure you're using words people will search for because the way YouTube suggests a video is via titles and tags. I can't emphasize enough the importance of crafting solid tags and titles. Before you write your own, search out highly trafficked videos that might share your same audience. Crib off their tags and titles. If you do it correctly, yours should pop up as a recommended video right after those traffic generators, allowing you to piggyback on their success. Don't forget to put in "short" or "short film" as part of your tags so people specifically searching for shorts will find you. If your film has a strong genre following (i.e., comedy or horror), the genre should be one of your tag words.

■ PICKING YOUR THUMBNAIL

The thumbnail is the still frame used to visually represent your film. Traditionally, YouTube automatically generates that image by isolating the image exactly midway through your upload. So if your piece is exactly five minutes, the image at 2.5 minutes is selected. Now you can have three randomly generated options to choose from, so make sure you pick the most alluring photo. A good image helps get some traction when it turns up in a search, but let's not forget it's less meaningful than tags when it comes to getting found in a search.

EMBEDDING IS EVERYTHING

The beauty of YouTube is that people can watch your film via outside sites, via embedded video. With the "share" button, YouTube makes it very convenient to post videos to MySpace, Facebook, and other platforms such as *Digg, del.icio.us, orkut, Bebo, StumbleUpon, Live Spaces, Mixx*, etc. Encourage others to embed, as well, using the html code provided.

Knowing that people will be watching your film outside the environment of YouTube, make sure you have a way to find you via your credits. Put your MySpace or dedicated website information in a readable-sized font at the end of your film.

BUILDING A CHANNEL AND A FAN BASE

As soon as you post your film, you get your own YouTube channel. As YouTube explains, "Your Channel's also an easy place for people to connect with you, to send you a message, share a channel, add you as a friend, or add comments to your Channel." Actively encourage others to seek yours out. Find other YouTube posters you like and subscribe to their channels. Pick favorite videos so people know what you're looking at and what you're into.

Build your subscriber base. Every time you post something new, your subscribers get a message. If people leave positive comments on your video, consider them part of your fan base. Don't hesitate to contact them and cultivate them. The YouTube audience loves interactivity. People love to know they're dialoguing directly with the filmmakers. Use your YouTube address book to keep a contact list, post bulletins, and send private messages. You want to make people feel like they are part of your journey as a filmmaker.

HOW TO BECOME VERY, VERY POPULAR

When it comes to numbers, popularity on YouTube is easy to track. Searching the most popular pieces "of all time," the top 10 are almost entirely music videos. In fact, the number one slot as of this writing is Avril Lavigne's *Girlfriend* with 102,054,384 views. Coming close on Avril's heels is one of the most famous user-generated pieces, comedian Justin Laipply's dance routine, *The Evolution of Dance,* which not only has 99,158,205 views but 229,553 comments. In comparison, a traditional narrative short film like *FCU: Fact Checkers Unit* (which, admittedly, is available on many different websites, so this is only a portion of its total audience) has 591,212 hits on YouTube and 1,620 comments. Although these aren't Avril-level numbers, how amazing to think over half a million people have seen your short film, and over 1,600 strangers cared enough to comment.

The fact remains that the true breakout stars from YouTube tend to be personalities rather than filmmakers doing traditional narrative work. You only have to watch Weezer's music video for *Pork and Beans* to be reminded of the most famous YouTube stars. Who are the big YouTube names getting deals with HBO? Video bloggers Kevin Wu (a.k.a. KevJumba) and Philip DeFranco (a.k.a. sxePhil). Michael Buckley of the *What the Buck Show* is another who has turned YouTube popularity into Hollywood deals.

One way to quickly increase your popularity is to get on the YouTube homepage as a featured video. Unfortunately, you can't suggest yourself — the featured videos are picked by YouTube Editors. I know a filmmaker who did an environmentally themed short film that someone posted on YouTube, without authorization, and without the filmmaker's knowledge — and the filmmaker only found out because the YouTube editors decided to feature his film on the front page on Earth Day. The filmmaker was completely flabbergasted by the whole experience — and ultimately thrilled that so many people watched his short film to celebrate Earth Day. If you have a film with a timely angle, you have a chance of being anointed with the front-page honor.

If you can't get prime placement, how can you increase your viewership? The harsh reality is your film's subject matter will dictate how big an audience you can attract. Chris Albrecht, who spent years programming shorts on *Atom.com*, sighs, "People prefer farts being lit on fire to artsy short films." He lists out what attracts online viewers: "animation, comedies, or anything that hints that there might be a bare boob."

It is possible to hire companies that can "guarantee" your short goes viral. But big businesses are trying to get in on this market, as well. How can you expect to compete with the big spenders? A more realistic plan would be to work the film yourself. Once you've notified all your personal contacts, it's time to reach out to strangers. See who has linked to YouTube films similar to yours and contact them, suggesting they might like linking to your video, as well. Use active sharing to see who else is watching when you are, then follow up by exploring users' recent histories. Click on play lists and use YouTube's "Watch" feature to reveal a list of all user playlists featuring the same video. Use the YouTube "Insight" tool to see how viewers are coming to your film. Troll message boards where potential viewers might lurk and post links to your film. As is always the case, the most dedicated promoter of your film is you.

Jennifer Chen from the Canadian short-movie channel Movieola has another suggestion. "You need somebody who is managing all the traffic, all the email blasts, all the communication — getting information out on all the different networking forums. Think about adding a dedicated communications person to your team. This doesn't have to be a professional publicist, just a person whose sole responsibility is promotion." Not a bad idea, especially since you don't want to spend all your time marketing when you should be making more films!

MAKING MONEY ONLINE

As YouTube continues to evolve, there will be more and more opportunities for short filmmakers to take advantage of. YouTube has recently opened a "Screening Room" to show curated shorts. These films are eligible for YouTube's revenue-sharing program, which is advertising based (the YouTube Screening Room also trumpets a "Buy Now" button, linking to websites selling DVDs and digital downloads). Of course, no one will publicly admit how much money can be earned from ad-share revenue. As of August 2008, YouTube was selling ads on fewer that 3% of its videos. But to give you a general idea of how much money you could potentially make, consider the fact that Metacafe was cited in a 2007 *Business Week* article as paying five dollars per thousand impressions to videomakers whose work passed the 20,000 views mark. Do the math.

Real money won't come from revenue splitting but from parlaying an online film or Web series popularity into other opportunities. Jennifer Chenn theorizes, "I think when anything's big on the Web, especially a Web series, what you want to do instantly is cash in with a broadcaster. Temporary take it off the Web and try to get a TV deal."

A QUICK WORD ABOUT PIRACY

Like the bigger studios, you should be concerned about fans who upload your film to YouTube without your permission. On one hand, you can consider any exposure good promotion. On the other hand, this unauthorized posting can torpedo potential television sales or ad-revenue sharing. YouTube does offer a video identification tool. If you're in the Partner program, you can set up a video-reference function where an automatic system will perform a search. If it finds pieces that match yours, you can have this bootleg posting left up (if you don't care), have it removed (if you want), or leave it up and claim it so you can receive ad-share revenue from that illegal posting, as well as your own authorized posting. As YouTube says, this tool gives you choices of how you want the piracy situation dealt with, as well as protecting the value of your piece.

BEYOND YOUTUBE

One of the most important words in the short filmmaker's vocabulary is "nonexclusive." When you decide to put your short on one website, make sure you're allowed to post it on others. If a website demands exclusivity, then you should be financially compensated. In today's landscape when new movie viewing platforms are bubbling up every day, you want to be free to put your short on all of them. The people who created the YouTube sensation *LonelyGirl15* made sure that their next series *The Resistance* could generate audiences across multiple websites including MySpace, Veoh, YouTube and Hulu, and of course their own website *LG15.com.*

There's an ever-expanding list of websites eager to share your short film with the world. If your goal is to make films seen by as many people as possible, then take advantage of every online distribution opportunity.

RECAP

• Words and images count. Make sure you've got the best title, description, tags, and thumbnail picture.

• Put your website or MySpace address in your credits so people can find you if they're watching your film via an embedded player on another site.

• You don't have to put your entire film on YouTube. Think about putting up a trailer, an outtake, a video diary, or a behind-the-scenes piece if you're not ready to host the entire film online.

• Work your YouTube fan base.

• Don't let YouTube be your only online platform. Once your piece goes online, post it on as many places as possible.

CHAPTER 7

RISING
TO THE
48-HOUR
CHALLENGE

YOU CAN SLEEP-IN NEXT
WEEKEND. THIS WEEKEND,
YOU'RE MAKING A FILM!

A student who took my online short filmmaking class sent me the following email: "Kim, I just wanted to thank you for inspiring me last spring. I entered the 48-Hour Film Festival and made a very good six-minute horror film. (We were unable to be judged due to late entry, our computer crashed for three hours!) Then I entered the National Film Challenge. I made a film in 68 hours and won Best Black Comedy! So thank you, Kim, for saying 'DO IT.' I did it, am doing it, and I LOVE IT!! With much appreciation, Michelle."

If you tend to procrastinate, or thrive under stress, or just love making movies quickly, you're a prime candidate for trying one of the many 48-hour-type filmmaking challenges. I guarantee you, too, are going to LOVE IT!

One of the most famous of these type of events, the 48-Hour Film Project, was started at the turn of this century and now takes place in over 70 cities worldwide, including Los Angeles, Salt Lake City, Amsterdam, Austin, and Tel Aviv. There are similar contests that take place in other cities and countries, and all pretty much run on the same set of rules. Before you plunk down your entry fee when such an event comes to your town, let's look at the pros and cons.

PROS OF DOING A 48-HOUR FILMMAKING CHALLENGE

- As long as you complete the challenge, you'll make a film and get another credit to your name, all within the time span of a weekend.

- You'll meet other local filmmakers and crew members who can be helpful to you in your future filmmaking career. For example, a 48-Hour Film Project in Pittsburgh had 200 actors, directors, and producers participate. What an amazing opportunity to meet everyone in your city who is interested in making shorts. In fact, if you don't feel up to directing yet, why not crew on someone else's film to get experience and meet people who can help you on your future film?

- Upon completion, your film will be shown in a movie theater and seen by a paying audience. Who knows where such a screening can lead?

- You could win one of the prizes at the contest, thus becoming an award-winning filmmaker. Traditionally, such contests give away a lot of prizes, so your chances are pretty good.

- You may get press coverage. Such festivals, especially in smaller towns, tend to get media attention. It's worth your effort to try to angle it so you and your film are featured.

CONS OF DOING A 48-HOUR FILMMAKING CHALLENGE

- There is an entry fee. If money is really tight, do you really want to waste money that could be better spent on your "real film"?

- There are mandatory story elements in a 48-hour film. We'll discuss this in more detail later in this chapter, but the 48-hour contests typically require you to include a specific line of dialogue, characters, and (most worrisome) a genre that may not be something that best represents you and your strengths as a filmmaker. For example, if your dream is to direct musicals, and you are given the genre of horror in a 48-film contest, will this be something you consider a worthwhile investment of your time and money? The concept of "You are the Studio" is definitely compromised by the mandates of the 48-hour filmmaking contest.

- The skills necessary in making a film in an insanely short time period might not be your strong point. Don't drive yourself crazy unnecessarily. If upon reading more about the ins and outs of the 48-hour contests you decide this simply isn't your type of thing, don't sign up.

- Most films made in a 48-hour film contest aren't up to the standards of other film festivals. It's more the exception than the rule that a 48-hour film (even a winning film) does well on the festival circuit.

- Many of the contests tie up the rights to your resulting film for Internet and/or television exhibition, especially if your film does well in the contest. This is not necessarily a bad thing (exposure is always good), but make sure you read the fine print regarding what you're giving up by making your film under the auspices of the contest.

SO, WHAT IS A 48-HOUR FILM CONTEST?

The contest is organized by a group that establishes the rules of the competition. Since the rules can change depending on who's organizing the contest, you should read all the specifics of your particular contest carefully. Generally, the contest begins with an opening ceremony of sorts on Friday night, at which time the teams that have signed up to participate are given their assignments. Usually the requirements include an assigned character, prop, and line of dialogue. Other variations include using a local landmark. How each team differs is by the genre of film, which the teams traditionally draw from a hat. The genre could be horror, science fiction, musical, etc.

For example, in the 2008 Quick Flix Challenge, the mandated elements were:

• Character: Radio Host/DJ

• Location: Dead end or abandoned road

• Prop: Takeout for Two box, containing a number of fortunes, mini-chopsticks, paper lanterns, and restaurant placemats with zodiac symbols on them

• Phrase: The game takes over your life

The winning film, *Takeout for Two*, became a tale of a Talk Radio host trapped in a time loop. (The film can be seen on YouTube)

Filmmakers are not allowed to do any "creative" preproduction before drawing the required elements/genre. Writing, costume/set design, shooting, editing, and sound design/scoring must occur within the contest's hours, which traditionally begin Friday evening at 7 p.m. and conclude with a race to deliver the master to the contest headquarters by 7 p.m. the following Sunday.

Each contest has its own specifics about how long the competition film can be, but generally it's less than 10 minutes. The length of credits is often also regulated.

Once the competition is completed, the public and the judges get to see the finished films at a celebratory screening in a local movie theater. Judging traditionally results in a wide array of awards, which may include Best Directing, Best Script, Best Cinematography, Best Editing, Best Acting, Best Use of Character, Best Use of Prop, Best Use of Line, Best Music, Best Sound Design, Best Effects. The "Best Film" prizewinner can go on to compete nationally if a countrywide challenge exists.

In each contest, the judging criteria should be clearly spelled out in the entry form, but usually it's a variation on these core elements:

- creativity/originality/entertainment value

- technical merit/production value

- adherence to the genre and assigned elements

Like "real" filmmaking, paperwork is a major part of the 48-hour challenge. Unlike "real" filmmaking, not doing the paperwork properly can disqualify you, so make sure you fill out everything correctly and clearly understand all the rules so you don't inadvertently break them. For example, some contests limit the number of cameras you can use during shooting. Almost all require you to use music that you have the rights to. Usually all permission forms are provided to teams in advance, or easily downloaded from the contest's website. If you're a teenage filmmaker, read the rules to see if you'll need a parental signature to participate.

In addition to the paperwork, delivery format is also crucial. Review the tech specs for delivery of your final product well in advance. Some contests will not accept DVD or QuickTime and will demand a tape format. There may be specifics regarding bars and tone and a countdown before your first frame of film. The ratio of final film may also be dictated, with 16:9 being the acceptable format or letterboxing being required. Most often, the festival will mandate that you include a statement that your film was produced as part of the contest in your end credits.

When you deliver your final film by the Sunday deadline, you won't be getting it back, so make sure what you deliver isn't your only "master." It's also a good idea (if the festival will allow it) to deliver two copies of your final film in case there's any trouble playing the master (better to be safe than sorry!).

THINKING AHEAD IS KEY

Even though you are restricted regarding what you can do creatively before you get your assignment on Friday, there are some simple things you can do that will give you a head start and a clear advantage over other "studios."

■ SOME PREPRODUCTION IS ALLOWED.

Double check the rules to make sure you are indeed allowed to do the following: organize your crew (including your postproduction folks), organize your cast, secure equipment, scout and secure locations, get releases signed.

■ IF YOUR HOST CITY HAS LIMITED FILMMAKING TOOLS, MAKE SURE YOU HAVE SECURED ESSENTIAL ELEMENTS IN ADVANCE.

For example, tripods are essential. If you don't own one and need to borrow one from the local school's equipment room, put your request in before anyone else does. If you think you'll want to borrow someone else's camera so you can have two cameras for your shoot, borrow it early and do tests in advance so you will be comfortable using it upon commencing photography.

■ TEST ALL EQUIPMENT AHEAD OF TIME.

This is especially true regarding your editing equipment. Make sure you know how to get the film from your camera into the computer, and then out again. Test and time the process so you'll know how much time you'll need to allow during the contest for such things.

■ SIGN UP A COMPOSER.

If you think you might want to include music (and you should — it adds a lot to your production value), find a composer ahead of time. Make sure you understand his/her technical and time requirements and he/she understands yours.

■ CAREFULLY CONSIDER YOUR CREW SIZE.

The 48-Hour Film Project reports that the smallest team they've had consisted of one person who set up the camera, then ran around to be "on-camera," while the largest team consisted of 108 people (let's assume most of those were actors!). You'll decide how many people work best for you. Just make sure that all know what they're supposed to do and are on the same page. This is supposed to be a fun endeavor, but it's a lot of pressure. You'll want your A-team on your side.

■ DO AS MUCH PAPERWORK AS POSSIBLE PRE-SHOOT.

Handle all administrative work while you're still thinking clearly and have time on your side. Get your potential cast and crew to sign the contest's release forms and get the correct spellings of their names for the film's credits.

■ MAKE ARRANGEMENTS FOR FEEDING YOUR CAST AND CREW.

Keeping everyone fed and hydrated is important on every production, but even more so on such a crazy breakneck schedule. You don't want to waste valuable shoot time trying to score food and beverage.

■ WATCH PREVIOUS WINNING FILMS.

Most contests will post the winning films on their websites. Additionally, YouTube is hosting many 48-hour films. See what others have done in the past in terms of production value, incorporating the required elements, and working out stories. This will give you a good sense of how high the bar is set.

BEING AN ORGANIC FILMMAKER IS KEY

When it comes to incorporating the required elements into your story, being an organic filmmaker works to your advantage here.

Before you even begin the contest, meet with your team and list out everything you have access to for free. List out locations, props, people/actors, etc. Make this list as long as possible because you never know what will work best with your assigned elements. For example, your little sister rides each week at a horse farm. The stable could be a great setting for any number of stories. Or perhaps you can use a horse as a character. Or a pitchfork and bale of hay. Secure permission to shoot there in advance (with the option to back out if the horse farm ultimately doesn't work for your needs), and be ready to pounce on your best elements. These are your assets.

Once you get your assignment, draw four big circles and put each element in a circle. For example, the most recent 48-Hour Project contest in Los Angeles had the following assigned elements:

• Character: Ronald or Rhonda Donnellson, Game Host

• Prop: 3 (or more) potatoes

• Line of Dialogue: "Leave it to me, I'm a professional."

So in one circle, you'd put "Ronald or Rhonda Donnellson, Game Host" — and then jot in the circle anything that you think would be part of the world of such a character. Let's say our team is going to use both Ronald and Rhonda Donnellson as characters. Judging from the names, they could be married or siblings. In their circle would be the career: the game show that they host.

In their personal life: their relationships. Then you'd list elements that might be part of either of those worlds. The more these elements are tied to the specific Game Hosts, Ronald & Rhonda Donnellson, the better.

In the next circle, you'd list the three (or more) potatoes — and list out elements that come to your mind when you think about potatoes. For example, they grow underground, they are bought at farmers markets, they can be peeled, they can be fried, they can be juggled, there are toy Mr. Potato Heads, Dan Quayle famously didn't know how to spell "potato," there was a potato famine in Ireland, etc.

Do the same thing with the line of dialogue and the genre you were given. Then take a look at all of your lists and see what kind of story you can come up with. Remember to keep referring to your "assets" list, so you don't settle on an idea that you can't execute quickly the following day. Since you have horse farm already lined up, how much intersection is there between your assets and your circles? In this case, not much, so you may have to scrap the horse farm location. Or you can commit to the horse ranch and decide Ronald and Rhonda Donnellson are divorcing game hosts who are arguing over every piece of co-owned property including their daughter and her potato-eating horse.

Another trick is to think about your ending first. A great ending will put you over the top, since most films made in a 48-hour time period (like skits on *Saturday Night Live*) tend to ramble on and then just stop. Having a solid open, middle, and ending will put you in good stead.

HOW TO MAKE A GREAT FILM IN TWO DAYS

While the limited time tends to encourage kamikaze filmmaking, it's important to retain control of the shoot experience.

■ AVOID BAD ACTING BY FITTING ACTORS INTO ROLES INSTEAD OF FITTING ROLES INTO ACTORS.

You're at a disadvantage since you don't know your characters ahead of time and you don't have time to audition. But as always, when working with actors, it's important to cast with an eye toward an actor's natural strength. Create roles that your pool of actors can handle. And don't give a role with a lot of dialogue to an inexperienced actor.

■ USE A TRIPOD.

Although the tendency is to go handheld, having steady camera work will give you technical superiority over the other amateurishly shot competitors.

■ KNOW WHEN TO STOP SHOOTING.

There's a reason why "real productions" have rules about limited shoot hours — exhaustion results in injury, faulty judgment, and often easily avoidable mistakes. If your Saturday shoot doesn't seem to have an end in sight, it's often smarter to call it a night and start up again on Sunday morning. Meanwhile, the editor works on what you already have shot overnight, while actors and crew can rest.

■ LEAVE TIME FOR TECHNICAL PROBLEMS.

Computers crash during editing. Traffic accidents happen on your way to delivering your master. Who knows what might go wrong? Don't sabotage everything you've achieved already by rushing to make the deadline.

■ FINISH THE FILM NO MATTER WHAT HAPPENS.

Read the rules, but some contests will let you screen at the big premiere even if you don't finish by the deadline. And even if the contest won't take your late submission, you'll want to finish anyway and post the result on YouTube. You've made a film, be proud of it!

RECAP

- Participating in a 48-Hour Filmmaking challenge can be a great way to tap into the filmmaking community in your town. If you're not ready to direct one yet, why not volunteer to be on someone else's crew to gain experience and network?

- Do as much preproduction as you can before the contest begins. Secure and test your equipment (especially cameras and editing systems) ahead of time.

- Make sure you read all the rules and have your paperwork properly filled out. Pay attention to delivery requirements beforehand.

- Creativity and originality count when it comes to making a successful 48-hour short. Don't take the obvious road when figuring out how to deal with your assigned elements.

- Use a tripod!

CHAPTER 8

BET ON ME: GETTING FUNDED

IF YOU CAN'T GET MONEY FROM OTHERS, RAISE THE CASH YOURSELF.

The question aspiring short filmmakers most often ask me is how can they get money to make a short film? Well, if you live in a country that actually cares about developing filmmaking talent, there is usually an entire government-supported grant system already set up. You may not be able to get all your funding from these organizations, but you can at least apply to get some of your budget covered. No matter where you live there are probably arts-oriented grants available to you. You just have to Google your way around the World Wide Web until you uncover them. Since free money is top on our list of free things, it's worth investigating what you can apply for. However, as Tricia Tuttle, editor of a U.K. guide to getting funding, reminded everyone on Film Network, "My advice would be to NOT expect to get funding and be prepared to make a short film without it. There are lots of filmmakers competing for very limited funds and you probably won't ever make a short if you wait for someone to give you money to do it. Shoo-ins? No, but the films which are more likely to get public funding are those whose makers have already made films on favors, gumption, micro-budgets, and credit cards."

"It's easier to find funding for a short film if the script is good," *Tanghi Argentini* director Guy Thys told the *Los Angeles Times* not long after his own short was nominated by the Academy of Motion Picture Arts & Sciences. "But if you get money from the government, it's not enough to make the whole picture, so you need to find more. And then that is more difficult when you make a short, because no one is interested."

So how do you get funding, then? It's easy.

GET MONEY FROM OTHER SOURCES

The first rule of filmmaking is don't spend your own money. Correction, that's the first rule of feature filmmaking. In short filmmaking, the director is usually bankrolling the project.

There are organizations that will give you money to make a short film. Because these opportunities come and go, do a Google search under "short-film funding" to see what's currently available.

Another thing to consider is corporate-sponsored films. Car companies like Ford gave filmmakers money to make short films featuring their Focus car. Jason Reitman made a terrific short called *Gulp* as a result. And, of course, BMW paid those big name directors to do flicks for their *www.bmwfilms.com* website. Quite frankly, who among us doesn't want a car company throwing money at us to make a film?

Recently, Xbox commissioned a series of horror mini movies to premiere on the game's live platform. The budget was a mere $10,000 and the directors had major credits: James Wan and Leigh Whannell (*Saw*), David Slade (*30 Days of Night*) and Andrew Douglas (*The Amityville Horror*). And for the past few years, Glamour Magazine has been laying out pretty major dough for female directors to turn reader's true-life stories into flashy short films. Again, it's been people who could afford to fund their own films who scored the Glamour funding: Gwyneth Paltrow, Kate Hudson, and Rita Wilson. If these sorts of commissioned opportunities are going to be snapped up by already established Hollywood heavyweights, how's a regular Joe supposed to compete?

The answer is you shouldn't waste time and energy worrying about sponsored gigs you'd never qualify for in the first place. There are plenty of other opportunities that will be geared toward everyday aspiring filmmakers like yourself.

As advertainment (as such sponsored pieces have been called) becomes more and more the norm, more opportunities will arise. If you can get such a gig, great! However, you must remember this paid-for piece will not reflect your personal vision; it will be a glorified commercial, with the money people's input overriding your creative voice. Still, it's somebody else paying you to direct, and isn't that what we all dream of?

If you discover a company currently funding shorts, your mindset should be, "They're going to give that money to someone, why shouldn't it be me?!" So go ahead and make a pitch, but don't sit around waiting for that money to land in your lap. Spending time researching sponsored programs and grants and then filling out the required paperwork can be an excuse not to cross the aspiring filmmaker/actual filmmaker bridge. So by all means, apply for funding, but also come up with a way that you can make the film you want to make on the money you, yourself, can raise. Maybe you need to put aside your big expensive sponsor-worthy idea and make a more modest alternative project, while waiting for that big money ship to come in.

APPLYING FOR GRANTS

In dealing with any kind of organization, you must read all the information available and pay attention to all rules and regulations (including deadlines). Take time to understand all the elements you are required to provide.

■ KEEP COPIES OF EVERYTHING YOU SUBMIT.

It's not only good to keep such paperwork as back up, you can cheat off this material when doing other applications.

■ SEND ALL REQUIRED MATERIAL, AND SIGN EVERYTHING.

Usually there's a checklist involved in the applications. Check things off as you complete them. Even something as stupid as forgetting to sign the printout can disqualify you.

■ ASK IF YOU CAN SEE AN EXAMPLE OF A PREVIOUS APPLICATION THAT WAS SUCCESSFUL.

If you think it's doable and suitable, it never hurts to contact the organization and ask. You'll understand if they say "no," but how helpful would it be if you have some sort of blueprint you could work off of?

■ MAKE SURE YOU ARE QUALIFIED TO APPLY.

Some funding requires previous work, others want newbies. Some will allow you to submit more than one project, others only one. Understand the parameters so you can take advantage of all angles.

■ HAVE A FLAWLESS PROJECT SYNOPSIS AND RESUME.

Almost every application will ask for a description of your project and a resume/bio of you and others involved. For description of the work, be specific and detailed. Ask someone not familiar with it to read it and tell you if they understand it. Often you're too close to your project to know if it is crystal clear to others who are unfamiliar with it.

■ HAVE A REALISTIC BUDGET.

Most applications will request to see your budget. Your budget doesn't have to be a multipage affair. Often a top-sheet summary is all that's required. But make sure it is accurate and professional. If you're asking people for money, they want to know that you know how to spend it wisely. Note: it's always fair to put in a fee for yourself as the director. Usually a percentage of the budget is the best way to go.

■ ADDITIONAL MATERIAL

Some applications allow you to add anything that you think will cause your proposal package to stand out (location photos, storyboards, past work, etc.). If you have such material, include it. Others won't want to see anything other than what's on their checklists. Don't risk alienating the organization by overwhelming them with material they aren't requesting.

■ LABEL EVERYTHING WITH YOUR NAME AND CONTACT INFORMATION.

Pieces get separated, and you don't want anything to be lost.

■ WHEN THERE'S A DEADLINE, APPLY EARLIER RATHER THAN LATER.

The majority of the applicants invariably wait until the very last minute to send in their proposals. In order to get the freshest eyes reading your proposal, be an early bird.

APPLYING FOR THINGS OTHER THAN MONEY

One of the biggest mistakes short filmmakers make is focusing on getting money rather than on getting free things. Rather than trying to raise enough money to buy or rent a camera, why not apply to the Panavision New Filmmakers Grant Program so you can be given a camera at no cost. Applying for grants that will give you free filmmaking tools (studio time, film, cameras, editing systems, sound-mixing sessions, etc.) are just as valuable as grants of cash. However, always read the fine print. For example, if you get the Panavision camera, you'll need to provide insurance (which costs money). Again, it's up to you to Google to find such grant opportunities, and it's up to you to decide if such applications are worth your while. Just don't overlook these grants because there's no actual cash involved.

WHO WINS GRANTS

Truthfully, many grants are political. The organizations have agendas, and they often award the grants to people they already have relationships with. An inside track is always a plus. As a general rule, grant-givers want to bet on someone who is so passionate he or she can't be resisted. This is where your successful filmmaker mantras come into play. It's just a matter of getting through the "noes" until you get a "yes." Make the heads of the organizations realize you're a talented filmmaker who is going to go far. Everyone wants to back a winner. Be the person they can't say "no" to. Be smart. Be courteous. Ask questions, but don't be annoying.

SPEND YOUR OWN MONEY

Everyone wants to use other people's money to make films. But realistically, you're probably going to fund your short yourself. It's time to look at your bank account or credit card limit and decide how much you can afford to spend right here, right now. Is  it $20,000? $2,000? $200? $20? If it's in the higher region, you can be more ambitious (shoot on film, shoot for several days, feed extras, etc.). However, even if it's $20, that's not going to stop you from making a film! With a $20 budget, your short might not be the grand opus you thought you were going to make, but you can still afford to run a tape through a borrowed mini-DV camera. You can still be a short filmmaker.

TEN EASY WAYS TO RAISE A LITTLE BIT OF CASH

Say you need more than twenty bucks. How can you get your hands on a little more dough?

1
GARAGE SALE

Time to turn purchases back into hard currency. Pick a good weekend to hold a garage sale, then ask your friends, family, neighbors, and coworkers to contribute their old junk. Before you put their things out for sale, go through the donations. Any good props or wardrobe you can use in your film? Anything that might fetch a better price on eBay?

2
EBAY

Sometimes junk that will go for $2.50 at a garage sale can be auctioned off for $25.00 on eBay. Why not give it a shot?

3
BAKE SALE

Set up a bake sale at your company's lunchroom. Convince your coworkers their money is better spent on homemade cupcakes than Starbucks. Earmark the money you raised for your production's future catering bill.

4
RENT PARTY

Think of it as a modest charity fundraiser. Or a house party with a cover charge. These parties have an additional benefit of being good networking opportunities. With friends bringing friends, who knows who will be hanging out in your kitchen? A musician whom you can talk into scoring your film? An artist who will help with set decoration? An actress who might be perfect for your lead? You never know! Bye the way, speaking of house parties, the feature film *House Party* was based on a short film. Bodes well for you, don't you think?

5
BENEFIT CONCERT

Ask the musicians who are going to do your film score to play the local bar as a fundraiser. It's certainly a lot less work for you than holding a garage sale or a rent party. And more fun, too.

6
FREE HAIRCUT DAY

Get inspired by Spike Lee's student film, *Joe's Bed-Stuy Barbershop: We Cut Heads*. The same benevolent hair and make-up artist who is going to volunteer to work on your film for free might be convinced to do a haircut marathon. The trick is to do men's hair only — much faster! With a suggested donation of $20 per head, those Andrew Jacksons can really add up.

7
SPONSORED STUNT

You know how you're always getting asked to sponsor someone's walkathon? It's payback time — their turn to sponsor you. You can do your own version of a walkathon, or you can do something more outrageous. It can be as silly as asking people to pay a certain amount per body you cram into a VW bug at the local Volkswagen dealership. Additionally, a stunt can be a priceless opportunity to get media attention. Let the local newspapers and television news stations know about your crazy event. Not only will local coverage give you something to put in your press kit, you never know what other opportunities might arise from having your community know about your project. Certainly it will be easier to ask favors later on when people have already heard about you and the outrageous things you'll do to become a filmmaker.

8
SELL YOUR BLOOD/SPERM

You won't even notice it's missing.

9
SELL YOUR DVD/CD COLLECTION

It's a tough bullet to bite, but you need the cash. You can always buy them again when you're rich. And, really, how many times do you need to watch *Reservoir Dogs* anyway? Follow the lead of Rab, who emailed me saying, "This weekend I bit the bullet, sold all my DVD collection, and game consoles, and such. I raised enough to buy a nice camera, and looked around and found a cheap 8mm camera in perfect condition. I found a place that turns the clips to DVD format, so I'm really excited to start playing around with that." This can be you!

10
SELL THANK YOU CREDITS

Otherwise known as asking your friends and relatives for cash. Time for those Facebook and Myspace friends to put a monetary value on that friendship. Work your networks, asking people if they will donate money in exchange for a credit in your film. Make it clear that their donation is neither an investment nor a tax-deductible charitable contribution. It is simply a gift that will be acknowledged with a "thank you" credit in the film.

MAKE AN "IN THE CAN" CONTRACT WITH YOURSELF

So how much money do you really need to make a short? This is where you have to change your way of thinking. Instead of thinking how much money you need, you need to think of how much you honestly can set aside for filmmaking, at this moment in time. Write that number down. Seal it in an envelope. Don't let anyone else know this magic number. Promise yourself you will not spend more than this number during production. No matter what!

What you have done by sealing that envelope is you've made a contract with yourself to not spend a dime more than that amount getting your film "in the can." By "in the can," I mean you have enough money to buy film (or tape), run it through the camera during production, and get the exposed film back into the can (or tape cassette box). Your next step is to move into postproduction (i.e., get the film out of the can). If you have enough money in that initial funding to get you through post and marketing, you're all set! If you don't, you'll have to raise more money. Time for another visit to the blood bank!

The good news is, unlike production, there's no real time crunch in post. Postproduction can take years (don't worry, yours won't). More good news: There are more opportunities to beg for free services in post and practically no people to feed (that's where the money goes in production). Plus, you'll be motivated by the experience of actually having shot your film. If you need to get a second job to raise the money, you'll do it. Or better yet, start right now sticking a little something away from each paycheck for your post budget. Don't forget that you'll need even more money for marketing. Some filmmakers advise setting aside at least $1,000 for playing the festival circuit. But let's not get ahead of ourselves.

You want to make a short film. With your envelope money, you now have the funds to make one. It may not be the grand opus you originally dreamed of, but you have enough money to make something. Congratulations!

RECAP

- When applying for grants, make sure your application is airtight.

- If you can find a company giving away money to make shorts, take the money! But, most likely, you'll finance your project yourself.

- Remember, you can apply for things other than money. Donated cameras, film, etc. all count toward reducing your budget.

- It may be hard to raise a lot of money, but it's not hard to raise a little.

- You don't have to raise your entire budget at once. Just set aside enough cash to get you through production.

PART II:
MAKING YOUR FILM

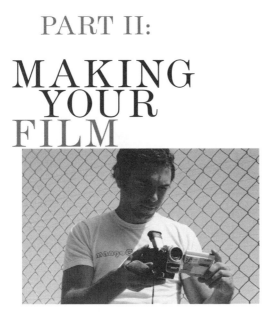

CHAPTER 9

FROM CONCEPT TO BLUEPRINT

WRITE SOMETHING YOU CAN MAKE.

Everybody has an idea for a short film. Take Lauren Beaumont. Lauren Beaumont came to visit her godmother in Los Angeles and was inspired to write a short. She set her story against the local landmarks she observed during her visit: Ralphs grocery store, Johnny Rockets, Jamba Juice, and Koo Koo Roo. For characters, she decided to include her godmother, Bear, and Bear's friend, Greg. Her stars, however, are five puppies who get free and roam the streets of Los Angeles. Her title: *Five Puppies on the Run.*

Lauren Beaumont is an organic filmmaker. She also under-stands the importance of fashioning a visual story that starts fast and strong. She, like many short filmmakers, ran out of steam before she came up with a killer ending for *Five Puppies on the Run*. But give her a break. She was only eight-years-old at the time. And give her credit: she picked up a pen (more accurately, a purple magic marker) and wrote and storyboarded her short, which is more than most wannabes do.

FIRST THINGS FIRST

Before you even begin writing a short-film script, take a few steps back and rethink everything we've covered so far. Your most important consideration is why — why make a short film? The reality is you don't have to make a short — there are more than enough of them already. Remember, you're most likely paying for the privilege of making your film. If you're doing something fairly big budget, you could probably buy a new car instead. Why not better invest your time writing a feature film screenplay? That doesn't cost anything, and you can potentially make a great deal of money as a screenwriter.

To make opening your studio worthwhile, you must be abso-lutely clear why you are making a short. If your motivation is to learn how to direct, then don't spend a lot of money. If your goal is to get a career as a Hollywood director, make something that will impress agents and studio executives. When I was produc-ing shorts for the Fox Movie Channel, our "Everything for Free!" modus operandi meant that we ended up shooting a lot of the shorts outside, in existing locations, in daylight. Although this didn't bother the filmmakers or anyone at the Fox Movie Channel, when I showed the shorts to an executive from Nickelodeon, she exclaimed in dismay, "All your shorts are shot on street corners!" Luckily, we weren't making shorts with the specific intention of impressing executives from Nickelodeon. Whatever your reason for making a film, don't lose sight of this original motivation.

YOU ARE GOING TO MAKE THIS FILM

"I'm always nervous about 'can I actually do it'... do I have the resources to make it?'" claims *Bad Animals* director David Birdsell. "Others write just whatever they want, and then worry about getting it later. Because they're good producer-types, they say, 'I can get 50 extras (or whatever).' For my first short, *Blue City*, I wrote it not knowing if I would ever be able to find streets like I had imagined. And I didn't really. But close enough." If you can't actually get 50 extras or the right streets, you need to rethink your story. When you write a short-film script, you're not fancifully sketching your dream house. You're carefully drafting a blueprint for a house you're building yourself.

HOW TO WRITE A GOOD SHORT-FILM SCRIPT

Just as a short story can't be constructed like a novel, a short film has to be crafted differently than a feature.

■ QUICKLY ESTABLISH YOUR SITUATION.

Look at Lauren Beaumont's script/storyboard. Her very first image is an establishing shot of the puppies in a cage. We don't need to know their backstory, why they're in a cage, who put them there, when that happened, etc. They're five puppies in a cage, and the film is called *Five Puppies on the Run*. The audience gets the point and is eager to get on with the adventure.

Danny Simon who, back in the day, wrote sketch comedy for Sid Caesar, had a good catchphrase to remind writers how important it is to immediately set up the situation and move on. His example was two men standing on a generic street corner. One man says, "Here we are in sunny Spain." Bam! The viewer immediately understands what the situation is and anticipates where the story might be going. Lauren's version of "here we are in sunny Spain" is the shot of the puppies in the cage.

▪ START YOUR STORY AS LATE AS POSSIBLE, AND END IT AS SOON AS POSSIBLE.

"A feature filmmaker has a long time to develop characters and to set the stage," remarks festival programmer Jennifer Stark. "A short filmmaker has to do that with an awful lot of economy. You have to be very focused and very succinct in how you're going to tell your story. Or you'll spend all your time just setting the stage and never actually doing anything."

▪ ALWAYS MOVE THE STORY FORWARD.

Every filmmaker encounters this universal problem: Scenes that you feel are crucial, that you insist get shot; you realize later in editing that those so-called essential scenes are superfluous. Be smart from the start. If a scene (or even a moment) doesn't move the story forward, cut it while your story is still in script form. Your goal should always be to make your plot as tight as possible.

▪ ADD A SENSE OF URGENCY.

If it seems like your story is moving slowly, think of a way to include a sense of urgency. Also known as a "ticking clock." In Lauren Beaumont's case, the adult characters of Bear and Greg should have a reason they have to recapture the puppies by a certain deadline. Or perhaps the puppies must reach a designated location before it's too late.

▪ USE DIALOGUE SPARINGLY.

You'll be surprised how many great short films have absolutely no dialogue. I'm not talking about the silent one-reelers of Laurel and Hardy. There are many modern day shorts that are dialogue-free. Why? Because shorts are such a visual medium that filmmakers can tell stories through pictures and actions instead of words. And because dialogue reveals the weakness of mediocre actors. Many a line has been spoken during production, then cut in editing in hopes of making the acting look better. "The first short I made was 12 minutes and there's no dialogue," remarks director Mat Fuller. "I know, it sounds like a boring art movie, but it's not. It has a climax. It builds. I've never had anyone tell me it's boring — even people I don't like!"

■ BE BRAVE IN YOUR CHOICES.

"In a short film, you can do things that a feature-length film just can't pull off," director Mark Borchardt reminds us. "You can ignore the three-act structure. You can break narrative rules. You can break a lot of rules. It's the arena of anything goes!"

■ END YOUR STORY WITH A BANG.

As you know from seeing countless bad skits on *Saturday Night Live*, it's crucial that you don't let your story limp to an ending just because you don't know exactly how to end it. In the case of Lauren Beaumont's puppies story, she can coast for quite some time with cute puppies racing through recognizable city settings, but for the short to really pay off, she needs a killer ending. In fact, killing the puppies isn't a bad way to cap that plot.

■ AVOID CLICHÉ STORYTELLING.

The war against cliché is something Fred G. Thorne fought stridently when teaching short-film screenwriting to university students. As a teaching tool, he created what he calls "a list of admonitions" to combat "the kind of subject a majority of contemporary university media arts students apparently find attractive. Following the imposition of new standards, my students became perennial winners of student national scriptwriting competitions." Thorne generously shares forbidden topics to help all of you avoid over-worn subject matter, advising "stay away from these subject areas. Find some other story to tell with interesting characters challenged by the circumstances into which they are propelled by story events and/or other characters in conflict."

• Student life, student parties, drug- or alcohol-induced events in sorority/fraternity life.

- Drunken trips to Tijuana to find sex as a 21st birthday gift for your bud or druggie trips to Las Vegas for a hot time or to help a friend find sex.

- Breaking up, dumb dates, or search for a sex partner.

- Sex as a weapon or habit, unnecessary/gratuitous violence (especially toward women), racism, or suicide.

- Rip-offs of TV shows.

Thorne adds, "Students collectively rolled up their sleeves and went to work when I asked them to explore their interests and hobbies as a starting point to the most interesting persons they know, themselves. It became a joy to be a teacher to help them fill their pages with stories of interest to other people."

TIME TO GET SERIOUS

Just because you have an idea and fleshed it out doesn't mean you have a script that you should make. Before your studio moves into preproduction, go through your screenplay and be your own harshest critic.

■ IS IT ESSENTIAL?

Your goal is to have the tightest script possible because — if you're like most short filmmakers — you, yourself, will have to materialize everything in that script. Is it essential the puppies run by Jamba Juice? Is it really worth your time and effort to get permission from Jamba Juice's corporate office — when in editing you're finally going to realize that puppies running by all those stores doesn't move the story forward fast enough and you'll cut back to only three stores anyway? Be ruthless, now, when it's all just theoretical.

■ CAN I MAKE IT BETTER?

Now that everything in your script is essential, you have to assess whether things could be better: more interesting, original, unique, unexpected, stronger, etc. Rather than just having Lauren's generic godmother and godmother's friend in the story, how could the "people" characters become more dynamic? How could they pump up the excitement factor of the puppies' adventure? Reexamine every element in the story to make sure it's the best it possibly can be.

■ DO I SEE IT IN MY HEAD?

After putting so much thought into your script, it's time to stop thinking and start seeing. Very soon you'll be storyboarding, but right now just stop and "see" your movie. If you're a good organic filmmaker, you probably already have locations and potential cast in mind. Close your eyes and run the movie in your head. Hopefully, you're already seeing specific shots, but it's okay if you aren't. After "watching" it, go back and re-read the script. How accurate was your vision? Are there things that you now can cut? Things that you might need to rethink, depending on the location? Things you need to clarify on paper so others will see what you see in your head? Now's the time to be specific.

■ CAN I REALLY DO IT?

Coming up with ideas is easy. Executing them is hard. You might have written a great script that you will indeed make into a short film — once you win the lottery. Right now, you're going to make

your script with the money you've set aside, and no more. Now it's time to do a little pre-preproduction. If Lauren is determined to have Ralphs, Jamba Juice, Johnny Rockets, and Koo Koo Roo, she needs to go visit those exact locations and talk to managers about how to get permission to include their stores in her film. If the corporations turn out to be uncooperative, she'll have to make some hard decisions.

■ WHAT CAN I CHANGE SO I CAN DO IT WITHIN MY
BUDGET AND RESOURCES?

If you don't want to give up, then you'll have to get creative. You
could write a script about a man on fire, but unless you know a guy
who can do the special effects for free, you really can't make the
film. *I'm On Fire*, in fact, is a short that writer/director Ryan Rowe
pitched to us at the Fox Movie Channel. My first concern was how
to do the extensive special effects of a man on fire — for no money.
The director, who is a comedy writer, said, "We'll just get a hobo
and light him on fire!" Joking, of course. We did call the fire expert
from the Spike Jonze Wax video (which consists of a guy on fire
walking down the street in extreme slow motion). Turns out it's
outrageously expensive each time you torch a stuntman. In the end,
the director found a guy who did special effects on the *Star Trek*
series who created the fire on his home computer after work.

■ AM I THE BEST PERSON TO TURN THIS STORY INTO A
FILM?

There's a reason that not all screenwriters are directors. You
might have come up with a great story and written the best
script that anyone has ever read, but that doesn't mean you're
the best person to direct the piece. As the studio, you must honestly decide whether you're going to hire yourself to direct. In
the case of little Lauren Beaumont, should she make *Five Puppies
on the Run* on her mom's home video camera right now or should
she wait until she grows up and goes to film school? No one can
make that decision except Lauren. However, I would argue that
a pre-teen would probably make a charmingly naïve film which
would most likely get a lot of festival play based on the little-girl-
filmmaker angle.

THINKING IN PICTURES

Okay, you've committed to this script. Let's jump forward to the
next step in turning your idea into a blueprint for filmmaking.
While the script can contain a general description of what you

have in mind, storyboards can make it specific. For example, for the Fox Movie Channel short *I'm on Fire*, the first shot reveals a typical Southern Californian suburban house with a convertible parked in the driveway. The front door flies open. A man, completely engulfed in flames, runs out, gets in his convertible, and drives away. Still on fire.

Do you really need to storyboard this? As with everything in short filmmaking, you can do whatever you want. But won't it help to know where exactly the car is parked in the driveway, which way the man runs to get into the car, and in which direction the car drives off? Are you going to shoot the scene entirely in a master shot, or you going to include some close-ups? The director wanted to shoot the entire scene in one uninterrupted master shot, with the camera observing the action from across the street. Here's the director's storyboard for this first scene:

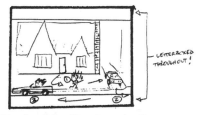

SC 1. MASTER ONLY. FADE UP ON HOUSE.
①GUY RUNS OUT FRONT DOOR, IN FLAMES.
②GETS IN CAR, BACKS OUT (POSS. OUT OF FRAME),
③DRIVES ACROSS FRAME R to L. FADE OUT.

HOW TO STORYBOARD

Because there are no rules, you can storyboard whichever way works best for you. The ones you see on DVDs or published in books are professional presentational storyboards. Short filmmakers have no need for such flashy artwork (unless you want it!). Some directors use stick figures, some do full-on illustrations. Some use computer programs, some do over-head camera plots. Don't let the fact that you "can't draw" stop you. Some directors go out to the location and take photographs with the appropriate lenses to previsualize. Even more popular are video storyboards

— using a home video camera to shoot scenes before you even begin production.

You are expressing visual information for the camera when you storyboard. This is the "composing" part of the director's job. Where is the camera in relation to the actor? What is visible in foreground and in the background? Is it a close-up or a master shot? Don't get trapped into thinking of static shots. Films are moving pictures. That's why arrows are your best friend when storyboarding. Express the action and camera movements with arrows. Don't forget transitions from scene to scene.

Here are a few tips for making storyboarding easier.

■ WHENEVER POSSIBLE, SECURE YOUR LOCATIONS FIRST.
Having the real location in mind can make storyboarding go much faster. Not having a location shouldn't stop you from doing drawings, but things will definitely change once you have the practical location.

■ TALK THROUGH THE SCRIPT WITH YOUR DIRECTOR OF PHOTOGRAPHY BEFORE BEGINNING TO STORYBOARD.
More than likely, while you talk, your DP will start making some preliminary sketches or ask you questions that will help clarify shots. Speaking about the pictures in your head before you document them will save you time and frustration.

■ IF YOU HAVE TOO MANY SHOTS TO DRAW, CUT BACK ON YOUR SHOTS.
If you feel like it's taking forever to storyboard everything you want to shoot, imagine how long it's going to take to actually shoot it. You're clearly being too ambitious. Scale back — now!

■ DON'T FEEL LIKE YOUR STORYBOARDS ARE SACROSANCT.
They're working documents. Feel free to use them however you want. Some filmmakers cut up the frames and put them on index cards, which can be shuffled around to make shot lists.

INSIDER INFORMATION ON THE
IMPORTANCE OF STORYBOARDING

In addition to being a talented short filmmaker, Robbie Consing is a storyboard artist who has worked on such major films as *Minority Report* and *Mission Impossible 2*. "If you don't storyboard your short film or have someone do it for you, you should be shot," Robbie proclaims. "You really should not even be allowed to do a short! Because this is your first film. You should not assume you know how to control a shot without having to have it already illustrated. Storyboarding forces you to think about your own movie. If you don't, if you don't come prepared, if you say 'I'll just tell them what to do on that day and we'll find it,' that's not exactly fair to your crew. Whatever inspiration you think you're going to get is going to kill them and you.

"Storyboarding is the way to get everyone started. The DP has to understand what you're talking about, and the actors have to know where they're blocking. If they don't know where they are going to be because you didn't take time to figure it out (especially since you're the one making up the schedule), what possible complaint can you have when things fall apart, organizationally? Storyboards are a shot list, first and foremost. The same way your script should be. If you're shooting junk, you're not going to have anything to cut when it comes to editing. Or too much to cut. With storyboarding, you can tell if your stuff is going to cut together.

"When it comes to directing, the only homework you really have as a short filmmaker (besides paying the tab) is storyboarding, rehearsing, and blocking. Because let's face it, what possible excuse do you have for not being prepared on your own set when all the elements, all the molecules, are all you?"

RECAP

- A good story is everything.

- Be ruthless about retooling your story and rewriting your script until every moment is the best it can possibly be.

- Before you sign off on your script, visualize the movie in your head.

- You don't have to be able to draw well to storyboard. Stick figures are perfectly fine.

- Don't be afraid to make changes as your start visualizing your story. Storyboarding should help you realize where you can cut back on your script.

BUDGETING: EVERYTHING FOR FREE

ONLY SPEND MONEY WHEN YOU MUST.

B udgeting is easy for short filmmakers who subscribe to the "Everything for Free! Everyone Works for Free!" mandate. We also know what our final production budget will be because we work backward from the amount of money we can spend — our "in the can" fund. Before we seriously dig into budgeting, we first have to breakdown the script to see what exactly we're going to be getting for free.

THINKING IN TERMS OF BIG TICKET ITEMS

Big ticket items traditionally refer to expensive items. Since, in theory, short filmmakers are not paying for anything, I define the term slightly differently. In the "beg, borrow, and steal" world, big ticket items are things you will not compromise on because you feel they are crucial to the success of your film — so crucial you may break your "Everything for Free!" rule to get them.

Guess what the two most essential big ticket items should be for every short film. Here's a clue: If they're sub par, they'll destroy your film. Yes, they are acting and sound. We'll discuss the pros and cons of hiring Screen Actors Guild talent in Chapter 11, but the reason why so many short filmmakers do sign with the Guild is they feel it's worth all the hassles SAG contracts entail to get the best actors they can. As for sound, sometimes you have to pay for good location sound. Any penny you try to save during production will cost you pounds in aggravation during post.

The third essential big ticket item tends to be a location. Ultimately, if you feel it's crucial your flick be shot on specific location but you can't get the place for free, you must decide how much you are willing to compromise or to pay to make it happen. Perhaps you can convince yourself to relocate your story.

If you can't achieve your crucial big ticket items, postpone production until you can. With *He Had a Hat*, the filmmaker's inability to get special effects for free killed the project. *I'm on Fire* would have been history if the director hadn't found someone to create fire effects on his home computer. For *Five Puppies on the Run*, Jamba Juice and all the other stores aren't essential. Without the puppies, you don't have a film.

Every big ticket item is a big decision. One of our Fox Movie Channel shorts called *Phil Touches Flo* featured a pug (Flo). My first question to the director: "Does it have to be a pug?" Yes, he felt quite firmly that the whole story wouldn't work without a pug. We lucked out and found the pug who had been in *Men in Black*. The dog was very well trained, and it saved us a lot of time on set having a pro. However, because there was a crucial scene in the film where the dog had to run on its own and turn a corner, there had to be two trainers on set — each of whom had to be paid. Let's just say that dog turned out to be a really big ticket item. But if you asked the director, he'd say it was worth every penny.

HOW MUCH FOR A PUG?

The story for *Phil Touches Flo* (a.k.a. the "pug" movie) can be summed up in four sentences: Flo is a dog. Flo's owner doesn't like people touching Flo. Flo's owner is not a nice man. Phil touches Flo. Inspired by the strange outcropping of two palm trees in an otherwise barren industrial section of downtown Los Angeles, the short takes place entirely on that street, where we shot for two days, with permits and a big crew, on 35mm. If we had done this truly as an "Everyone Works for Free!" budget, the only crew who were paid would have been those we couldn't get away with not paying, i.e. the dog/trainers and the police.

The dog had a flat rate, but the trainers went into overtime after eight hours.

Since we were shooting in downtown Los Angeles, we had to get a permit from the city. The permit office decides what will be required after reading your script. In our case, not only did we have to pay for the permit ($385), spot check ($85), and postings ($72) fees, we had to hire two police officers, who got paid overtime after eight hours (police x 2 x 2 days = $1,107). Notice how the location — being the second big ticket item we're willing to spend money on — is spinning exponentially out of control.

Then, when we did a tech scout of the location during preproduction, the "free location" was so filthy that the unit production manager was seriously worried it might be a health hazard for the actors and crew to spend two days there. Not to mention the very expensive "star" pug, who would be sniffing those potentially toxic street-level odors. We ended up having to hire two different private companies to hose down the street and sidewalk, and then do trash removal. That cost us $455.

119

Our "free" site turned out to be pretty expensive. However, the fact that it came pre-art directed with amazing graffiti should always be taken into account. Another plus: because the street was deserted, we had no problems with neighbors, traffic, or noise.

And shooting outdoors in sunshine meant natural lighting, so no electricity or special lighting was necessary. We did have some bounce boards, which grips manned.

A filmmaker named Tommy emailed asking, "When you were shooting *Phil Touches Flo* on that street corner in downtown L.A. where did people pee? The reason I ask is, I am about to begin shooting a short film and I am planning on shooting on one street. But neither myself nor anyone I know lives on it. Did you have porta-potties? Where did you set up base camp?" Before I answer his question, I will now admit that we snuck back to the downtown location for a half-day additional shoot with a bare minimum crew, no police, and no dog. That stolen half day was the way a true "Everything for Free!" shoot should go. For the main two-day shoot we rented a Winnebago that functioned as wardrobe, dog holding pen, and bathroom for everyone. But on the half-day shoot, I personally drove anyone who needed to use a restroom to the nearby Burger King.

As for equipment, it's easy to work your "Everything for Free!" motto if you try hard enough. But you will discover expendables are a hidden cost in professionally crewed shorts. Each crew member who uses his or her own supplies will ask you for a kit fee to cover out-of-pocket expenses. The camera guy charged us for his personal supplies, sound guy charged us for batteries, the make-up woman for her kit. It's true, they are using material that will have to be replaced, so it's hard to argue with them.

Food was also a major expense. We had a professionally catered shoot, feeding 40 people x 2 days x $11.50 per head, plus extra miscellaneous charges. The total catering bill came out to be $943 — which is relatively cheap. Food is always where the bulk of your money goes during production. If you have the time, you can try to make everything yourself ahead of time, but you don't want to be like a team of directors I know, one of whom had to step off set to make the peanut butter and jelly sandwiches. We had second meals of pizza one day on *Phil Touches Flo*. We only had to do second meal once, but you should have a little extra tucked away for a pizza run, should the shoot day extend into night. You can see how food bills will mount. This isn't even taking into account craft service!

Other charges that might surprise you:

- Runner's Mileage/Gas
  You can refuse to reimburse for gas/mileage, but if you do, make sure everyone understands this upfront so there's no misunderstanding later.

- Loss & Damage
  It's amazing how often things get broken on shoots. You need to be clear what your policy is. If you shoot in a friend's house, are you really going to refuse to repair or replace something your production clearly broke?

- Dry Cleaning
  If actors wear their own clothes, it's common practice to offer to pick up the dry-cleaning costs. If you're not offering to cover such bills, make it clear in advance so there are no hard feelings once principal photography wraps. Another way to go is to convince your neighborhood dry cleaner to donate services in return for a credit in the film. Another tip regarding costuming: if you buy new clothes from department stores and plan on returning them when the shoot's done, don't clip the tags. Lastly, don't overlook neighborhood thrift stores. Sometimes you can make a deal to borrow clothes off their racks for free as long as you promise to return them dry cleaned.

MAKING A BUDGET

Unlike a feature, you don't need to do a big fancy budget for your little film. A simple item-by-item listing in Excel will do fine. Most things are for free anyway! If you're dealing with the Screen Actors Guild or an insurance agency, they will request that you submit your budget, but they're used to seeing informal ones from short filmmakers, so don't think you have to fancy it up for them.

The most crucial thing about budgeting is to remember the amount you promised yourself you wouldn't exceed. If your budget before production is scarily close to that number, you're in trouble because production always ends up costing more than you expect. You need to spend more time trying to get everything for free so you won't blow your budget. Don't forget to budget in a contingency fund for anything unexpected!

HOW MUCH FOR A CHICKEN SUIT?

As a case study, let's breakdown a simple one-day production like *Bad Animals*. First a little back story. When I was putting together the DVD short-film collection, *Short 10: Chaos*, I commissioned filmmaker David Birdsell to make a short film with the theme of "chaos." He came up with the following story. A man waits for the bus. Across the street, a person in a full-on chicken costume stares relentlessly at him. The chicken crosses the road, and continues to stare at the man, who is getting progressively freaked out. Luckily, the bus comes, and the man makes his escape. A few stops later, a person in a full-on mouse costume boards the bus and sits down, staring at the man. The mouse is so bold as to move to the seat right next to the man. Desperate to escape, the man jumps out at the next stop. Exiting onto the street, he's confronted by a person in a bear suit. The mouse also exits the bus, and the mouse and bear start shoving the man. The man runs away, pursued by the mouse and the bear. All of a sudden, his path is cut off by a huge 1970s-era convertible — driven by the chicken. The three animals wrestle the man to the ground, chloroform him, and dump his unconscious body into the convertible's trunk. The bad animals hop into the convertible and drive away. The end.

Because the DVD company was giving him a grand to make the film, Birdsell didn't feel like he had to operate under the "Everything for Free!" mandate. He had cash to dispense, so he paid everyone who worked on the film, rented the car and costumes, and even splurged on a few toys. If you were producing this short for no money, you would have called every car rental place until you got the convertible for free, every costume shop until you got the costumes for free, etc. And of course everyone would have worked for free. Now, if you were shooting it with a 35mm camera, you'd have to call the bus company, see if you could rent the bus for the day, pay the driver, get friends to be extras, lug the 35mm camera up into the bus, etc. But David Birdsell knew he was going to borrow a mini-DV camera and be his own crew. David was willing to risk boarding a real bus and use the real passengers as extras. Mind you, not only did he have to board a real bus as the camera operator (depositing his bus fare without taking his eye off the camera's viewfinder), he also had to ask an actor dressed in a full-on mouse suit do the same.

In preproduction, David Birdsell rode the bus several times to map out his route and see how doable his plan was. Deciding early Sunday morning was his best bet, he also realized the logistics of getting his actors off and on the bus required an assistant to help with transportation. Because there was no dialogue in the film, he figured he could augment whatever production sound he captured easily in post; therefore, he decided to forgo a sound person and use the in-camera microphone. As for actors, David knew a guy whom he thought would be great as the man. However, anyone could be in the animal suits. It was a real education about friendship when he had to ask a trio of good buddies to spend a sweaty Sunday inside huge animal outfits and "act" in a guerilla-style production. The guy who played the chicken also had to drive a huge car while wearing a costume in which sight lines were a little scary. Needless to say, there was no special insurance taken out for this shoot.

The filmmaker's two previous short films had debuted at the Sundance Film Festival. When he submitted *Bad Animals*, the DV piece didn't get in. *Bad Animals* did, however, get accepted into the highly prestigious Clermont-Ferrand festival — and it even won a prize. On the basis of that French award, the flick got invited to show at Cannes during the International Critics Week. For Cannes, Birdsell had to provide a film print. Having shot on tape, his only option was to do a tape-to-film transfer. Because this money was going to come out of his own pocket, David called around to the various companies that do tape-to-film, explaining his short was going to Cannes if he could get a print made. One company agreed to do the work for a discount in exchange for logo placement in the film's end credits. The going price was $350 a minute, and *Bad Animals* runs four-and-a-half minutes. Birdsell talked the transfer company into matching his production cost. After Cannes, the film got picked up by Res Fest, where it went on an extended theatrical tour and was issued on one of their DVD collections. It's also played a host of other film festivals, won a few more prizes, garnered some nice reviews, and ultimately ended up on a revenue-sharing website. Not bad for a $2,000 film!

So let's breakdown the film.

CAST (LEADS):
• Man
• Chicken
• Mouse
• Bear

CAST (EXTRAS/ATMOSPHERE):
• People on the bus
• People on the street

WARDROBE:
• Man's casual work clothes
• Chicken suit

- Bear suit
- Mouse suit

LOCATIONS:
- Street w/bus stop
- Bus
- Street

PROPS:
- Bus fare
- Chloroform
- Rag for chloroform

VEHICLES:
- Bus
- Chicken's car (convertible to accommodate chicken costume height)

CREW:
- Camera operator
- (No sound, no lighting)
- Assistant to transport actors/take behind-the-scenes photos

EQUIPMENT:
- Camera – a borrowed Canon Optura
- DV tapes – 2 (free from production company)
- Camera mount (for car shots)

INSURANCE:
- None

POSTPRODUCTION:
- Editing system (free from the production company)
- Editor (he edited it himself)
- Sound Design (none)
- Score/Music (none)
- Master tape (free from production company)
- Tape-to-film film print

What are the big ticket items? The obvious one is the bus. However, the director knew he was going to guerilla that. For him, the costumes were the most crucial thing. He dragged his friend around from costume shop to costume shop until he found  the right chicken outfit. Unfortunately, at the "chicken" shop, he couldn't find another outfit he liked, so he continued going to wardrobe houses until he found the other animal outfits. At the second shop, he used the price paid for the chicken costume as his benchmark, talking all the shops into matching it.

Here is how the director accounted for his $1,000 production budget.

PRODUCTION COSTS:
ACTORS (4) + CREW ASSISTANT (1): 5 x $50 = $250.00
Because he did have a grand to spend, the director paid everyone who worked on the film. If you're going to break the "Everyone Works for Free!" rule, pay everyone the same amount as a flat fee to avoid any complications.

DIRECTOR: $100
He allowed himself 10% of the budget as a fee. Taking a percentage of the budget is always a good strategy if you're asked to name your fee.

FOOD: $80
Since it was a one-day shoot, no catering was necessary. The director took everyone out to lunch and picked up the tab.

COSTUMES (RENTAL): 3 x $100 = $300
Thus it was established that a hundred bucks will cover a weekend rental charge for a chicken outfit.

COSTUMES (DRY CLEANING): $25

The animal outfits didn't require laundering (which is why they smelled terrible, especially inside the heads), but the actor playing the man wore his own work clothes, which did get taken to the dry cleaners.

CAR (WEEKEND RENTAL) $150

The original thought was just to borrow a friend's car, but the chicken head was too large to fit inside a traditional car. Once again the director decided to spend some dough rather than seeking out a free car. Since he was paying for it, he rented the largest car possible for $100. If had tried to get it free, he would have done the "Want to be in pictures?" note under the windshields-in-parking-lots technique. Or he could have asked the car rental place if they'd lend it to him for free if he cut the short down into a promotional piece/spec commercial for them featuring the car, which they could play on their website or use as a local cable ad. The car rental company would be extremely foolish to pass up an offer to get a free commercial made for them.

PROPS: $5

Yes, he paid five bucks for a chloroform-looking bottle and rag. Robert Rodriguez would not approve!

BUS FARE: $30

This amount included checking out the possible bus routes during preproduction.

CAMERA: FREE

You can always find someone's camera to borrow. In this case, having such a small mobile camera allowed the director to mount the camera all over the chicken's convertible, giving the film an invaluable sense of motion.

TAPE: FREE

Finally, here's something done in "beg, borrow, and steal" style!

CAMERA CAR MOUNT (RENTAL): $15

Best $15 ever spent!

LENS (RENTAL): $30
If you do shoot mini-DV, being able to add a lens gives you more options.

BEHIND-THE-SCENES STILL CAMERA FILM & PROCESSING: $15
The photos you see throughout this guide were paid for by that fifteen bucks. Of course, the film was made before high-quality digital cameras were so common. If his photographer had taken digital stills, this budget could have been $15 less.

POST COSTS:
EDITING: FREE
Because the filmmaker is also a professional editor, he edited the film himself on a borrowed system. Although he added some simple sound effects during editing, he chose not to include any music.

MASTER TAPE: FREE
TAPE-TO-FILM PRINT: $1000
TOTAL COST: $2,000

RECAP

- Breakdown your script to see what you need to make your film.

- Evaluate what you can get for free.

- Put your effort into securing necessary big ticket items. Don't compromise on these most essential elements.

- If you want to pay people, pay every person on the crew the same amount.

- Even with the cheapest shoot, you'll have to pay for food.

CHAPTER 11

WHY CASTING COUNTS THE MOST

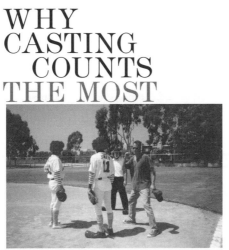

DON'T LET BAD ACTING KILL YOUR FILM.

If you read no other chapter in this book but this one, you'll be miles ahead of most filmmakers. Because the two biggest sandtraps in short filmmaking involve actors. One is bad acting, which, along with bad sound, is the artistic downfall of many a potentially good short film. The second hazard is signing a contract with the Screen Actors Guild (SAG) without really understanding all that it entails. Before we get tangled up in SAG issues, let's look big picture when it comes to working with actors.

"Often I get so caught up in the logistics and camera angles and lighting and time schedule that I always forget, or give virtually no attention to, the most important element of all: the acting," reveals filmmaker Jordan Horowitz. "People will forgive almost everything but bad acting. That's what everyone watching the film will use to size up your skill as a director. I don't care how fancy you are with a camera; if your actors suck, then so do you."

HOW TO AVOID BAD ACTING

Hire good actors. Direct them well.

HOW TO HIRE GOOD ACTORS

Finding your actors is the fun part of preproduction. Think of it as a shopping spree that won't cost you a penny. You may be thinking of casting yourself or friends, and that can be a very good option. But if you want to hire people you don't know to portray the characters in your piece, there are many ways of finding them.

■ WATCH SHORTS AND FEATURE FILMS MADE BY FILMMAKERS IN YOUR TOWN.

Are there any actors that interest you? Track them down via the filmmakers. This is a wonderful way of shopping for actors, because not only do you see how they look on film, you can get the real skinny from their previous director on what it's like to work with them.

■ RUN AN AD AND THEN HOLD A CASTING SESSION.

Ah, the casting session. Casting can be a lot of fun because it can open your eyes to an entire range of possibilities. Perhaps you always pictured a small man in a role that really comes alive when portrayed by a fat man. Not only will you benefit from seeing different people, auditions are a great opportunity to polish your "working with actors" directing skills. Ask actors to tackle the material in different manners. Can they stretch their interpretation? Can they give you what you want? Better to know now rather on the set if someone is a one-trick pony. You'll also get a sense if this is an actor who will take up a lot of your time on set with needy behavior.

Casting sessions are also a wonderful opportunity to test out your material. Are lines falling flat no matter who says them? Are actors telling you they don't understand what the scene is about or why their characters act certain ways? You need to go back and fix the script.

As to where to run an ad, organizations like Craigslist are an obvious place to start. Or search MySpace and Facebook for actors who are advertising themselves. As to where to hold the casting sessions, local theaters that are dark during the day are an ideal choice. But you can even cast out of a corner table in Starbucks if you need to.

CASTING STARS

Believe it or not, it's relatively easy to cast stars in your short. It helps if you know them. Grant Heslov got George Clooney to appear in his 30-minute romantic comedy, *Waiting for Woody*. Of course, Grant happens to be one of George's best buds. But you don't have to have already shared a beer or two with Clooney to get him to be in your movie. All you have to do is call the Screen Actors Guild, ask them to tell you the star's agent, call the agent, and ask that your project be considered.

Why should George Clooney's agent take your call? Three reasons. Because you're going to be the next Spike Jonze, and George Clooney likes to work with on-the-cusp, extremely creative filmmakers. Because everyone knows shorts are where the really adventurous filmmaking takes place. And because you've got a project that is one hundred times more exciting than most of the run-of-the-mill features he's offered every day.

Mat Fuller had a former pop star in his film: Danny Wood from the New Kids on the Block. "I don't have this cool story about how I sent a script to his agent or anything," says Fuller. "When we were casting *Deveria*, the production coordinator on my film knew Danny. She's from Miami, and he was her neighbor. She asked if I would be interested in using him because he wanted stuff for his reel. That's the key. It sounds stupid, but I think the easiest way to get someone who has any kind of name is to get a guy who is trying to transition from TV to film. Danny did it for free. Find a guy whose looking for stuff for his reel. That's what I gave Danny. He got an agent out of it, so he was happy with me. And I was little bit lucky with the timing in terms of the New Kids thing. My short came out at the time that Mark Wahlberg had a big movie coming out, Donnie Wahlberg was on *Band of Brothers*, and Danny Wood had just done a short! So there was some value there."

There are additional values to having a name in your film. "Mark Wahlberg saw my film. He hasn't asked me to do his movies yet," laughs Mat, "but having Danny in the film got me that exposure. And the cool thing is — on top of that, forget the good it does your movie — I know Danny now. He has a CD coming out, and I get first pitch on his video."

Meanwhile David Wain, who created and stars in the web-series *Wainy Days* has been able to attract high-profile guest stars such as Elizabeth Banks, Jonah Hill, and Paul Rudd to be in his series. Wain's pitch is the minimal time commitment and the fact the stars can do things they normally can't do in feature films.

One of the best stories of how to secure a major star to be in a short was told by animator Bill Plympton. When asked how he got Paul Giamatti to narrate his *The Fan and the Flower* animated short, Bill explained he happened to find himself at a lunch gathering that included Mr. Giamatti. So he got up from the table and made his way over to talk the actor. Of course, that gathering was the official Oscar nominee luncheon (Plympton was there for his animated short *Guard Dog*). I guess the moral of that story is if you find yourself nominated for an Oscar, work the room!

The point being, "name" actors of all levels are attainable. But do you want them?

PROS OF HIRING NAME ACTORS

• They're much better actors than your Uncle Charlie.

• The other actors' performances will rise to a higher level as a result of working with a better "player."

- People will be impressed that you have someone they've heard of in your movie.

- The name actor could potentially hire you in the future.

- Your work gets shown to their high-powered friends in the industry.

CONS OF HIRING NAME ACTORS

- They're used to professional productions. Stars don't understand the realities of no-budget filmmaking. Let's just say they're not too happy about public restrooms doubling as dressing rooms.

- They're used to unlimited takes. They're looking at your film as a chance to stretch as actors, and they'll want to experiment with their performances. You, on the other hand, have a busy day to get through. Neither of you will be happy with the results.

- You will be intimidated. They do have much more experience than you do and have worked with the best. The last thing you need is to feel inferior on your own set.

- If you get George Clooney, you'll discover it will be hard to get people to focus on your contributions when all they'll want to talk about is the former *ER* hunk.

- You're a victim of their schedules. Stars have very busy and unpredictable lives. You may be prepared to start filming on Saturday, but if they get a last-minute invitation to fly to Aspen for the weekend, they'll expect you to wait for them to return. Or if they have to leave early to attend a premiere, you'll have to shoot around them. In the balance of power, they're doing you a favor by being in your film.

CASTING FRIENDS

Why ask strangers to act in your project when the perfect person to portray your character might be right under your nose? Robbie Consing decided to cast his good friend Guy Dyas as one of the two leads in his Fox Movie Channel short, *Beeker's Crossing*. He knew Guy had the right look for the part and wrote the role with Guy in mind. The only problem: Guy is not an actor. "Writing the short film," Robbie muses, "when you visualize somebody who you think might be right, you corner yourself. Which, of course, is good when you're writing because the more corners you have, the easier it is to let things flow out. It gives you more inspiration to do certain things. Having the person be a friend whose personality and look are perfect, the advantages are plentiful. Number one, he's a good friend of mine. I know what his strengths and weaknesses are. Number two, he won't mind the long hours — which any filmmaker will definitely appreciate! Number three (and this is very crucial), you can be honest with him. And friends usually understand what their limits are. Now if you have friends who are dying to be actors and they're not very good actors, that can be incredibly hellish. Do not ever, ever, ever promise parts to friends who are dying to act until they either audition or do a tape to see for themselves whether they are right for the role. Because you will know right then and there if they are. I would never ever, ever again promise friends roles unless I taped them first. Because my friend was more terrified about it than I was, I later found out."

Would he recommend hiring non-actors? "It just depends on what kind of short it is," replies Consing, "what characters they are playing, and how much is it about their look or their presence. Guy has enough charisma to power any 10 short films. Can he act? I think he can, and I think I got a great performance out of him."

Filmmaker Mark Borchardt also hires non-pros. "Sometimes a non-actor can bring charisma to screen that an actor cannot," says Borchardt, "because an actor is a trained professional with a certain flow of instinct bred through instruction in the craft, where a non-actor can bring a sense of aliveness and spontaneity because that's all he knows. It can be quite charming on screen. Working with professional actors, it's far more technically easy to deal with them because they understand about hitting marks and this and that. Whereas people off the street who are quite adept at adapting, they immediately get it, too. But real actors have a sense of shedding self-awareness so they're acting as a job, where people off the street might obviously overact, trying to figure out how to act. I tell anyone who is nervous about acting, 'Don't act, man, be.'"

CASTING YOURSELF

"It's easy to get too overwhelmed if you want to be in it as well as direct it," advises Tara Vernerso, who played the lead in one of her experimental films. "Also you don't have the same vision when you're in it as when you're a voyeur, looking at the action from the outside and directing it. If you're in your short for an artistic reason beyond vanity, then you might consider it. But if you are directing just to pursue your acting career, perhaps you should hire a director. And if you are directing it only because you can't find a director to do it, you might want to reevaluate your acting ability!"

Heath Mensher, who starred in his own short *He's My Dad*, counsels, "You have to do everything really well, or one little thing that isn't done well is going to cut your lights off. So if I was a great actor, but I wasn't really paying attention to the direction — screwed! If I was a great director but I wasn't really focused on the role — screwed. If you're prepared, if you thought everything out, storyboarded everything, and learned your lines, you can be in the character and make sure everyone is doing his or her job. If you're prepared, there are fewer things that can addle your brain."

Greg Ivan Smith also starred in, as well as directed, his short, *The Back Room*. "I found very early on in my directing that I completely trusted my amazing DP and  my co-director/assistant director 100%," says Smith. "I would set up the shot with a stand-in, then I stopped watching every take because it would have just been too time consuming. You're trying to stay in the moment with your other actors, but there's a little portion of your brain that is always in director mode, going 'oh, the line wasn't really right,' and 'did my sound guy hear the ice cream truck go by, because I heard that.'"

Greg also advises, "Make sure that your acting is not the primary focus of the filmmaking process, unless it has to be. You can't be worried about your lines on set. I didn't have a lot of lines in my own film although I'm the lead character in it, which made it easier for me because I did a lot of listening, a lot of reacting — which I would be doing as a director anyway. I also made a conscious decision to not make this process about me judging my own acting work."

TEN TIPS FOR GETTING GREAT PERFORMANCES

1. REHEARSE.
Work as much as you can with your actors in preproduction. Recording your rehearsals on video is also highly recommended.

*2. DON'T GET OVERWHELMED BY THE MYRIAD DETAILS A DIREC-
TOR IS SUPPOSED TO SUPERVISE ON SET.*

Remember that it's the actors' performances that will make your film. Pay attention to the on-screen drama, not the petty behind-the-scenes dramas.

3. PLAY TO YOUR ACTORS' STRENGTHS.

Don't ask inexperienced cast members to reach outside of their natural way of doing things, where they are forced to "perform."

4. LESS IS MORE.

The camera catches more than your naked eye. A deadpan performance can read on film as something real and emotionally deep, whereas theatrical-style acting will seem too big and unnatural.

5. DON'T RUSH TO CALL "ACTION" OR "CUT."

You'll be grateful in editing when you can steal little moments the actors take while waiting for action or the little things they add on before you can say cut. One good technique to force yourself not to rush is to say "And... action."

6. SHOOT ACTORS LISTENING OR REACTING.

Great actors always swear that the secret to acting is listening. During each take, make sure your actors are listening to each other rather than just waiting to deliver their own lines. During editing, you're going to want to be able to cutaway from the actor speaking to show others reacting — especially if you have an actor delivering a large chunk of dialogue.

7. WHEN POSSIBLE, HAVE THE ACTORS SPEAK AT A QUICK PACE.

Movies move faster than real life. If you don't want scenes to drag, your direction to sluggish actors should be, "Once more, only faster."

8. RECORD WILD TRACK LINES OF DIALOGUE ON THE SET.

If you don't think you'll be able to do decent ADR (automatic dialogue replacing, or looping) in post, consider doing a down and dirty version on set. While rolling sound only, let the actors try different ways of delivering their dialogue. You never know what you'll need during editing, and it's nice to have some options at your fingertips.

9. IF YOU CAN AVOID IT, DON'T HAVE CHARACTERS TALK ON THE PHONE.

Actors are better and scenes more dynamic when the characters interact face to face.

10. IF YOU'RE WORKING WITH KIDS OR ANIMALS, SHOOT THE REHEARSAL.

Understand that they both have limited attention spans. And when they're tired, you might as well just call it a day and send everyone home.

LET'S TALK ABOUT PAPERWORK

Anyone who appears on camera must sign a personal depiction release. You could get a lawyer to draw up a document for you, or you could just use a generic release you find on the Internet. In general, the simpler the better. A long and complicated release can scare some people away, whereas a few simple paragraphs spelling out everything makes people more inclined to read the entire document and understand what they're signing without feeling like they might have to consult an attorney.

If the film stars your best friend, you might be tempted to skip the paperwork. Don't. Because when you later try to sell your film, no potential distributor will touch it if you don't have all your actor releases signed. You can always go back to your stars after the fact and get them to sign releases, but it's easier to do it during production when you have guaranteed access to everyone.

Remember, even if you're doing a short for a 48-hour film contest or an Internet website, you still need releases from your actors.

AND NOW LET'S TALK ABOUT THE SCREEN ACTORS GUILD

Whether you're making a short film for the festival circuit or for the Internet, if you want to use Screen Actors Guild talent you will end up dealing with the Guild. And, yes, SAG does offer agreements specifically for short films and Internet/Online pieces.

Up until this point, you've controlled everything about your film. When you sign with the Screen Actors Guild, you give up a huge part of that control. Now you are a SAG signature company, and you must play by their rules.

A filmmaker named Kim emailed me, worried, "I am currently weeks away from shooting a short I am producing, directing, and acting in. The process to become a SAG signatory seems endless. When you shoot with SAG actors, do you need to provide both 1) insurance and 2) worker's compensation? The last thing I want is for them to ride me after our production for not having it." I replied that one should never be afraid to talk to SAG, that they are more than glad to answer any questions filmmakers have. Kim emailed back to say, "All is good. My producer talked to them, and we were given a SAG rep. They made it all nice and easy and we are gonna shoot hassle free."

The thing you have to remember about SAG is that if you plan on being a professional filmmaker in America, you're going to be dealing with them for the rest of your professional life, so you don't want to get on their bad side. The good news is they recognize you are indeed a studio just like a major studio, and you are treated just like any other SAG production. The bad news is SAG demands you to play the game just like the big boys do, and that means professional working conditions, hours, paperwork, and payments.

The many things they require you to be professional about include:

■ COPYRIGHT REGISTRATION

SAG demands you to register your film script with the copyright office — not for your protection, but for theirs. The Guild recognizes that you are starting to build a property that has value, and that value starts with the copyright.

■ WORKER'S COMPENSATION

You must prove to the Guild that your actors will be insured. This is, in fact, a good thing for everyone's protection. However, if you weren't planning on getting insurance, you are now.

■ SAG WORKING CONDITIONS, PAPERWORK, AND HOURS

You are agreeing to run your set in compliance with all of SAG's rules and regulations. Again, this is a good thing for everyone involved, but it means someone else is dictating how you run your show.

■ DON'T FORGET ABOUT SAG — PRODUCERS PENSION AND HEALTH PLANS AND ROYALTIES

The SAG headaches just keep on coming.

■ SAG: FRIEND OR FOE?

Don't be afraid of dealing with SAG. The reps are wonderful people who do understand that you are a talented director who is going far. They also understand you're a novice learning the ropes of film production. They want to help you do everything right (right, according to SAG, that is).

But make no mistake. SAG is very up front about whose side they're on: their members, the actors. SAG is not your guild — it's the actors' guild.

If you do go the SAG route, you must begin conversations at least a month before you plan to begin shooting in order to do your paperwork in the proper amount of time. There are several types of agreements. If you are a student currently enrolled in film school, you may do a student contract. You will need to produce a letter from your instructor confirming that you are indeed enrolled in a filmmaking class and that you are making the film as part of the course. If you're not a student production, then you'll probably sign the SAG short-film agreement.

When you first begin dealing with SAG, you will have to submit to the representative assigned to your project a full packet of information including the following material:

■ YOUR SCREENPLAY AS YOU PLAN TO SHOOT IT.

SAG will not accept first drafts or treatments. Problem areas your rep will be looking for include hazardous situations or nudity.

■ A COPY OF YOUR ACTUAL BUDGET, INCLUDING ANY PAYMENTS YOU PLAN TO DEFER.

For features, a professionally prepared budget is expected. With a short, you can get away with a relatively informal list of categories and costs. Be very liberal with your use of "Ø" in filling out how much you are paying for people and things. SAG wants to make sure that everyone else isn't getting paid big bucks while you ask the actors to work for reduced fees. Your rep will look at the bottom line to make sure you fall within the defined short-film budget limit of a maximum of $50,000.

■ A COMPLETED INFORMATION SHEET CONTAINING THE FOLLOWING INFORMATION:

1. Title of your short film.
2. The date you plan to begin production (i.e., start date). Make sure this is indeed at least 30 days from the day you meet with your rep.
3. Your estimated wrap date. It's okay if your wrap date is the same as your start date if you're doing a one-day shoot.
4. The total shoot days. Note: 30 days is the Guild's maximum allowance if you plan to use the short-film agreement. And frankly, what legitimate short film shoots for 30 days?
5. What format you plan to shoot on (HD, 35mm, etc.).

6. Current expenses, crew salary deferrals, above the line (other than performers) deferrals, equipment/stock/processing deferrals.
7. A summation of your budget.
8. The source of your financing ("self" is a perfectly good answer).
9. Intended distribution ("festivals").

Once you begin the process, the Guild will supply you with production paperwork including sample performers' contracts, cast list information, and daily production time report forms. If you are negligent, delinquent, or don't comply with your production paperwork, SAG can fine you.

"Working with SAG seems overwhelming, seems like a hassle," remarks filmmaker Amy Talkington. "The best thing is not to be afraid of them. You need to call them, talk to them, and they generally will work with you. But if you cross them, it's a mistake that will come back and haunt you for the rest of your life."

RECAP

- Bad acting must be avoided at all costs.

- You don't have to hire professional actors. But there are definite advantages to working with pros.

- If you are acting and directing in your film, doing your prep work is key.

- Look at dealing with SAG on your short as a learning opportunity so when you make your feature you'll already be a pro at SAG rules and regulations.

- Do not lie to SAG. This is an organization you will be dealing with for the rest of your filmmaking career, and you do not want to be on their bad side.

CHAPTER 12

ESSENTIAL PEOPLE AND PAPERWORK

WHETHER YOUR PRODUC-
TION CONSISTS OF FIVE OR
50 PEOPLE, YOU NEED TO BE
ORGANIZED.

When it comes to deciding how you're going to run your production, the concept of "you are the studio" comes heavily into play. You can have a completely anarchistic/guerilla attitude, not bothering with talent releases, location permission forms, workers' comp, or insurance of any kind. You can incorporate television shows taped off TV and include any music you want without asking for permission. You can do whatever you want because no one can stop you — you're the boss.

This route certainly allows complete creative freedom. It also makes it impossible to do anything with your film once you decide to enter "the real world." If you don't have the rights to the material contained within your film, cable channels, DVD companies, and even discriminating Internet sites won't touch your film with a 10-foot pole.

In contrast, maybe you are the kind of studio that is very meticulous, dotting all your "i"s and crossing all your "t"s. You'll file a copyright on your script and the resulting film, create production reports, get signed releases from everyone involved, get insurance, pay for permits, negotiate music rights or hire a local band to compose music in a "work-for-hire" situation.

You might find that playing it straight may force you to artistically compromise your film. For example, you're not going to be able to include that Rolling Stones song you dreamed of. But if you plan on making features, it's great training to do things the way "real" filmmakers do. And most importantly, if you've done everything correctly and have no clearance issues with your final work, you can commercially exhibit your film. Translation: make money off it.

Those two models, of course, are the extremes. You will find a happy balance that works for you. Having produced shorts for the Fox Movie Channel, I come from the get-a-permit, get-permission school of filmmaking. I know a lot of filmmakers who never permit locations and have never been busted. If you do get in trouble, you just claim to be a dumb short filmmaker who doesn't know better. Even people in authority know that shorts are a learning experience for everyone and that there's no money involved, so most will cut you some slack.

PAPERWORK IS SEXY

Okay, it's not sexy, but it is important.

■ COPYRIGHT

In the United States, you can file copyright paperwork for your script and your final film. Even if you skip copyrighting the script, you should definitely copyright your final film. This will start a chain of title that you will need to produce for sales later on. To file, go to the United States Library of Congress Copyright Office website at *http://lcweb.loc.gov/copyright*.

■ INSURANCE

Because you can't get it for free, ideally you'd like to avoid insurance. However, when it comes to securing the many things you want to get for free (such as equipment or locations), the owners won't give them to you unless you have the proper insurance. Additionally, the Screen Actors Guild won't let you use their actors unless you have workers' comp. So unless you're using your own equipment and locations, hiring non-SAG performers, and are confident you won't be sued by someone, you probably will need to secure some sort of insurance policy. A quick search of the Web will give you a listing of insurance brokers. Be careful about getting too large of a deductible because things do get broken, lost, or stolen. One filmmaker I know came back to set one morning to discover the dolly had been looted — and with it went the $1,000 she had to pay for the deductible. As for worker's compensation insurance, even if you don't do it because SAG demands it, you might consider it just because people do get injured on set.

■ PERMISSION TO RECORD LIKENESS AGREEMENTS

No one (except SAG!) is expecting you to do extensive paperwork for your short, but you do need some sort of agreement with your actors giving you permission to record their likenesses. You don't want agreements so complicated that people feel like they have to consult with a lawyer before signing. A better choice than generating your own agreements is to use pre-existing generic permission forms – for talent, location, and even composer agreements – which can easily be found with a quick Internet search. If it's clear that you haven't generated the agreement (i.e., tampered with it to your advantage), most people are willing to sign without hesitation.

If you're doing behind-the-scenes on your short (and you really should — ask a friend with a mini-DV camera to go around and do a little "making of" — you might want to put it up on YouTube or your MySpace/Facebook page), it's good to get everyone on the crew to sign a permission-to-record likeness release.

If you're shooting in a heavily populated area where real people are doing everyday business, put up signs warning the general public that there is filming going on and their likenesses may be used in a short. For your protection, have your behind-the-scenes video camera document the sign so that you have proof a sign was posted.

■ LOCATION RELEASES

Once again, a generic pre-existing form will do. Although it's easy enough to find proper location releases via a quick Google, I've seen some people use the personal depiction release, scrawling "for house" and having the home owner sign and initial. However, if you're dealing with a more established entity like Jamba Juice or Ralphs grocery store, you'll want to present a more professional release.

■ TRADEMARK RELEASES

Some studios are very careful about clearing everything, others figure as long as it's not used in a derogatory way they're safe using trademarked products, as long as such products are not the main point of the scene. If it becomes a problem later on, you can always do the reality TV solution: blur out the trademark or logo in post.

On the other hand, you can emphasize the logos in exchange for product placement. Tell Coke you'll use only Coke products in the restaurant scene if they give you free drinks. Unfortunately, most companies know that shorts aren't seen by millions of people so they'd rather save their placement for features. But you can always try.

PRODUCTION PAPERWORK IS EVEN SEXIER

There are computer programs that will generate breakdown sheets, shooting schedules, call sheets, production reports, etc., or you can find blank generic forms on the Web. It's always good to do the work yourself, but if you can hire a line producer or a first assistant director to do production paperwork for you, do so! Paperwork can bog you down and sap all your creative energy. Leave it to the pros.

WHERE TO PUT ALL THIS WONDERFUL PAPER

Make a production book that you will have with you during preproduction, production, and post. Some people prefer the accordion style binder, others an old fashioned three-ring notebook. It is your office in a box, and you'll find, even years later, you'll pull it out to refer to something. Paperwork is always important!

SECURING THE ESSENTIAL PEOPLE

How do you get people to work on your film — especially if you're not paying? The simple truth is everyone wants to be involved in good projects, and everyone likes to work with a talented filmmaker who is going to go far.

All you need is one crewmember to sign on and start the ball rolling. Hopefully, that crewmember will have worked enough productions that he or she can recommend others who might like to join your show. The person to begin the process  with is the person you will spend the most time with from start to finish: the producer. However, it's hard to get someone to produce your film because anyone who has produced a short knows how hard it is and is reluctant to do it again for no money. More than likely, you'll be doing the producing yourself. Or you'll ask someone close to you who has no experience but is willing to share the workload with you.

The second best person to start with is your director of photography, who should be able to recommend people he or she has worked with in the past. How do you find a good DP? Watch short films made by filmmakers who live in your town. Note who shot them. Track down the filmmakers and ask if they would recommend their DPs. While you're at it, ask for any other crew recommendation. Other methods: ask students in the local film school to shoot your project. Or ask the camera rental house to make recommendations. Asking the rental houses is also a good way of finding other crewmembers. Soundmen can be found at sound rental houses, gaffers at lighting warehouses, etc.

"Work with people whom you really like," counsels NYU film school student Rashaad Ernesto Green. "If you're trying to fill up positions with people just because you think you need them, it's going to wind up taking away from your production because they're the ones who are going to be upset with you or frustrated in wanting that break. If you have people you know, trust, and love, then I'd say have a skeleton crew rather than a big production crew."

ONE-MAN-BAND STYLE OF FILMMAKING

Like the director of *Bad Animals*, you might decide that you can borrow a hand-held camera and shoot the short yourself. You might even forgo any additional crew, such as a soundperson or an art director. It's true, you can do everything yourself — but do you really want to? Actor/filmmaker Matthew Modine thinks so. "We were able to get into a hedge fund office on the Upper West Side without disturbing them," Modine explains, regarding his short *I Think I Thought*. "It was just me, Adam (who produced it) was the cameraman, and I did the costumes and direction. The beauty of HD is you don't need lights or cables or anything like that — it's just a tripod, a camera, and a lavaliere."

Jennifer Chen, who spent years distributing short films, strongly counsels not being your own director and producer. "I think it's part of the director's learning curve — just like they're honing their craft working with the actors — to hone their working relationships with producers."

PROS OF DOING EVERYTHING YOURSELF

- No workers' comp insurance necessary.

- No need to set aside money to feed the crew.

- You don't have to waste time communicating with other crewmembers.

- Without the distractions of others asking you production questions, you can put your full concentration on your actors.

- It's easier to get away with guerilla filmmaking if it's just you and a discreet camera rather than a full movie crew.

CONS OF DOING EVERYTHING YOURSELF

- It's a false reality. You're not learning how to deal with others, which is what you will be doing when you direct a bigger piece.

- No benefiting from the knowledge and experience of those crewmembers who know more than you do.

- You're so busy doing everyone else's job (producing, lighting, arranging props) that you can't concentrate on doing your job: being a director.

- You can't do those other jobs as well as professionals can.

- You're overworking yourself when there's no reason to. Other people will be glad to crew your production for free if you ask them.

ASSEMBLING THE BARE MINIMUM CREW

Remember, the two things that kill most films are bad acting and bad sound. If you only have one other crewmember, hire a sound mixer. You'll never regret having a good sound guy on set.

If you're going to layer in another crewmember, and if your film is very visual, consider passing off the cinematography duties. Not only will a good director of photography know how to operate the camera better than you, he or she will light it more professionally than you ever could.

Lastly, if you can throw one other person into the mix, get someone to help you with production needs. This can be a producer, a coordinator, or a production assistant. It will make your job so much easier if there's someone to handle the myriad things, big and small, that production entails.

STAFFING A "REAL" PRODUCTION

If "Everyone Works For Free!", why not expand into a properly staffed production? If you're not paying anyone, it's tempting to keep on layering in the people. "I had 50 people on my flick," reports filmmaker Mat Fuller. "It was like a real movie for eight days." True, you're not paying them, but you do have to feed them, so it's not entirely a free ride. And if your crew

gets too big, a lot of people sitting around chatting because they have nothing to do will kill your momentum. Better to have a lean, mean, fighting machine. Of course, if it's too lean with not enough hands to do things quickly, that's a problem. You'll find the correct balance for your project.

Here's the 26-person crew (not including the director) I used when doing two-day productions with a 35mm camera. You can decide for yourself how many positions you can eliminate on your own project.

PRODUCTION STAFF:

- Producer/UPM (Unit Production Manager)
  It's nice to have someone handle all the production details for you.

- 1st A.D. (Assistant Director)
  The assistant director runs the set, keeping everything and everyone moving along. You'll find the only way to make it through an ambitious shoot schedule is to have a good first, who can keep you and the crew cracking along.

- 2nd A.D.
  If you must economize, try to get away without having a second A.D.

- Script Supervisor
  Another job that you might be tempted to axe, but think carefully before you do. Not only is the script supervisor there to take script notes, she is the director's second pair of eyes. While the director is thinking "big picture," the script supervisor is trained to keep an eye on details. She'll notice errors in continuity, crossing the line, etc. You'll regret it in post if you cut this crucial safety net.

- P.A. (Production Assistant) x 3
  These are the hard workers who will be assigned to do anything and everything, on set and off. Because you'll always need an extra set of hands, legs or wheels, hire as many P.A.s as you can.

SET OPERATIONS:

- Key Grip
  Grips are the ones who move the equipment and do the work that doesn't involve lighting (that's the gaffer's department). I always try to hire a key grip who comes with his own grip truck.

- Grip
  Usually, you need more than just a key grip.

- Dolly Grip
  If you have a dolly, you need someone to push it. A good dolly grip does it effortlessly and smoothly, while a bad one will render your dolly shots useless.

SET DRESSING & PROPERTY:

- Art Director
  Many of our Fox Movie Channel Shorts were shot on street corners where the real world was our art department. However, every production benefits from having a designated person making the location look good for camera. If you don't have a lot of money to spend, a good art director can whip up miracles you never would have expected on your limited budget. And production value does count for a lot in a short film.

- Props Person
  A heavily art-directed short will require more than just one person in the art department. If you have many locations in your short, a props person will be assigned to keep everything straight on the hot set while the art director is off prepping or tearing down another set.

- Lead Man
  Works with the art director to get things ready ahead of time.

- P.A. (ART DEPT)
  A designated art department production assistant will move things along considerably.

WARDROBE:

- Costume Designer
  Quite often, the person in charge of wardrobe requires assistance. If your costumer asks to bring along his or her own assistant, only agree if this will help move things along. You

don't want to be stingy, but every additional person is another mouth to feed. Perhaps the art department P.A. can help out.

CAMERA:

- DP (Director of Photography)
It's standard operating procedure on shorts for the DP to also function as the camera operator.

- A.C. (Assistant Cameraperson)
With film shoots, it's all about servicing the camera. The DP mostly likely has a team of A.C.s he or she likes to work with.

- 2nd A.C.
If it makes the camera department work better and faster, let them have as many people as they need. Also, be prepared to be hit up for expendables from the camera department.

- Loader
If you are using recanned film or short ends, you'd be wise to have someone dedicated to loading the camera magazines.

PRODUCTION SOUND:

- Sound Engineer
Do not forget that the engineer is the second most important person on set. Make sure you pay attention when he or she suggests you do certain things for sound. Most sound engineers come with their own equipment, which they request you rent from them. Even if they donate the equipment (good luck), they'll charge you for the DATs, CDs and batteries used.

- Boom
Usually the sound engineer has someone he or she is used to working with. If not, a P.A. can be recruited to handle the boom microphone, but be prepared for a lot of mistakes and inconsistencies.

LOCATION:

- Location Manager

If you have a lot of locations, having someone scout, make deals, and be the liaison can be a wonderful thing.

MAKEUP & HAIRDRESSING:

- Makeup & Hair Artist
Have one person do both, unless it's a very makeup-oriented project or there's a big female cast. If your film requires a lot of makeup or hair, pile on the artists to keep things on schedule in the morning, then release them before lunch so you don't have to feed them. Because they are using up their own supplies, your hair and makeup people will probably ask you for a kit fee.

LIGHTING:

- Gaffer
A well-lit film is worth its weight in gold. A DP can often act as his or her own gaffer, but everything will take longer (tweaking the lights always seems to take forever anyway!).

- Electrician
Runs the power for the lights.

- SWING
Does both gaffing and gripping.

TOTAL CREW: 26

RECAP

- Ignore doing proper paperwork at your own peril.

- At the very least, get your actors to sign releases.

- Assemble your crew by recommendations. Ask your DP to help you.

- There's real learning value in doing many jobs yourself when making a short.

- Don't let your crew size get too big or you'll find yourself feeding an army!

CHAPTER 13

FINALLY, YOU'RE DIRECTING!

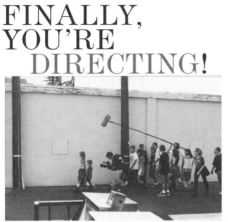

REMEMBER SOUND IS AS IMPOR-
TANT AS PICTURE!

Even if you went to film school, inside every director is that gnawing doubt that says, "Who am I to be claiming to be the next Spielberg? I'll never be as talented as Wes Anderson. How can I call myself a director? I don't even own a baseball cap!" Don't panic. Remember, you don't need a diploma or a license to be a director. You're the studio. You've decided hiring you to be the director is a good decision. If you believe in you, others will follow suit. Don't worry, you'll be fine.

WHAT EVERY DIRECTOR SHOULD KNOW

There is no real rulebook for directing, but if you want to act like a real director, here are some helpful tips.

■ ALWAYS REMEMBER YOU'RE NOT CURING CANCER.
Obvious, but easy to forget.

■ BE PREPARED. BE ORGANIZED.

Yes, being a director is a lot like being a boy scout. So many things can go wrong in production, the only preventative thing you can do is be as ready as you can be. Don't let the problem on the set be you.

■ BE AN EGOIST.

"The thing I've learned about directors is you have to have a massive ego," reports Robbie Consing who, in addition to being a short filmmaker, has worked as a storyboard artist for major directors such as Steven Spielberg, David Fincher, Michael Bay, and John Woo. "You don't have to display it, but you have to have it. Because you have to make these crew people and actors suffer endlessly to achieve your vision. If you're doing your own short with your own money, the one thing you want to be able to do at this point in your life is tell your story your way. Even if you don't know how to do it. Even if you're fudging your way though it. The point is, this is the last time that you can call your own shots because you're the director and the producer. Once people start paying your tab, that's it. It becomes a question of how much are you wanting to fight for your own art. Making shorts is not the time to start chickening out. Because that doesn't say much about the rest of your life."

■ BUT DON'T BE A JERK.

Filmmaking is a communal activity in which your job is to interact with, inspire, and energize a whole host of people. Mat Fuller reminds us what's important. "I'm all about the thanks — 'Thanks, man!'," yells Fuller. "I can't remember ever in my life going, 'Thank God I was a jerk to that guy or I wouldn't have gotten what I wanted!' Until that happens, I'm not going to use that method. Just because you get to play director for a few days, don't be a jerk."

■ DON'T TRY TO DO EVERYTHING YOURSELF.

Why bite off more than you can comfortably chew? "It's essential that you have a great producer, and I would recommend not doing that yourself," advises filmmaker Amy Talkington. "It can be done, but it doubles the stress and it takes away your focus from directing. I worked as an assistant director on a short a friend of mine was directing and producing. As she was also the line producer, in between directing the actors she had to dole out petty cash. No. Not a good idea."

■ MAKE SURE YOU HAVE ENOUGH "ME" SPACE.

Madeleine Olnek remembers, "My apartment was used as a holding pen for all the equipment during my shoot. And with my second and third films, it was also the set of my movie. I now think it's very important for filmmakers to keep a little pocket of sanity for themselves throughout the shooting experience. It wasn't helpful that I was sleeping among craft-service garbage. That definitely wears on you. It's important to have some separation. So while you save money shooting in your own house, you lose intelligence. You want to make the film with your real brain, not your broken/fragmented self."

■ PICK YOUR PEOPLE WISELY.

Moviemaking is not a solitary proposition. Cast everyone — actors and crew — with care. "I was co-producing an ultra-low-budget film several years ago, and we saved money by getting much of our crew for free," shares producer Melissa Brantley. "One of those free crewmembers was our script supervisor, who had never done a film before. When we interviewed her, we were not 100% comfortable with her abilities, but because we were excited about saving money and pushed for time, we hired her anyway. After a very long fifth day of filming when the crew was wrapped and we all were exhausted and had gone home, the producer and I get a dreaded call. On her way home, the script supervisor had put her notebook containing all of the script notes from the days before on top of her car and didn't realize it until she was going down the freeway, looked in her rearview mirror and noticed papers flowing in the traffic behind her. I learned the hard way to always follow your gut, don't scrimp on the most important elements, and interview, interview, interview until you find qualified people. Qualified people do work for free if they know you are loyal and will take them with you when you succeed. Also, I learned not to push the crew so hard that they are completely exhausted and can't do great work."

■ INVOLVE YOUR CREW.

"Nobody's getting paid. They're just wanting to make a movie," Mat Fuller points out. "If you get everyone stoked, it's not like the director is over here and the grips are over there. On my shoot, the grip department had a full storyboard and shot breakdown showing what to do three weeks before we rolled film. A day we didn't get a shot, there were grip guys who were bummed."

■ DON'T LOSE CONTROL.

The egoist in you will remember that this is your movie. By all means, be open to suggestions from others during all stages of production. But don't allow anyone more opinionated or more experienced to undermine you and take over your movie. If you give in to others, you'll end up with a movie you feel is comprised and doesn't represent your true vision.

■ ENJOY THE PROCESS.

Life After Death director Jordon Horowitz is the first to admit that he gets "so freakin' stressed out making films that I almost find myself paralyzed on set, unable to accomplish what needs to be done. I think if you don't love the actual process of making the film, then there really is no point to doing it. It's very important how the finished product turns out, but remember, it's not where you are when you die, but how you enjoyed the process of living."

You'll always be your own harshest critic. The trick is to not dwell on what you did wrong, but credit yourself for what you did right. Rashaad Ernesto Green says, "My film was six days, plus a pick-up day. It was too long. I should have had it more structured and more concise. But we definitely got done what we needed to get done."

■ TAKE CARE OF YOURSELF PHYSICALLY.

Directing means being on your feet all day, usually outside, in changing temperature. Even if you're only doing a one-day shoot, you'll be much sharper if you don't exhaust yourself. I don't want to sound like your mother, but don't forget to eat. Drink plenty of water. Faithfully apply your sunscreen and lip balm. Wear comfortable shoes and layers. Whenever you can, sit down. You want to live to direct again, don't you?

■ WEAR A BASEBALL CAP.

Not only because a hat will protect you from the sun. Not only because you'll be so focused on directing you can't spend extra time worrying about your hair. Wear a baseball cap because you've watched enough of the behind-the-scene pieces on DVD to know wearing such a hat really does make you look like a director!

READY, STEADY, GO!

Every director will tell you that you can't spend enough time in preproduction. "I see a lot of people going into short filmmaking on a 'let's make a film!' whim," remarks Brian McDonald, who wrote and directed the mocumentary, *White Face*. "They get a lot of friends together, and it's 'let's put on a show!' That's not what I did. I approached my short no differently than I did the feature project I'm doing. I made sure the script was solid. I made sure

I had really good actors. They were auditioned, and they were good. I worked for years on my directing skills — still do." But sooner or later you're going to have to put on that baseball cap and say "action" and "cut."

MARKETING BEGINS NOW

Many short filmmakers put on their marketing hats after they have finished films. Wrong. You should be calling attention to yourself and your film during production. "I was given your book at Xmas," a filmmaker named Ray wrote me, "and I have finally gotten off my rear and am about to shoot my film here in England. I've used your advice and have attracted the attention of the BBC, who are coming to film us in production for the news here."

Especially if you live in a town where filmmaking isn't an every day occurrence, the fact that you are standing on a set and yelling "action" can be newsworthy. Notify the local press. At the very least, make video diaries and post them online. Encourage your actors to do the same. Blogging is also good.

TEN COMMON PRODUCTION PITFALLS TO AVOID

Although every production is unique, every filmmaker comes away with a "I'll never do that again" moment. Learn from our mistakes!

1

NOT PREPARED.

"The most important thing — and it's not redundant, it's not beating a cliché — you have to be prepared," warns *Coven* director Mark Borchardt. "I mean, there's no way around it. The more prepared you are, the more focused you are, the better results you'll see on screen. That goes for anyone, but it goes massively for people without any money. Because you can be a drunken lout if you got a hundred million dollars, the crew's going to do all the work for you; you're just going to incoherently point, and they'll bring you a masterpiece. Filmmakers without any money have to live off their means, their intelligence, their drive, their ambition. Because if they don't have a sterling professional crew, they have to fight to invent that quality in order to get it up on screen. And if you're slacking, man, if you don't get a proper microphone or stuff like that, it's going to show, it's going to damage you. Whatever or whoever you are as an independent filmmaker is going to show up on screen."

2
OBSESSING ABOUT THE WRONG THINGS.

Bad Animals filmmaker David Birdsell warns against "getting off track and getting overwhelmed by things that don't really matter, that aren't going to end up on screen. Usually there are so many logistics to deal with during production. The danger is that you spend all your time and energy fixing little things or moving a prop in the background, and forget that the whole focus of the scene should be on an important look on a character's face or the way a line is directed. When people watch the short later, they'll say, 'Did you see how bad that actor was?' No one will say, 'But the props were excellent.' So look out for logistics getting in the way of right priorities."

3
TOO AMBITIOUS FOR YOUR MONEY.

Don't try to stretch your production beyond what you can realistically accomplish. I know a directing team who jokingly referred to its extended and overly ambitious production and postproduction experience as "the *Apocalypse Now* of short filmmaking." Don't let this be you. If it's clear in preproduction that you're over your head and sinking fast, call a halt before you move into production. If you're already in production, scale back as you go. For example, extras — don't think you need 50 if you can get away with 30. Or locations. Rather than going from location to location, reutilize the same location to avoid a series of moves.

4

CREW: A) TOO FAT B) TOO UNSKILLED OR C) TOO SKILLED.

I was shocked when Mat Fuller told me he had 50 people on his crew. I thought my productions were fat with 26. That's a lot of mouths to feed, and a lot of people just sitting around. Mat admits he had "about 20 too many, but in eight days we did 160 shots, and a 120 set ups with a 35mm Panavision camera. That's a lot. Considering there wasn't one pro on the crew!"

Yes, shorts are a learning experience for everyone. But you don't want everyone to be at kindergarten level when you need high school seniors to make it through your day. "If you're not paying them, anything goes at any time," prompts Mark Borchardt, whose production woes were documented in *American Movie*. "I have some professional people who work with me recording sound, etc., who give up their time because they believe in the work. And then there are other people who are passed out in the kitchen by 11 a.m., you know, from drinking. It's quite a polar experience."

Conversely, be wary of pros used to big-budget extravaganzas who can't go back to guerilla-style filmmaking. Directors of Photography who work extensively on high-profile commercials are particularly worrisome. They'll want all their toys, and can even help you get them, but sometimes you won't want them. I've been on sets where precious time was wasted waiting for the crane operator to get ready, when there was no need for a crane in the first place.

5

SKIPPING ESTABLISHING AND CUTAWAY SHOTS.

It's easy when you're trying to make it through an ambitious shot list to try to skip over things you'll need later for editing. Like cutaway shots. Or even worse — establishing shots.

6

SLOPPY SHOOTING.

Fans of *American Movie* send Mark Borchardt their own work to watch. "Half of the people haven't even heard of, or understand, what a tripod is," Borchardt laughs. "It's amazing and bizarre at the same time. You would have doubled, tripled your production value by simply putting the camera on a tripod. I don't understand that! Also they haven't studied enough film to understand how to shoot, and how that shooting is going accommodate the editing process. The shots don't match, the shots jump. They don't understand the 180-degree rule, they don't understand the 30% change rules. These are not rules for rules' sake. These are rules that give quality and flow and natural velocity to images on screen. You have to educate yourself. For example, the 180-degree rule is that when characters face each other and you're doing reverse shots back and forth, the camera has to stay on a chosen side of both of the actors so on the screen it looks like they're actually talking to each other. I've seen horrible Christian films where these guys are talking back and forth into outer space, it's bizarre!"

Filmmakers who don't pay attention to crossing the line also irritate *Beeker's Crossing* director Robbie Consing. "Motion has to be kept consistent," Consing points out. "So basically if the good guys are charging at the enemy left to right, and the enemy charges right to left, you have to keep it that way. Let's say you're depicting a football game in a movie. Yes, the camera will go handheld. Yes, you'll have shots from the stadium and the blimp. But if it's not made very clear that left to right means losing, and right to left means winning, you violated a simple part of film vocabulary."

Other mistakes include getting the actors' eye lines wrong, which becomes obvious in editing when the direction a character is looking doesn't match the reverse angle or a POV shot, or not framing the actor with enough head room (not enough space between the top of the frame and the top of the actor's head) or nose room (from the tip of the actor's nose to the edge of the frame).

7
SHOOTING TOO MUCH

For *I'm on Fire*, director Ryan Rowe had a 10-to-one shooting ratio. Because most scenes were locked-down master shots (he had to do that for special effects reasons), Rowe decided to use his 10-to-one ratio by shooting each master shot 10 times. When it came to editing, he couldn't decide which one of the 10 was superior.

I've also seen filmmakers fall into the trap of "shooting one more for safety" early in the day, taking up so much time that by the end of the day, to get all their scheduled shots they had to do one take only and move on. So much for one more for safety!

Don't let actors burn through tape (or film) doing different takes. Get what you need, then move on.

However, don't make the mistake of being so conservative with film or tape that you don't let the camera run a little extra before you call "action" or call "cut." Not only is that where you'll find some crucial footage you'll need in editing, it's where some of the most spontaneous elements will happen.

8
NOT PAYING ENOUGH ATTENTION TO SOUND.

Viewers forgive bad lighting but hardly ever forgive bad sound. During the shoot when so many people's attention is focused on the visuals the camera is capturing, it's equally important to capture good sound.

Getting good sound from a camera microphone is a losing battle. However, if you must, make sure the camera microphone is close to your actors. If you're using a boom or a lavaliere, make sure the microphone isn't in your shot. Whenever possible, wear headphones so you can hear what the camera "hears." And lastly, pay close attention to background sound. You don't want a refrigerator hum. (And speaking of turning off the refrigerator during filming, a good trick to remind you to turn the fridge back on, when you're finished filming, is to put your car keys in the freezer. This guarantees you can't leave without remembering to check the fridge!).

Let's not forget the importance of room tone. You'll kick yourself in editing if you don't record some clean room ambient sound at every location. Yes, you can always scrape around and find suitable moments in editing if you forget, but how much easier is it if you just make a practice of having everyone cease moving to allow your sound person to capture some accurate "empty" sound before you move on from each location. You'll never regret spending those extra moments.

9
SAYING YOU'LL FIX IT IN POST. OR COUNTING ON RESHOOTS.

If you always think you can go back or fix it later, you'll get sloppy. It's cheaper to do things right the first time. If you're shooting digitally, review footage before wrapping a location. That's the beauty of digital — you don't have to wait for the film to come back to the lab to discover if anything is wrong. However, it's tempting to waste time viewing and reviewing what you've already shot. Operate under the assumption that things are fine, but do your "idiot check" before you move on and can't go back.

10
FORGETTING TO TAKE STILLS OR BEHIND-THE-SCENES.

Director Beth Macheleny reminds us, "There are two things specifically that you need. One is publicity stills, which are taken from the POV of the camera without any equipment in the shot, as if it were a still directly from the edited film. Two, behind-the-scenes stuff." Make sure you get a decent photo of you posing near the camera, looking like you're directing. Pointing also seems to be a good pose indicating "director at work." And of course, wearing a baseball cap is essential.

RECAP

- Shorts are a learning experience for everyone.

- Directors must have egos, but shouldn't be jerks.

- Pay attention to sound.

- Don't plan on reshooting. Get what you need during production.

- Enjoy the process!

CHAPTER 14

POSTPRODUCTION
WORKFLOW
MADE
EASY

YOU "MAKE" YOUR SHORT THREE
TIMES. FIRST IN WRITING. THEN
IN SHOOTING. AND FINALLY, IN
EDITING.

L et's be honest — postproduction is a hideously painful
process. Every step takes longer than you want it to.
Things go wrong all the time, and everyone blames someone else for the problems. Worst of all, you're forced to face the
film you actually did shoot rather than the film you thought you
shot. Fortunately, it all comes together in the end — when you
see that you really do have a film that you can be proud of. Then
you'll forget about all the pain and suffering of post, just like you
did with all the pain and suffering of preproduction and production. And you'll want to do it all over again.

The most important thing to remember about post is that,
unlike production, you have no concrete time frame. You can
take your time arranging for freebies. However, whenever you
are paying (especially by the hour), you need to go as fast as
possible.

HOW TO GET YOUR FILM FROM "IN THE CAN" TO "IN THE EDITING SYSTEM"

If you shot film (as opposed to video), you need to find a lab to develop the negative and prep it for telecine. Because labs charge by the foot, if you have very little footage, you might be able to beg for free processing. Perhaps your DP has a lab at which he or she has done a lot of jobs and therefore can ask a favor or two. If you have to pay the lab, take consolation in the fact that developing and prepping the footage for telecine aren't your biggest expenses in post. Also, the future of your entire film rests on the continued wellbeing of your negative. Don't risk mishaps occurring at an inexpert lab. Better to beg a discount at a professional lab than risk an unmitigated disaster at a fly-by-night company.

Once the negative has been developed, in order to see your footage, you need to do telecine. During this process, your negative is run through a machine, a color timer makes adjustments, then the image is laid down on tape. A good timer can perform miracles in telecine. If there is something that is terribly wrong with what you shot, mention it to the colorist and see what he or she can do.

However, be aware that such magic has only been done on your video footage. Your original negative is in the same shape it always was. If you want to go back to print, you'll be dismayed when you discover that those problems remain.

The telecine step is a prime example of how things in post can be done for free or can cost outrageous amounts. I've paid as much as $400 an hour for telecine, and I've also gotten free service (although tape is rarely free). That's why it's so hard to budget for post. Three hours of telecine could cost you $1,200 or $∅ (plus tape).

If you have extremely limited telecine time, you might be forced to lay down only your preferred takes or skip syncing up sound at this stage and wait to marry sound with picture during editing. Don't allow yourself or your DP to get lost in the magic of telecine. As you know from shooting, some DPs will tweak forever. If you're paying by the hour, you need to keep the workflow going. Sometimes to get the best deal, you have to agree to unsupervised telecine. Meaning you and your DP can't be there. If this is your only option, take it.

If you do get free or severely discounted telecine time, you'll probably be working late at night and on bumpable hours (meaning if a paying client comes, you're bumped) and with the less experienced color timers. If you're never planning on going back to your original negative, it's worth paying for a good color timer who can work fast and give you the best results. After all, this is the stage where your film's look is being solidified. Why suffer with five free hours with a lame colorist when one paid hour with a kick ass miracle worker is worth its weight in gold? Another option is to do unsupervised telecine for your raw footage, and then book time to color correct after editing, when you have a locked picture.

Be aware that you can beg free telecine, but quite often the tape stock isn't free. If you lay your footage down to DigaBeta or HD Cam, it can get pricey fast. Speaking of tape stock, you should have already chosen your editor (even it's just you) so you'll know what format you'll need for editing.

FROM "IN THE CAN" TO "IN THE EDITING SYSTEM": DIGITAL

How easy is this? If you shoot digitally, you don't even have to take the stock out of the camera! Just wire your camera up to the computer and begin to edit.

TIME OUT FOR EDITING

Before you begin editing, know your footage. This is definitely a "free" step that you should spend a lot of time on. It's time to make a log of all your footage. Note the time code, the scene and take number, what works, and what doesn't. This is you putting the film together in your head. During this process, refer to your storyboards, script supervisor notes, and any notes you might have scribbled down during telecine. You might even go as far as making a paper edit — listing the takes in the order you'd assemble them if you were doing a linear edit. Not only does this help you become familiar with the footage you actually did shoot, it will save you invaluable time in editing.

With the proliferation of desktop editing systems such as Final Cut Pro or even iMovie, you really can edit your film yourself on your home computer. But just because you can do something doesn't mean you should. Many short filmmakers edit their own work. This is the reason why too many shorts are too long. You don't have the distance to be objective. "A lot of people opt to edit their own movies," points out filmmaker Amy Talkington. "On one level, that's great, you learned a lot about editing. On the other hand, it's very valuable to learn how to work with an editor. When you make a feature, you're going to have an editor." A good editor is like a good DP — they'll make everything look better than you ever could, doing it yourself.

Greg Ivan Smith did his own postproduction because he wanted to learn how. "If you had told me that I would be premiering my film two years after I shot it, I would have cried and run away from the camera! But I really, really wanted to edit it myself because I had edited as an undergrad in art school and loved it, loved the process of it, and really wanted to learn Final Cut Pro. So I taught myself editing for six to eight months. Now I feel really confident with editing, I actually find it almost the most fun part. I realize I also have new appreciation for it. If you're working digitally, it's easier to do it well — and easier to do it badly, I think. I always notice if people are clearly going through the list of available filters in their films. It's easy not to have a unique film or a specific look to your film because everyone has so many standard options. I would recommend editing down, editing cleanly. Because less is more."

When I asked Robert Arentz, who has seen literally thousands of short films as the head of L.A. Shorts Fest, if he could tell filmmakers one thing, he immediately replied, "Edit your film down.

I think a lot of times filmmakers will get in there, they'll make their points, but then will linger. It lingers on, and it loses its power and effectiveness. Whereas if they could just get in and get out, it makes it a much more powerful story and film."

TEN COMMON EDITING PITFALLS

1
FEATURE-FILM PACING.

I'll say it again: you are not making a feature!

2
STARTING A SCENE TOO EARLY, ENDING IT TOO LATE.

Remember back when you were writing your script you tried to start each scene as late as possible and end it as soon as possible? The same thing applies in editing. If you start a scene with a character walking somewhere, know that one day Noah Edelson is going to see your short and yell at the character, "It's a short film — you should be there already!"

3
FALLING IN LOVE WITH YOUR TEMP MUSIC.

It's perfectly acceptable to use pre-recorded music as a temp track during editing. Problems arise when you get so attached to that Stones song that you can't imagine any other kind of music ever being as good. We'll cover music in more detail in the next chapter.

4
SUFFERING FROM TIRED EYES.

Even if you're working with an editor, you're too close to your material to be the final arbiter. Throughout the editing process, bring in people who aren't familiar with your film to give you a fresh perspective.

5
NOT LISTENING TO HONEST CRITIQUES.

"What I've noticed is most filmmakers want advice," remarks director/editor Tara Veneruso, "but when they get it, they're like,

'Oh, but you don't understand why we did it like this.' They're not actually open to listening. So many people get into that over-defensive mode, which is a mistake. Usually, people will only give you advice if they actually want to help you!"

6
HAVING A TITLE SEQUENCE.

Features have time for a fancy title or opening-credits sequence. Shorts don't. Every filmmaker who loads the front of his or her film with an opening-credits sequence regrets it. Don't do it. However, it isn't a bad idea to make a quick logo that plays in front of your film. The reason being, a short film is usually the first thing projected in a festival situation, and if the projectionist is a little slow in doing everything right, the very first few seconds of your film can get cut off, or have sound that is too loud, or no sound. A very quick logo can be your sacrificial victim. With the Fox Movie Channel shorts, our logo was eight seconds long — and that was much too long.

7
TOO-LONG END-CREDIT SEQUENCE.

If you feel like you must thank anyone and everyone who had anything to do with your film in the credits, consider doing an alternate version of your film that has the never-ending credits roll. For the "real world" (festivals and potential television sales), keep your end credits to a reasonable length.

As for the order of crewmembers in your ending-credit sequence, there are no rules about that. If you want your credits to look like a feature film, cheat off the way credits are organized on a Hollywood movie.

8
NOT INCLUDING A WEBSITE IN YOUR CREDITS.

Put your film's website or MySpace page at the very end of the credits and leave it up long enough for people to remember it. That way anyone watching your film can contact you.

9
INCORRECT COPYRIGHT NOTICE.

Don't forget your copyright notice at the end of the film: "© 2010 Jane Filmmaker." If your film is finished at the tail end of one year, chose the following year as your copyright.

10
EDL NOT CONFIGURED FOR NEGATIVE CUTTER.

If you shot on film and are going back to film, make sure your editing system can generate an EDL (edit decision list) that a film negative cutter can use. Have your editor consult with the negative cutter if you're not sure.

MOVING ON TO SOUND

It doesn't matter how pretty your film looks — if the sound is sucky, people will think your film is sucky. Spend the time to do this right. Great sound will add so much more production value. For one of our Fox Movie Channel shorts, we got to spend a day with professional Foley artists. Wow! I can't tell you impressive that short's sound is! In fact, I don't think I'll ever want to go back to lesser quality sound houses. I know another short filmmaker who got free sound work at Lucas's Skywalker facility (he had connections). Use your short filmmaker selling points ("one day you'll be a paying client," "it's less time commitment than a feature") to see what you can beg for free. Don't be afraid to aim high.

NYU student filmmaker Rashaad Ernesto Green, who spent five months in post, wisely points out that you can approach post people even during preproduction. "Get people like a sound designer signed on as early as possible, even before you start shooting. Because especially in film school, once you wait until postproduction, everyone is seeking the same people. By the time you got around to them, they're already booked solid. Get them early." Asked how to convince people to sign on before they can see a cut, Rashaad reminds, "You sell them on it. You're the number one promoter of your film, so promote."

When you're doing your final sound sessions, make sure you create a Music and Effects track (commonly known as an M & E track). Having a dialogue-free track is important for foreign television sales, where certain stations won't take your film unless they can dub it into their own languages. If your film has no dialogue to begin with, you've got a de facto M & E track, and this is a non-issue for you.

BEHOLD YOUR FINAL VIDEO MASTER

Your video master should be on the best format you can achieve. In some cases, it might be a mini-DV tape or a DVD. If you can swing it, DigiBeta is your best master format, for now. However, HD is quickly becoming the new standard. If you have an HD master, you'll be in a great position for future sales.

You can have a "letterboxed" master, but also make sure you have a full screen version for television sales (many networks won't take anything but full screen).

Your master should begin with 60 seconds of bars and tone, followed by 30 seconds of black. When you make DVD screeners, leave off the bars and tone and black leader. Your picture should start at even time-code hour. Non-drop frame time code is preferred.

Your audio should be:

Channel 1: stereo mix
Channel 2: stereo mix
Channel 3: Dialogue (if at all possible)
Channel 4: Music and Effects (if at all possible)

ONE LAST WORD ABOUT PAPERWORK

There are two very important documents you need to collect during this phase of post, and because they are time-code oriented, it's easiest to generate them during the last phases of post.

■ DIALOGUE LIST

This is a basic time-code referenced listing of every piece of dialogue in your film. You'll need to provide this list to foreign festivals and foreign television stations if they are going to translate your film.

■ MUSIC CUE SHEET

This is a time-code referenced listing of every piece of music in your film. You'll need to provide this list to television stations who will pay royalties. We'll go over the music cue sheet in more detail in the following chapter.

DON'T FORGET TO FILE A COPYRIGHT ON THE FINISHED FILM

Visit the Library of Congress Copyright Office website (*http://lcweb.loc.gov/copyright*) for specifics.

FINISHING ON FILM

Because very few shorts have any hope of theatrical exhibition, the only reason you need a film print is to screen at festivals. "If they can afford it, most filmmakers want a film print," sighs short-film distributor Carol Crowe of Apollo Cinema. "For them, it's like a romance. The best thing in the world is to sit in a dark room, see the flicker and hear the sound of the projector. And most of the film festivals right now — in a couple of years, it will totally change — but right now, most of the festivals still screen film. But they also screen off of DigiBeta masters. In the future, it will be more digital projection. The thing filmmakers need to be open to, and a lot of them aren't right now because they're in love with film and very stubborn, is digitizing their shorts to be projected digitally. Think about how much you're going to save on print trafficking and wear and tear!"

There's no stigma attached to not having a print. "We show films that were shot on video, then transferred to film," says Sundance Film Festival senior programmer Trevor Groth. "We also show films shot on video and projected on video. We also have shown work shot on film but then transferred to HD, and projected on video. Whatever works best for the filmmaker, whatever makes the most sense, aesthetically and financially, we accommodate." Rather than investing time and money in getting a film print, you might better invest that money in getting a great video master.

MAKING A FILM PRINT

If you're going back to film, there are quite a few more steps after you've completed your video master.

■ TITLES CREATED — THEN SENT TO NEGATIVE CUTTER TO BE CUT INTO THE FILM.

Anything that isn't on the original negative has to be created if you're going back to film. So your credits that you created on the editing system need to be created on film — and it's very expensive if you don't get it for free. A better option is to figure out a way to shoot your own titles and credits. I've seen film titles and credits written in sand on the beach, embroidered on clothes hanging on a clothes line, arranged with magnetic letters on a refrigerator door, and even done up with ransom-note-style clippings.

■ OPTICALS CREATED — THEN SENT TO NEGATIVE CUTTER TO BE CUT INTO THE FILM.

Any digital wizardry you did in editing that doesn't exist on the negative also has to be shot on film — it's called an optical. Those slow motion shots you did in the computer? Opticals. The split screen? An optical.

■ COMPUTER-GENERATED SPECIAL EFFECTS OUTPUT TO NEGATIVE — THEN SENT TO NEGATIVE CUTTER TO BE CUT INTO THE FILM.

All those "free" special effects you generated in the computer? No longer so free when you want to output them to film. For the Fox Movie Channel short *I'm on Fire*, we did the fire digitally. Then we went to a high-end special effects house that outputs to film negative — and charges per frame. Yes, per frame. As in 24fps. We ended up paying thousands of dollars for our "free" fire.

■ OPTICAL SOUNDTRACK CREATED FROM YOUR FINAL SOUND MIX. THE OPTICAL TRACK AND THE CUT NEGATIVE CAN BE MARRIED AT NEGATIVE CUTTER OR AT THE LAB.

Remember your sound doesn't exist on film yet. You need to have an optical track created. This is another step worth trying to beg for free but ultimately isn't that expensive if you have to pay for it. I never had any trouble with sound not synching, but other filmmakers have. If you're begging, it's harder to get your problems fixed in a timely manner.

■ THE NEGATIVE CUTTER GOES TO WORK.

The negative cutter assembles negative and attaches an Academy leader to the front of your film. You can try to beg for free negative cutting, which usually is billed per 10-minute reel with a maximum amount of cuts. But do you want some trainee potentially ruining your irreplaceable negative when negative cutting isn't that expensive for one-reel films? If your short is five minutes long, try to pay half rate. For *I'm On Fire*, we did beg free negative cutting since we already had the bulk of the film assembled when we did that super-expensive special effects output. All the negative cutter had to do was splice the opening and closing credits on.

■ COLOR TIMING OF PRINT

The cut negative and optical track are sent to your lab to strike a film print. Now comes the fun part — seeing your film projected for the very first time on the big screen. Similar to the telecine step, once again there's a color timer who makes adjustments. Unlike the digital wizardry of telecine, there are only so many adjustments your timer can make with film processing.

While it's easy to get obsessed with unfixable details as you finish the last step in creating your film, it's important to stop and appreciate the fact that your film is now being projected on the big screen. Your little idea is now a movie. This is a very big deal!

■ WALK OUT THE DOOR WITH AN ANSWER PRINT. ORDER MORE RELEASE PRINTS AS NEEDED.

Sometimes you walk away with the final answer print and never order more release prints. If you become successful on the festival circuit, you'll need more than one print. For some of our most popular Fox Movie Channel shorts, we had 11 prints in circulation all over the world.

A WORD ABOUT DVD

Right now DVD is going to be the format on which most people will be watching your film — if they're not watching it online. If you're making your own DVDs on your computer, don't obsess about making fancy DVD menus. Simple and clearly functional is the best way to go. Festival programmers who will be judging your films for possible inclusion in their festivals hate fancy menus. They'd prefer the films play as soon as they are plopped in the machine.

If you want a professional company to make your DVDs so they can be eventually sold in stores, museums, on Amazon, or via your website, you might want to look into having a service handle the work for you. Amazon's CreateSpace service will handle all the details for you, including getting a UPC barcode and number so your film can be sold in stores. This is something to think about as you're nearly ready to embark fulltime on the next phase of making it big in shorts: marketing your film.

RECAP

- Post can be time consuming and frustrating.

- Start working on making your post arrangements during pre-production.

- Just because you think you can edit yourself doesn't mean you should.

- Don't have an opening-credit sequence. Or excessively long end credits.

- Short films can always be shorter. Be ruthless during the editing phase.

CHAPTER 15

WHY
MUSIC
WILL
KILL YOU

WHEN IT COMES TO MAKING THE
SOUNDTRACK OF YOUR DREAMS
A REALITY, YOU MIGHT HAVE
TO MAKE A FEW ARTISTIC AND
FINANCIAL COMPROMISES.

The simplest thing to do is to hire a composer to make an original score. Find a blank composer agreement on the Internet. Have your composer sign it. Your composer creates a killer score from scratch and turns in a music cue sheet — and you're done. Easy. No outstanding licensing fees. You're free and clear to sell your film anywhere.

Unfortunately, most filmmakers want to include already existing music, to have a hit-filled soundtrack like feature films have. It's true, "real music" adds so much more production value to your film. Many of my favorite short films incorporate already existing songs. And that's why you'll never see them on iTunes or television — the filmmakers couldn't afford the music rights for commercial exhibition.

Music is such a tricky issue for all involved. I got an email from a filmmaker who worried, "I'm searching for a final definitive answer on music clearance for FESTIVAL USE ONLY. Some people say you need it. Others say you don't. Who's right? I'm now an official selection for a fairly high-profile fest, so I've got to get this resolved." As many of you may have noticed, when you send in an application to a film festival, most of the festivals require you to state that you have all rights to everything in your film. You're telling the festival you have done so, and they're taking your word that this is so. You could, of course, be lying. And I guarantee you most of the short filmmakers are, because very few really do have festival music licenses.

Short filmmakers risk screening without festival rights all the time. If you were ever to get caught, you'd say you didn't know you needed permission since you aren't earning any money on the film, but of course you would be glad to do clearances now that you know. Those in the music business always caution that music people attend festivals and might catch you using uncleared music, and I have heard a few horror stories.

When I was putting together the short film DVD compilations for Warner Bros., we had an incident with an NYU filmmaker. He approached the Hank Williams people to clear two songs for festival use, found out it would be $500 each, and decided not to go forward with licensing the music officially, but used the songs anyway for his festival run. He was never caught — until we tried to clear the songs for the film for DVD. We sent the publishers a copy of the film so they could see how the music was used, and they saw it was already in the film despite the fact they had never finished the deal for festival clearances. They were so furious that they hiked the rates tremendously (ultimately the filmmaker just changed the music for the DVD).

"You've got to have your music clearances," emphasizes Megan O'Neill of Atom. "And that doesn't mean just for festivals. If you want your film to be sold — and I've never met filmmakers who, afterwards, didn't want their films to be sold — do not use music you haven't paid for. If it's too late and you've already got festival-only rights, then change the music. Maybe not necessarily in your festival screening master, but certainly in everything else."

Film sales agent and distributor David Russell of Big Film Shorts stresses the importance of not tying up your film's future with bad choices during postproduction. "The thing I wish I could get across to filmmakers," Russell says, "especially if you haven't made your film yet, is ask yourself truly and honestly why you are making the film. If it's just to have a calling card so you can get a meeting with a studio executive or an agent (or try to, anyway!), then use music you don't own. It's not legal, but you aren't going to get busted for it. Put anybody on the soundtrack if you think it's going to goose up the watchability of your film. Go ahead and put the Rolling Stones on the soundtrack. They're only a million dollars a song, no matter how you use it. But if you think at any point you'll want to make a dollar on your film (and I think all filmmakers do nowadays), you have to make the film legal."

Director David Birdsell was put in a situation where he had festival rights for two crucial songs in his student film, *Blue City*, but he couldn't license his short to television because he couldn't afford the rights to those two crucial songs. He ended up substituting two alternate songs for television. Nobody who hadn't seen the original would ever realize the televised version didn't showcase the director's first choice in music. But the filmmaker knows that version is the "artistically compromised" version of his film. "Music can be one of the most important things in a film," says Birdsell, "so don't run away from it because you think there will be a problem. Everything in making a film is a problem. If there's something that is really going to help your film, do your best to get it. Music is important. All things being equal, it will make your life easier if you can wrap up the music rights beforehand."

Mark Osborne's short, *More*, is set to an entire New Order song. Did he secure the music in advance? "I got the permission after I made the film," Osborne admits. "I got permission from the band, but I didn't know until way late in the game that I needed permission from the label. It was a big pain."

Whether you do the legwork in advance or late in the game, securing music rights will be a big pain.

HOW TO GET A FRANK SINATRA SONG

In fact, it is annoying but fairly easy to score free (or very cheap) festival licenses for pretty major songs. Just like your dealings with the Screen Actors Guild, the people who administer music licenses will treat you professionally if you deal with them professionally. If you have your heart set on including Frank Sinatra singing "My Way" in your film, here's how you do it.

First, you have to realize that you're actually asking for two licenses. One is the right to use the song, the other the performance. For example, the song "My Way" has been recorded by many acts including Sid Vicious, Elvis Presley, and Frank Sinatra. You need to secure the rights for the song itself (the sync license). Then you have to get permission to use the Frank Sinatra recording of it (the master license). If you want one of your characters to sing the song himself in your film (rather than using the already recorded Sinatra version), all you need is the sync license. But for Sinatra's version, you need both.

To find out who controls the sync rights, look on the CD — the publishing company is usually listed right under the song title. As for who controls the master rights, it's usually the record label itself.

So you're approaching two different organizations. The way it usually works is you can get the master rights for the same amount you're paying for the sync rights. Start with the sync rights since there's no point in getting the label to say "yes" if you can't get permission to use the song.

There are two terms you need to master before you begin this adventure:

■ GRATIS

A fancy way of saying our favorite word: "Free."

184

■ MOST FAVORED NATION

Which means no one will be paid more than this company. In other words, if the publishing company agrees to a $500 most-favored-nation license fee, and the record label holds firm at $750 for the master rights, you have to go back to the publishing company and give them another $250 to equal what you agreed to pay the record company.

INSIDER INFORMATION ON GETTING WEEZER SONGS

Filmmaker Karl Hirsch made a short called *Media Whore*, which featured Weezer's hit "Hashpipe." "Our short is essentially a series of interview clips with an idiot VJ," Hirsch explains. "We wanted to cut it together as hip, cool, and MTV-like as possible. In editing, we used temp music — the latest, hippest, coolest music from Fat Boy Slim, Weezer, and everybody you can think of. When we were all done, we knew we had to replace all the temp music with music we could realistically afford the rights to. What we did for most of the music is call a couple of composers and ask them to take a song and copycat it so it sounds close but it isn't really the original song, it's actually a brand new song. However, one of our songs was crucial, a song by Weezer, and we wanted to get temporary festival rights for it. I ended up finding the publisher, sent him the movie. It took him forever, but he came back and approved it. Universal approved it. We paid $2 for a one-year festival-run only. One dollar each for sync and master use. Not bad considering 'Hashpipe' is Weezer's biggest hit song! The paper on which the sync- and master-use agreements were printed on is probably worth more than a dollar each! One thing that I found out is a lot of artists are retaining their own publishing. So when I found the publisher, it was essentially a publishing agent who handles people like me for people like Rivers who, as the songwriter, owns Weezer's songs. So all I had to do is call this guy, and he called up Rivers and said, 'You want to do it?' It was that easy. It probably took about five weeks. My experience is you usually have to go to the publisher first, and the record company will match whatever the publisher says."

IT'S EASY TO MAKE A LICENSE REQUEST

When you're approaching publishers and record labels to request a music license, it's important to be professional. Mara Schwartz, who licensed music for the DVD series *Circuit*, suggests you prepare a memo with the following information:

■ YOUR CONTACT INFORMATION

Your name, relationship to the film (producer, director, etc.), and contact information.

■ DESCRIPTION OF YOUR FILM PROJECT

Including the title, log line, and the fact that it is a short film.

■ INFO ON THE SONG

The title of the song you are requesting permission to use. The songwriter/publisher. (You get this information from the CD.) The record label.

■ TYPE OF USE

How the song is used in the context of the scene, whether it's in the foreground or background, etc.

■ LENGTH OF USE

How many seconds of the song you are using.

■ TERRITORY

This should always be worldwide unless you want restrictions on where the film can be shown, which you don't in the age of the Internet.

■ RIGHTS

Wherever you want the film to potentially be shown: festival only or television, Internet, DVD, etc.

■ TERM LENGTH

This should be "In perpetuity" unless you want to limit the length of time your film can be shown.

■ LICENSE FEE REQUESTED

How much you're willing to pay. Your obvious first choice: gratis. If you'd rather not name a number, you can wait to get a quote from the publisher or record company first — but don't be surprised if it's higher than you expect. Best to give them a ballpark figure in the beginning. A few hundred dollars can be reasonable, but it depends on the artist.

■ DEADLINE

By what date do you need a response? Give them at least a month to process your request. Allow yourself time to choose another song if the one you want doesn't work out.

This seems like a lot to think about, but all this information needs to be put in writing to avoid problems later. You can always hire a music clearance company or music supervisor to do this legwork for you, but somebody needs to make sure music is cleared properly or there will be headaches and hold-ups down the line.

DO IT YOURSELF

With computer programs such as Apple's Garageband, it's not inconceivable that a complete novice could build up a suitable score for a short film. Just like you can teach yourself editing, you can teach yourself to do your film's soundtrack. But just like editing, just because you can doesn't mean you should. Creating an effective score is a skill, which is why you probably should ask someone with real musical ability to do the job for you. But if you insist on doing it yourself, investigate computer programs designed to help you build off of looped musical tracks. However, beware of preexisting royalty-free tracks on Garageband because, as you might imagine, they are used by so many people that they have become clichés.

INSTEAD, HIRE A COMPOSER

"Here's my big advice: use original music," counsels *Breezeway* director George Langworthy. "The world is filled with amazingly talented musicians. They're right around the corner, they're cool, and they're dying to do great work. If you say you need a film score, even people who are very successful musicians will do it. I've had amazing luck with very big bands."

As with every step in the filmmaking process, you need to choose your people wisely. *Life After Death* filmmaker Jordan Horowitz had a telling experience. "I knew my last film would be heavily music driven, and therefore hired a composer at the very beginning of post-production," recounts Horowitz. "I wasn't impressed by his reel but thought he had a good attitude and would be easy to communicate with. Eight months later, on the day he was to deliver a music cut, I discovered how wrong I had read him. He was completely condescending, and told me this is his cut, and if any changes whatsoever were needed, I would need to hire someone else. With that said, I prayed he had composed something at least decent. It was total crap. Looked as if he hadn't even watched the film for which he was composing. So I left the music with him, and walked out. It did work out for the best as later I found an inexperienced but talented kid with the right attitude who composed a terrific score."

Don't be afraid to approach anyone. "I knew I wanted to have this sort of goofy, charming story song at the end of my film," says *Second Skin* director Amy Talkington, who is fearless about tracking down people. "And something I thought of was *Welcome to the Dollhouse*, the music in that movie. So I looked at that movie's credits, I saw the woman's name. Called information. She was listed. Called her up. She loved my movie and wrote a song. She also did the music for another short of mine that had a goofy song. She did them both for a tiny deferred fee."

AND THEN THERE'S MOBY

Moby's MobyGratis program allows filmmakers to use his music in their films for free. In the music man's own words, *"mobygratis. com is for independent and non-profit filmmakers, film students, and anyone in need of free music for their independent, non-profit film, video, or short. To use the site you log in (or on?) and are then given a password. You can then listen to the available music and download whatever you want to use in your film or video or short. The music is free as long as it's being used in a non-commercial or non-profit film, video, or short. If you want to use it in a commercial film or short then you can apply for an easy license, with any money that's generated being given to the Humane Society."* Let's hope others follow this bald creative genius's generous lead!

DON'T FORGET ABOUT THE MUSIC CUE SHEET

Whether you use pre-existing songs or new material composed specifically for your short, you'll need to keep a record of how much music was used in the film and where it was used. "A music cue sheet," explains film sales agent Carol Crowe, "has the title of the song, the cue in the movie where it comes in, the name of the composer or publisher, and who to pay music royalties into (BMI or ASCAP). If your composer isn't a member of BMI or ASCAP, he or she should join. Or you can write on the music cue sheet that no royalties are owed anywhere because no one is affiliated with any societies." This information is given to television channels that license your film for broadcast and therefore must pay music royalties. "Most filmmakers think this is going to cost them money," remarks Crowe. "It doesn't cost the filmmaker. It's the TV station that pays. For the composer, if it turns out to be a hot short film, I'm sure over time it can actually add up!"

RECAP

- To license already-recorded songs, you need to secure both a sync license and a master license.

- You can get major recording artists to give you reasonable licensing fees if you ask for festival-only rights.

- However, it's nearly impossible to get those rights for any kind of commercial sales.

- Consider having an artistically compromised version of your film for television sales.

- Music cue sheets are necessary for royalty payments.

PART III:
MARKETING YOUR FILM

CHAPTER 16

CREATING A FOOLPROOF GAME PLAN

TIME TO LAUNCH YOUR FILM AND YOURSELF.

Now what? Now comes the marketing and distribution plan for not only your film, but for yourself and your future career. It can be overwhelming, but remember you didn't sacrifice all that blood, sweat, money, time, and tears for nothing. The whole point was to make something you wanted to show to other people.

"The term I came up with after doing all this press and promotion was 'prestitute' — that's what I felt like," jokes filmmaker Roy Unger. "But the reason I made my film, *Requiem*, was as a calling card. The concept of the film was to promote me as a director, not just the film. It goes hand in hand. I mean, I am my film. If important people like the film, they might hire me to make another one, which is the whole point. When you market yourself, you need to get yourself out there. Nobody else is going to do it. You're basically a press agent. I didn't fully understand what a press agent does until I became my own."

Short-film programmer Joel S. Bachar adds, "What I see is that people end up with a short film, and they don't know what to do with it. Of course, everybody wants to get into Sundance, and you know most people don't. Make up a target list of festivals, and think of the costs of submitting not only entry fees, but also all the ancillary materials that go with it. People don't realize it adds up: The cost of the DVD, stamps, and puffy envelopes. What if you actually do get into Sundance? The cost of the flight, the hotel, all the marketing swag, travel, press kits, the DVDs — you can fill in the blanks. If you've got a hot film on your hands, multiply it by 10, 20, 100 festivals."

A veteran festival attendee, Roy Unger stresses that "the festival circuit's going to eat up another year of your life. Be ready for it. Put some money aside. Budget $1,000, and that doesn't cover airfare." Shane Smith of the Sundance Film Festival adds, "Take time to travel with your film. Budget travel in."

Filmmaker Heath Mensher reminds us, "It's incumbent on you to overcome shyness, talk to everyone possible, hit every possible avenue, and hustle. Take every opportunity to hustle. Use MySpace. I don't know if anything comes from it, but you have to sit at the table."

HOW TO SUCCESSFULLY LAUNCH YOUR FILM

Now that you've finished making your film, it's important to sit down and create a game plan. Think of it as a marketing plan or a launch strategy for you and your film. Ultimately, you want to be like Jeff Bemiss, who made a short called *The Book And The Rose*. "We've managed 57 film festivals worldwide," reports Bemiss. "Twenty-seven awards. Academy Award semi-finalist for Best Live Action Short. We've found a boutique distributor that loves the film and has started selling it on DVD and for broadcast, premiering it recently on the two largest PBS stations in the country — WGBH Boston and KQED San Francisco." This can be you, too. If you follow the following game plan.

■ DURING EDITING, HAVE MULTIPLE PRIVATE TEST SCREENINGS BEFORE LOCKING PICTURE.

Get feedback from people who will honestly tell you how good your film is. By the time you're ready to officially send your film out into the world, you should consider it as good as it's ever going to get.

■ MAKE POSTCARDS.

Forget about doing posters or fancy press kits. All you need to market your film is a strong postcard.

You'll use postcards at every step of marketing your film. Make them in time to be given out at your first screening. How many postcards should you order? Most filmmakers do print orders for 1 to 5,000. Other filmmakers skip the formal printing and do them as needed on their computers. Whatever works for you!

■ HOLD AN INFORMAL CAST AND CREW SCREENING.

For this screening, your film is shown in an informal setting like someone's house with a big screen TV or a neighborhood bar that can project DVD. Provide cheap food and lots of liquor. Don't worry about working the room — you are allowed to get drunk and have fun. Notify people of this screening by phone calls, texts or email, not by postcard. Obviously, the people you're inviting are already familiar with your work and aren't impartial, but this screening is your first time to see how your short plays in front of an audience. Listen to what people tell you. It's not too late to make changes before officially launching the piece.

This gathering is also a chance to have fun and celebrate everyone's achievements. When you give an introduction, your speech can be sloppy and your list of thanks elaborate. Collect everyone's contact information so you can send information on the formal premiere. Have stacks of postcards to pass out so your cast and crew can invite VIPs to the premiere.

■ MAKE DVDS.

Don't make tons of DVDs of your film until after your first screening — just in case you do want to make a few minor tweaks. Ultimately you're going to be making a lot of DVDs. You never want to be stingy, calling around to ask to get your DVD back. Don't forget to make copies for your cast and crew. If you figure you will be submitting to 30 film festivals, plus fielding various requests, you'll be surprised how many you'll go through.

Make sure the actual DVD is labeled with your film's title and your contact information. Regarding cases, those with full sleeves are nice because you can showcase your postcard artwork. The sturdy casing also adds a little more protection during mailing. Nevertheless, a simple paper cover works just as well.

As for labels on the DVDs themselves, be wary of putting a sticker on the DVD. Avery stickers are notorious for jamming up DVD players and laptops. I constantly hear festival programmers begging filmmakers to just write the film's title, running time, and contact info on the DVD with a Sharpie.

■ ASSEMBLE MAILING SUPPLIES.

Here's something that will endear you to everyone you mail your film to: never, ever use those jiffy-padded envelopes. When those devils are opened quickly, shredded padding goes everywhere. If you want extra padding, spend a little extra to get the bubble-lined envelopes.

■ PUT TOGETHER A PRESS KIT, WEBSITE, MYSPACE/ FACEBOOK PAGE, REGISTER WITH WITHOUTABOX.

This will be discussed in detail in the following chapter.

■ BEGIN FILM FESTIVAL SUBMISSIONS.

As soon as you can, begin to submit to festivals because there is a lag time between the entry deadline and when your film is accepted. Your goal is to have a major festival lined up before your self-organized premiere.

The festival circuit is vitally important to the short filmmaker for many reasons. Unless you luck out and get some sort of theatrical distribution, the only time your film will play on the big screen in front of paying audiences will be at a film festival. Secondly, festivals are a priceless networking opportunity. In no other context are you so clearly identified as a filmmaker. In no other context will you meet so many other filmmakers and professionals in the film industry. Work every angle you can to meet people, make connections, and perhaps get a gig. Thirdly, buyers scout for product at festivals. If you want to sell your film to foreign television (that's where the real money is), your film needs to show at a festival where foreign buyers go.

However, be smart about your plan. Robert Arentz of the L.A. Shorts Fest muses, "Usually after their films are done, filmmakers don't think of a master plan for submitting it. They just think 'when's the next festival coming up?' They just start submitting, just to see what festivals they get in. If the ones they really want to get in have restrictions of where the films have previously played, they've blown their opportunities. So really think about what festivals you play in first. Have your top five festivals that you want to get in first and focus on those. If you get in those top-tier ones, other festivals will come to you."

More about festivals in Chapters 18 and 19.

■ HOLD YOUR BIG PREMIERE.

For this screening and this screening only, try to get a proper screening room. This can be your school auditorium, a local art house, or even a private screening room. One of my former students who lives in L.A., but is from Belgium, got the Goethe Institute to host his premiere.

If your film is very short, consider pairing with one or two other pieces by other filmmakers. However, if you do a co-screening, make sure the other pieces are not as good as yours — you should be the filmmaker everyone fawns over! The advantages of screening with someone else are many. First, another filmmaker will have different people to invite, so the circle of VIPs at your screening grows exponentially. Secondly, sharing the event helps defray the cost. Split all charges down the middle ahead of time to avoid later arguments of who had more guests attend and therefore should pay more. Lastly, people are more likely to attend if you offer more than 10 minutes of programming. Guests don't want to spend more time parking their cars than sitting in their seats!

Compile a massive invitation list for this premiere. Work your MySpace/Facebook friends. Invite anyone and everyone who might possibly help you with your career (including press). Remember, you're a major talent who is going to go far, and they should know about you! This is the screening that officially launches you and your film. If you have an upcoming festival already scheduled, promote it with this mailing. For example, slap on a sticker saying, "Catch it now before it debuts at Slamdance in January!" This makes people think they're getting a sneak peek at a hot film. Some bigwigs won't actually make the effort to come to the screening, but they will call asking to see a DVD screener. Tell them you'll send copies after the screening.

A director named Paige emailed with the following concern, "I will be hosting a premiere party this summer once postproduction is complete. Since I adhered to the mantra 'everyone works for free!' how do I handle the 'ticket issue?' Do I comp each cast and crewmember a ticket to the event or do I charge them for the party, but perhaps give each cast and crewmember a DVD of the film instead? I don't want to go cheap on everyone, but in an effort to throw a great party at the right place (easy access, screening room, etc.), I need to make sure I sell a certain amount of tickets to cover the cost of the party, food, alcohol, etc." One way to solve this problem is to share the bill with other films, so you can split the costs. Or you can have a cash bar, assuming that might cover some of the screening room rental costs. Lastly, you can charge for tickets, explaining that the screening is designed to raise funds to send the film on the festival circuit. Then think of other ways you can turn the event into a fundraiser — maybe you can hold a silent auction in the lobby, etc.

■ AS YOU EMBARK ON THE FESTIVAL CIRCUIT, UPDATE EVERYONE OF YOUR SUCCESS.

Roy Unger says, "When I was having a festival screening, I would send out an update sometimes before, sometimes after, sometimes both! Even if people couldn't come to my screening in Germany, they knew I was going to Germany, and when I came back, what the experience was. Invariably different people would be interested."

Working animator Eileen O'Meara sent out missives specifically targeting companies that have hired her in the past. "Whenever I got into a few festivals, I'd send out a postcard saying 'Coming in June' and list all the festivals my film was playing, plus my name and phone number," reports O'Meara. "The idea being that a client I might not have heard from in a while would get it and go, 'I forgot about her!' then call me up and say, 'Hello, I'd like to pay you a lot of money!'" O'Meara laughs. On a more serious note, she adds, "Also send notice of your success to any people who helped on your film so they're glad they helped."

■ PROMOTE, PROMOTE, PROMOTE.

Now is not the time to be shy. You've got to make a little noise to be noticed. Ari Gold, director of a very short short called *Culture*, made promotional shirts. "Selling the T-shirts, I lost money, because I gave enough away to counteract my sales. But the film cost only a few hundred dollars, all the way to a print, so a few sales to TV and I was profiting. While I wouldn't necessarily recommend T-shirts, it was fun and added greatly to the publicity hype. I ended up being the first filmmaker being written about in the Sundance wrap-up article in the *New York Times* that year, I think in large part due to the shirts and posters. The over-promotion, for me, was a big part of the joke of having a one-shot, 60-second film that I'd made in about two hours."

■ WIN AWARDS.

Not every film wins awards. Of the 19 shorts we produced at the Fox Movie Channel, a few consistently won prizes, while others never won anything.

The most high-profile award you can win is the Oscar. Yet winning one award at a festival in Nowheresville makes you an award-winning filmmaker — and you should always describe yourself thusly. Very few people will ever ask you which award your film actually won. However, since it is relatively easy to earn an award, no awards except at the most major festivals mean anything in terms of advancing your career.

Obviously, the number of festivals you play increases your chances of being awarded a prize, but no one really knows what makes one film award worthy over another. I will say, however, that comedies have a hard time winning jury prizes. Juries seem more inclined to honor "serious" or "weighty" films. Having been on several festival juries, I will admit that if the filmmaker is present at the festival and available to pick up the prize at the award ceremony, this is sometimes taken into consideration.

If you do win an award, make sure you send a thank you note to the festival's organizers. Update your press kit and website. And then send out a charmingly humble note to your email list, thanking all for their belief in, and support of, this now award-winning film.

■ QUALIFY FOR AN OSCAR NOMINATION.

God bless the Academy of Motion Picture Arts & Sciences. Every year short filmmakers get to accept Academy Awards on national television. While big companies like Miramax and Focus spend millions on marketing their films to earn a nomination, you can qualify for one with very little effort on your part. And if you win, you can be seen on TV holding that same statue that turns major Hollywood players into blubbering idiots.

Although the rules can change from year to year, there are four ways for a short filmmaker to win an Oscar. One is to win the Student Academy Award. It's true, student awards aren't televised, and, even worse, the award is not the Oscar statue (it's a medal designed by Saul Bass). Still, you can claim you are an Academy-recognized filmmaker if you win one of the student awards, which also come with cash grants.

The second Academy Award category you can win is the live-action narrative short film. Amazingly, less than 100 films qualify each year, and the Academy can nominate up to five. Those are pretty good odds! How can you qualify? Two ways. One is to win a top prize at a festival that the Academy officially recognizes (a complete list of those festivals can be found in on the *www.oscars.org* website). The festival fills out the qualification paperwork, then you summit it with your application paperwork to the Academy — all of this at no cost to you! If you don't win any of the qualifying festivals, have no fear. You can buy your way in. All you have to do is have your film screen commercially in Los Angeles or New York for three consecutive days in front of a paying audience. Of course, there are some theaters that will legitimately want to show your film in front of paying audiences as a real screening. But the way most filmmakers make this three-day screening happen is to pay a theater to play their films (a.k.a. four walling the theater). In Los Angeles, the Laemmle Theater makes a tidy little profit doing this.

When I was producing shorts for the Fox Movie Channel, we did the Laemmle route for each one of our 19 films. Consequently, all were eligible for Academy consideration. Not a single one got nominated.

Just because you qualify doesn't mean you'll be a contender. The Sundance Festival winners, for example, rarely seem to get nominated. Having seen every year's Oscar selection, Carol Crowe reports, "Across the board, the live-action short films seem to be very different from each other, which is refreshing. There is no rhyme or reason to the Oscars."

It seems lately like it's the well-funded European films that get nominated and win. To get a sense of the Academy's taste, you can download recent nominees and winners from iTunes or watch the DVD collections Shorts International and Magnolia have produced. Fred Joubaud, who represents many Oscar winners, says, "I think the Academy members have a very good eye. They pick very original stories." While there have been exceptions, what the Academy is generally looking for is a film that feels like a "movie" — that is, a big, expensive production that just happens to be 30 minutes or less. They also like longer films, which I know flies in the face of my "shorter is best" philosophy.

My usual recommendation about the Oscars is if you think your film has a chance, then it's well worth the odds to qualify it and submit it. Even getting nominated is enough to kick your career in high gear.

The other two short-film Oscar categories are animated shorts and documentary shorts, which have different rules than live action. Interested filmmakers should visit the *www.oscars.org* website for up-to-date qualifying rules, regulations, and paperwork.

Recently the Academy has been taking out full-page ads in short-film festival programs with the following statement "Please note: previous television or Internet broadcast will disqualify a film from consideration." Clearly, this is something to keep in mind. Your film cannot be broadcast previous to qualifying for nomination. However, you are free to televise after qualification. The Academy always finds out if you try lying about your film's broadcast history. Never lie to the Academy.

■ **FIELD OFFERS FROM PEOPLE WHO SAW YOUR FILM ON THE FESTIVAL CIRCUIT.**

If your film has strong potential for Internet or TV sales, within six months on the festival circuit you should be fielding offers directly from buyers or from sales reps wanting to broker deals for you. Time to decide if you are going to rep the film yourself or have others do it for you.

■ **SIGN WITH A SALES REP, OR DO IT YOURSELF. LICENSE YOUR FILM TO INTERESTED COMPANIES.**

Whether you sign with a rep or make a sale yourself, send off an email notifying your fan base of these exciting new developments.

■ **PUT YOUR FILM ON THE INTERNET.**

Not all shorts are festival-appropriate. Some flicks are better suited to becoming Internet sensations, garnering a huge following over the Web. In terms of achieving maximum eyeballs, the Internet is the way to go. "I had 260,000 people look at my film in the first four weeks it was up," marvels filmmaker Amy Talkington, whose shorts *The New Arrival* and *Our Very First Sex Tape* debuted on *www.Atomfilms.com*. "I got emails from all over the world, which was really an amazing experience."

One thing you should be aware of: putting your film on the Internet can ruin other opportunities. Some festivals won't show your work if it has already played on television or the Internet. Additionally, the major television channels won't buy your film if it's been on the Internet. We've already discussed how Academy Award consideration can also be kiboshed if your Internet debut happens before qualifying for the Oscar. If you want to play it safe, hold off Internet exhibition until after you've tested the marketplace for your short. Only after you've exhausted all other venues should you allow your film to be shown on the Web. However, once you're completely done exploiting your film, definitely make it available on the World Wide Web. Who knows what unexpected opportunities might come your way?

RECAP

• Launch yourself with your own premiere.

• Build a fan base and notify people of your film's continuing success.

• Playing the festival circuit should generate offers from television networks to license your film.

• If you think your film has Oscar potential, qualify it for Academy consideration.

• Consider the Internet the last stop on your short's exposure tour.

CHAPTER 17

PROMOTION IN THE ERA OF MYSPACE AND FACEBOOK

A STRONG SYNOPSIS AND ARTWORK ARE CRUCIAL.

W hen I was producing short films, I made paper press kits which I dutifully sent off to festivals. I assumed those press kits were given to the press covering the festival. Imagine my horror when I became a reporter covering short films for *indieWIRE* and discovered the press was almost NEVER given the press kits. When I cover festivals, I am usually given the shorts in advanced as screeners, but no press kits. I end up doing what everyone does — I Google when I need some background info on a film.

The same goes for programmers. Shane Smith, one of the programmers of short films for Sundance says, "Don't waste your money sending in fancy folders, swag, and all that stuff. Make a press kit, absolutely. Better yet, make a PDF and put it on your website. Save trees and save money. All I see is the film, cold. I don't see the packaging, the case, nothing. The guys entering the submissions at the festival, doing the database, they're the ones that see it and get it."

The truth about press kits is very few people ever see them. It's your Withoutabox page, postcard, MySpace page, and website that everyone who counts checks out. Those are your real press kits.

PROVIDE USEFUL INFORMATION

Whether you're putting the information up on Withoutabox or MySpace, let's rundown the information needed so that it will be functional for festivals, press, or potential buyers.

■ YOUR CONTACT INFORMATION

If you set up a specific email account for all your film-related matters, make sure it's an email account you check regularly. When people are contacting you for a professional reason, it's usually a matter of some urgency and if you don't reply in time, you could miss out.

■ TITLE OF YOUR FILM

The wonderful thing about short-film titles (as opposed to feature-film titles) is there is no fear of having one so long that it can't fit on the movie theater marquee — because short-film titles never appear on marquees! Your title can be as long and as funky as you want. In fact, a unique title sparks interest. Would you want to see a 15-minute-long short called *I Killed My Lesbian Wife, Hung Her on a Meat Hook, and Now I Have a Three-Picture Deal at Disney*? Probably so. And I didn't even have to tell you that Ben Affleck directed it! Not that your title has to be a block long. It just has to be memorable. Noah Edelson's short had a main character who spent the first minute of the film jumping up and down on a manhole cover chanting "78." Noah called the piece *78*. Andrew Busti and Sebastian del Castillo did a super cool experimental film consisting of faces and hands pressed against the Xerox machine glass. The title *deleriouspink* ("delirious" intentionally spelled incorrectly) makes that short even more memorable.

■ LENGTH (TRT)

This is the total running time from the first image on screen to the last. You may want to adjust your reported TRT for various purposes. Some filmmakers subtract the running time of their credits to make their films more eligible for festival play.

■ FORMAT

Format is tricky. It may mean what you shot on, not what your final exhibition format is. If you shot 35mm, but don't have a 35mm print, say 35mm. If you shot DV or Super-16, but bumped up to a 35mm print, say 35mm. It's always better to be 35mm!

■ ASPECT RATIO (E.G., 1:85, 1:33)

Your film's aspect ratio matters for projection.

■ COLOR

Whether your short is color or black and white matters for television sales.

■ SOUND (E.G., DOLBY SR)

Another projection issue.

■ COUNTRY

Another tricky category. If your film was shot in Israel, but you are an American and funded the film, your film's country can be either Israel or USA. Adjust to whatever works to your advantage. However, the Sundance Film Festival is definitive about how they define foreign versus domestic films: American shorts must have at least 50% U.S. financing.

■ YEAR

This should mean year of completion, but sometimes it means year of production. In general, you want your film to be as current as possible, so the latest date you can claim is your best choice. For instance, if you shot your film in August, completed post in November, but didn't start exhibiting it until January of the following year, the January date should be used as your year.

■ LOG LINE/SYNOPSIS

Can you describe the plot in a sentence or two? That sentence-long description is known as a log line. Sometimes it's hard to boil down a complex short into one utilitarian sentence. But even the most complicated feature film has to be cut down to a one-sentence description. Here are some examples of short-film log lines from the *Short* DVD collections:

Franz Kafka's It's a Wonderful Life (Director: Peter Capaldi). Richard E. Grant stars as a tormented writer who cannot complete the first sentence of his novel.

Boundaries (Director: Greg Durbin). A desperate woman is pursued from Mexico to San Diego by a musician who pokes her relentlessly in the head with his trombone.

More (Director: Mark Osborne). An elderly inventor works on a secret project that could bring bliss to the world.

Having read these simple log lines, do you have a fairly good idea of what the films are about? More importantly, do the descriptions make you want to see the films? If so, they've done their job. Although these particular log lines don't include genre and character names, many do (e.g., "a darkly comic tale of a bank robbery gone horribly wrong." Or "Karl is a man on a mission — a mission to bring his wife to her senses."). There are no real rules about what you should and shouldn't include; if it helps to be specific, then do so. One thing you should think twice about doing is using adjectives that sound like you're praising your own film. It's okay to say "darkly comic" because that helps clarify the tone, but including descriptions like "visually ravishing" could be considered self-praise. Someone reading "visually ravishing" will immediately start judging the film — is it, indeed, as visually ravishing as the filmmaker claims?

Coming up with a good log line is hard. With a short, sometimes it's extremely hard to sum up the film without giving away the entire plot. Take for example, *I'm on Fire*. As you may remember from the storyboard in Chapter 9, the film begins with a shot of a house on a suburban street. All of a sudden, the front door flies open. A man completely engulfed in flames runs out. He fumbles around on the lawn like men on fire in movies always do, then flings himself into his baby blue Mustang convertible, which is parked in the driveway. Still on fire, he drives off. Still on fire, he arrives at a flower shop, buys flowers, then drives to his girlfriend's house to pick her up for a date. She opens the door to reveal she's also on fire. Obviously, fire is a metaphor for love, and the short is a comic love story. We struggled and struggled to come up with a decent log line. Finally, the filmmaker came up with the following log line: "A very short film about a guy on fire." It pretty much sums up the film without giving away the entire plot, doesn't it? Hopefully, it makes you want to watch it. Certainly it's more intriguing than my long, detailed explanation of the plot, isn't it?

For a feature-length film, it's important to come up with a log line and also a longer synopsis. For shorts, unless your piece is a mini-feature, there's no need to create a separate synopsis. It's perfectly acceptable for your log line to function as your synopsis on any form that requests a synopsis. However, your log line does need to convey the story if it is to function as a synopsis. Some filmmakers come up with very arty log lines that they use as synopses. For example, for his film *Culture*, Ari Gold wrote, "This is culture." His film is only one-minute long, so you could argue there isn't much more to say. But it isn't really a plot synopsis, is it? Don't mistake taglines for log lines. Taglines are catchy attitude phrases that you will see at the end of movie trailers or on posters. For example, one of the most famous taglines ever created is "In space, no one can hear you scream." Does that line tell you what the film *Alien* is about? No. But it's a cool line that makes you want to see the film, right? Here's another cool log line — from Arayana Thomas' short *Epiphany*: "Peace by way of Hell."

While undeniably cool, taglines can't function as your log lines. A log line has to answer the question, "What's your film's plot about?" "An elderly inventor works on a secret project that could bring bliss to the world" is a suitable reply. "Peace by way of Hell" is not.

Crafting a good log line is essential because if you come up with a particularly apt one, festivals will use it in their programs. Not every festival which played *I'm on Fire* printed "a very short film about a guy on fire," but several did. Whom would you rather have write the description of your film — an overworked, underpaid festival flunky or you? If your log line is especially solid, everyone will repeat it practically verbatim without even thinking about it. If you were asked right now to tell someone what *I'm On Fire* is about, wouldn't you more or less parrot our wording?

There's nothing wrong with changing your log line if something strikes you as better. Many festivals will use your log line, but some will write their own. If you like theirs better, there's nothing wrong with appropriating it. Sometimes outsiders are better at crystallizing plot than filmmakers who are too close to their own work.

■ FESTIVALS/AWARDS

Don't feel bad if you don't have any festivals or awards to list. In fact, a virginal film is more attractive to programmers who want their festival to have world premieres. By the way, you can fudge this list if you feel it will help. For example, if you get into a smaller festival first, then play a bigger one, put the biggest one first on the list. And don't include an awards category if your film hasn't won any yet.

■ CREDITS

Credits can be reduced to just the main players, e.g., director, writer, producer, cast, DP, editor, composer, or you can print out a full listing. Whatever works best for you.

■ DIRECTOR'S BIO/FILMOGRAPHY

Most short directors don't have other credits. Just write up a quick charming paragraph about yourself. If you have any local ties to specific film festivals, sell it in your bio ("A Park City native...").

■ OTHER BIOS

If anyone else on your production is noteworthy, include that. "No one will know you got this incredible cast and crew, if you don't tell them," points out filmmaker Amy Talkington. "If you have elements to sell, put the information out there." In one of our Fox Movie Channel shorts, the lead dog was the pug from *Men in Black*. You better believe the dog got his own bio!

■ PRODUCTION NOTES

No need to do full production notes like you see in feature-film press kits, but if you have anything noteworthy about your production, mention it here. Often it's impressive how many days you shot, where, etc. These are the kinds of tidbits that might intrigue someone. I know when I'm covering films for *indieWIRE*, I'm always desperate for anything behind-the-scenes-related I can include in my articles.

Culture director Ari Gold took a unique approach to production notes. Playing off the infamous Dogme95 vows, Ari Gold created his own set of rules, which he put in his promotional material (it's even on the back of the *Culture* T-shirts):

1. The film must be exactly one minute in length.
2. The film must have no cuts.
3. The number "3" must not be mentioned.
4. The film must have live sound only (no post).
5. The film must have no dialogue.

6. Only black, white, and primary colors may be used.
7. The film must be shot in one take, with no rehearsals.
8. The film must be projected in 35mm.
9. The camera must not move.
10. Ari von Gold must perform in the film.

■ REVIEWS

It's very hard for a short filmmaker to get reviewed, but if you do, make the most of it. Any reviews or testimonial quotes from someone noteworthy who said anything nice about your short should be heralded. Blurbs not only help you feel validated as a filmmaker, they can attract attention from other festivals. "Thanks to you," filmmaker Gayle Knutson wrote to me after I wrote an *indieWIRE* article mentioning her short when it played the Aspen Shortsfest, "*Green Jell-O* keeps getting calls from festivals! I think a lot of folks saw it listed in your column. Sure makes it easier to get waived entry fees when you've had a bit of good press."

■ DIALOGUE LIST

For foreign festivals and television sales, you'll need to include a dialogue list which notes every word spoken in the film and the time code when it appears. The resulting rundown is used for translations. If you can put this up as a PDF on your website, you'll be ahead of the game.

■ PHOTOS

JPEGS are the way to go. "The best piece of advice that I could give anybody," whispers filmmaker Roy Unger, "would be get some production stills. In my particular case, I had a friend come out to my set and shoot some key images. One of those became the image that has represented *Requiem* — the *Requiem* guy in close-up. The best $40 I ever spent! It became my poster, it became my postcard. It's gone on festival flyers around the world. I've been on magazine covers and all sorts of things just because I gave them the artwork. If you give them the artwork, and it's cool, they're going to use it. It's free, they don't have to do any work." Needless to say, always label your JPEG with the film's title.

AND NOW TO THE POSTCARD

Some filmmakers print up posters for their shorts. If you have posters, festivals will display them, but they tend to get lost among the feature-film posters. They also tend to disappear — as Roy Unger well knows. "I had done these really expensive *Requiem* posters, glossy, cost me $35 each to make," reports Unger. "I took a couple with me to a festival screening in Hamburg. When I went from one screening room to another, I realized someone had stolen one of my posters! I thought 'that's cool, someone liked it enough to steal it' and now it's probably hanging in some German kid's apartment, but that cost me $35!"

Postcards are a better investment than posters — and more multi-purpose in their uses. "The postcard is the most impor-tant thing," swears filmmaker Amy Talkington. "The postcard is everything," agrees consultant Thomas Harris. "That piece of art can generate validation and interest. A perception and belief system is created by what people first see — and that tends to be your postcard. It's on the outside of your press kit for the few people who get to see that. It's the thing you're mailing and hand-ing off as your business card. If there's ever a place to spend money, it's that. This is the worst thing that I can tell any film-maker, but the bottom line is nobody really wants to see your film. You have to create the desire in people to see it. And what ultimately opens the door first is your postcard."

HOW TO CREATE A KILLER POSTCARD

"With really inexpensive software, it's easy for anyone to make a really sharp looking postcard," declares filmmaker Karl Hirsch. "In the case of *Media Whore*, the photo was taken on a 35mm still camera, and I used PhotoShop to alter the colors and create depth. It's very basic stuff. I'm not a graphic artist at all, but I've seen what movie posters look like. We made 5,000 postcards. Without counting the time that it took to put it together, the actual hard cost ended up being $500 or $600. A bunch of people have now seen that image, and if they were to see it again, there would be a certain amount of recognition, and that's a really difficult thing to achieve with a tiny little movie that cost under a grand. So it was the best investment of anything we did. And it was easy. It was really easy!"

■ THE DESIGN OF IT SHOULD CONVEY THE FEEL OF YOUR MOVIE.

"Remain true to your picture," Thomas Harris reminds us. "Whatever your movie is, do not advertise it in a different way than what it really is all about."

■ EVERYTHING ABOUT THE POSTCARD SHOULD APPEAL TO YOUR AUDIENCE.

Film sales agent Carol Crowe loved the postcard for *Greggor's Greatest Invention*. "I saw the postcard at a film festival here in Los Angeles, and I picked it up," recalls Crowe. "I kept looking at it and thinking I've got to call this guy because the postcard just told such an interesting story. I was pleasantly surprised to find out that the film definitely backed up what the postcard was telling. It was a great story. And it got nominated for an Academy Award. I kept telling the filmmaker how great that postcard was. He got a lot of calls from it."

■ USE A STRONG SINGLE IMAGE.

"The way I like to do things is based on a single recognizable image or design," states marketing-savvy filmmaker Roy Unger. "It should represent the style of your movie, it should be attractive to an audience. And I think the last thing is probably the most important thing of all."

■ THE TITLE NEEDS TO BE PROMINENT.

You need people to remember the title of the film. Don't bury it.

■ USE A TAGLINE IF YOU HAVE ONE.

If you have a great tagline, by all means use it on your postcard (and website). But don't worry if you can't come up with one. Very few films have great taglines. If you really want one, sometimes a line of dialogue from the film will suffice.

■ INCLUDE A BILLING BLOCK.

Cheat off of feature posters to see how to build a block of credits at the base of your card. Note that they are usually written in a highly condensed font size.

■ PUT CRUCIAL INFORMATION ON THE BACK.

If you want to have something printed on the back of the card, include your film's stats (i.e., USA, 35 mm, 15 minutes). Make sure your contact information is printed in a readable font. And of course, your website or MySpace address should be prominently displayed.

■ ADD STICKERS WITH RELEVANT INFORMATION.

When you play a festival, customize your card by adding a sticker listing your screening information. This sticker can go on front or back. If you've recently won a prize, make a sticker with that information as well.

HOW TO USE YOUR POSTCARD

"Whenever we go to festivals, we give tons of postcards away," *Media Whore* filmmaker Karl Hirsch states. "We leave stacks of them at parties. We hand them out to people. Whenever we send screener DVDs, we include a postcard in the sleeve. If you make press kits, take a postcard and glue it to the front. Now you have a personalized press kit. Our film has been finished for a year and a half, and we've given out 4,995 postcards — we're all out!"

AND LAST BUT DEFINITELY NOT LEAST: YOUR WEBSITE AND MYSPACE/FACEBOOK PAGE

In the Internet age, a website is a film's most practical press kit. "It's a way for people to reach you, it's a way for people to know more about your movie," says design guru Karl Hirsch. "Having a Web presence is never bad."

If you are going to build a website, it's best to do the film's title, but certainly a production company or even your own name will suffice. Then put this www address on everything — including the end credits of your film. That way, when your short plays on TV, on a DVD collection, as a press screener at festivals, or on the Internet, people can track you down.

"I've already registered the website address for it," says John Halecky when his most recent short was still in postproduction. "I've been working on a MySpace page. I consider social networks more the emotional, self-promotional aspect of the film, it's not distribution of the film yet. Use online as a tool for the promotion for the film — you know, publicity — rather than putting your film online."

NYU filmmaker Rashaad Ernesto Green has a Facebook page and his own website. "I'm one of these people who accepts any friend. I live in New York and have a bunch of contacts in Los Angeles, as well. So if I have a film festival coming up in NY, I just go down the whole NY list, place everybody from the NY list on the events invite, and invite them. With these new social networks, it's a lot easier to stay in contact with people. If it's Facebook and they're looking for things to do, they see 'my friend Rashaad's got an event coming up' — and they can just click and see a trailer, people can post comments up there, and all of a sudden their friends see 'Douglas posted a comment on Rashaad's video,' and they go and they look and say, 'I want to see this, too.' So it is a social network that attracts people. Sometimes I don't even know their names, and they're leaving comments on my videos. It's great. And the website is a big plus. On Facebook you can only do so much. On your own personal website, it can look nice, be artistic, have trailers of everything, and your contact info. It's a one-stop shop."

Your website can be as simple as your postcard imagery and an email button. Or it could be your entire press kit online, including links to the festivals screening your film, reviews, stills, filmmaker's blog, or podcast, etc. Always keep your website up to date — you have no idea when people will see your film and want to reach you.

As with any material you generate to promote your film, your website should look professional. If you don't think you can do it yourself, think about taking a class on website design. Or just leave the page "under construction" with nothing but your email address for people to contact you. "I did the website myself," says can-do guy Karl Hirsch. "I'm not a Web designer person. I figured out how to do it because I didn't have any money to pay any one else to do it. Learned how to do it with a program called Dreamweaver and a lot of trial and error! Because I'm not a designer I purposely made it look really simple and easy — like a bank. I found a free Web-hosting service. From there, I could create an email address. Makes it seem like we're professionals. We constantly update the site. It is an extremely helpful tool — and essentially free."

There's no limit to what you can do with your website. For the short *Three-Fifty*, the filmmakers offered branded ringtones and cell phone wallpaper!

RECAP

• A good log line is perhaps your most useful tool.

• Be very liberal with your postcard distribution. If you're very ambitious, 5,000 postcards can go quickly.

• The most functional press kits are online.

• It's never too early to establish a presence on the Web. Make a website, a MySpace page, a Facebook page, and anything else you can think of.

• Use social networks to promote screenings.

CHAPTER 18

FESTIVALS THAT MATTER

YES, IT IS ALL ABOUT SUNDANCE.

Picture it. There you are at Sundance. Chatting with Robert Redford at the filmmakers' reception. Rubbing shoulders with Hollywood agents and studio executives at over-crowded A-list parties. And best of all, having total strangers line up in the snow to pay money to see your little film. It could happen. It really could. All it takes is $35.

WHY YOUR IDEAL FESTIVAL CIRCUIT BEGINS WITH SUNDANCE

Everyone is familiar with the festival heavyweights: Cannes, Berlin, Venice, and Toronto. But countries like Belgium, Egypt, Finland, and Taiwan have film festivals, too. Here in the U.S., Philadelphia, Sedona, Dallas, and Fort Lauderdale are lesser known stops on the festival route. Faced with an overwhelming array of festivals to choose from, how can a filmmaker with a modest budget allocated for festival exhibition decide what's worthwhile and what's a waste of time?

The most important question to ask yourself is what exactly do you want out of a festival experience?

■ AUDIENCES APPRECIATING YOUR WORK.

You made your film to be seen, didn't you? Seen by people other than your friends and family, right? Festivals are the venue where that's going to happen.

■ VALIDATION AS A FILMMAKER.

You validated yourself with your own premiere. Having a festival programmer agree that your film is worthy of endorsement is your next major step.

■ OPPORTUNITY TO MEET PEOPLE WHO CAN FURTHER YOUR CAREER.

You want people to be so impressed by your work that they'll hire you to work for them. You might not meet these potential employers at every festival, but they'll definitely be at the biggies.

■ EXHIBITION/DISTRIBUTION/LICENSING OFFERS.

If you want sales offers for your film to materialize, you need to have your work seen by acquisition executives. Such executives are trolling the festivals, looking for fresh meat. Make sure your film is on their radar!

■ LIFE-ENHANCING EXPERIENCES.

Also known as fun.

You can achieve all of these goals in one swoop — if you get accepted into Sundance. "The reason the Sundance shorts get seen a lot is not because they're better," points out former L.A. Film Fest programmer Thomas Ethan Harris. "It's simply the perception the festival holds that these are the best shorts." That's not to say that if you don't get into Sundance you are doomed as a failure. "I've met so many filmmakers through the years whose whole thing is about Sundance," complains Megan O'Neill. "Sundance is great. They play a ton of short films. It's a great place for industry meetings and the possibility to have your film sold. But it's just one festival. There are 5,000 festivals out there. Maybe you want to be the big fish in a little pond."

Have no fear, your film can be very popular and successful on the circuit without the Redford endorsement. In fact, there are many festivals that will treat you much better than Sundance. At Aspen Shortsfest, the short filmmaker is treated like a celebrity. You won't find that to be the case at Sundance (unless you really are a celebrity!).

So why should Sundance be your primary focus? Three big reasons. For films of all lengths, being an "Official Selection of the Sundance Film Festival" means something. That brand has value in the festival world, the industry (indie and Hollywood), and the universe at large. Think about it: Even your grandmother knows what Sundance means. Sure, it's great to play the Crested Butte Reel Fest, but it doesn't really impress the neighbors, does it? Secondly, knowing that Sundance gets first crack at most films, programmers from other festivals go there to scout. You'll be surprised by the number of invitations that will come your way after your Sundance debut. When festivals solicit your film, you don't have to pay entry fees. Score! Less work, no cost! Lastly, Sundance is very good to its alumni. Your subsequent short or feature will be given special consideration by the programmers, who have already endorsed you as a Sundance-worthy filmmaker. Being in the festival can also create inroads to the Sundance Institute's writing and/or directing labs. Your future's looking bright!

INSIDER INFORMATION ON GETTING INTO SUNDANCE

Just apply. Every single short that is submitted to Sundance is personally watched by at least one of the Sundance short-film programmers. So what type of shorts does Sundance program? The festival showcases an array of genres: live action, animation, documentary, experimental. "There's not a set sort of criteria as to what makes a 'Sundance short,'" explains Sundance senior programmer Trevor Groth. "We've shown everything from a minute-long film to 50 minutes, and everything in between. For me personally, as a programmer, I want a wide range — in terms of where the films are coming from, what the aesthetics are, what the themes are. If someone were to look at the entire shorts program and watch all the films, you would hopefully see a little of everything in there."

Groth adds, "People always ask me if I need world premieres for Sundance, for the shorts. No. It's not like that with shorts. I would never want someone to not show his or her short at another film festival — just to wait for Sundance — because I think short films need to be seen in as many theaters as possible. Make the festival route. Show your film in as many festivals as possible because that's where people are going to have a chance to see your work in the format you want it to be seen." Filmmaker Amy Talkington certainly found this to be true. Her Columbia student film, *Second Skin*, played over a dozen festivals before it got into Sundance. And the 2009 Sundance application clearly spells out, "Short films may have screened at any number of other festivals or on the Internet. As of this year, short films submitted for consideration are also still eligible if they have been broadcast on television or released on DVD prior to the Festival."

More good news: You don't have to have a print to play Sundance. "At the festival, in all our sections, we project both film and video," explains Groth. "For video, we have to have it transferred to a specific format, which is the Sony HD Cam."

It's only $35 to apply. What are you waiting for?

AND THEN THERE'S SLAMDANCE

Slamdance is held in the same city as Sundance, at the same time of year. Although your film can't play both, you can apply to both. If you get accepted first by Slamdance, and then Sundance, congratulations! You've made a very special film that's going to do very well on the festival circuit. And don't worry, you aren't the first to pull out of the upstart in favor of the more established 'Dance.

Slamdance, in fact, has become prestigious in its own way, marketing a "more cutting edge than Sundance" vibe. Doing well at Slamdance means good things will happen to you. *White Face* director Brian McDonald reports, "We went to Slamdance and won the audience award. And that helped a lot."

HOW MANY FESTIVALS SHOULD YOU APPLY TO?

In addition to Sundance, there are a number of "gold standard" festivals that every short filmmaker should enter, knowing that if your film gets in and you win a major award, your career is set. Among the gold-standard festivals: Cannes, Berlin, Venice, and here in the U.S., Telluride. However, these festivals fall into the "miracle to get in" category. Not only do they accept very few shorts, the focus of these festivals is certainly not on short films. Cannes, of course, is changing because of its Short Film Corner, but that's a different category than the official competition.

Don't obsess about getting into these impossibly difficult fests. All over the world there are many other wonderful festivals — if your film is invited to screen in any of them, many great things will happen. "Great things" can mean great treatment as a film-maker, great audience turn out, great networking opportunity, great prize money, or even great sales offers. You never really know where opportunity may be knocking. It's worth your while applying to a wide variety of festivals.

As to how many festivals to apply to, 30 seems to be the magic number. Filmmaker Beth Macheleny says of her recent film *Still Me*, "So far, I've applied to almost 30. That's about a grand. For my last one, I only spent $500." Rashaad Ernesto Green chimes in, "I applied to a good 30 festivals so far, and I've had a pretty good start. I won the HBO Short Film Award at my premiere at the American Black Film Festival, so I started off with a bang. I feel like other festivals are now going to start seeking the film from that. So even though I only applied to 30, it may end up being more than that."

Obviously there are hundreds and hundreds of festivals around the world that accept shorts. How can you be discriminating in your choices so you're picking the right 30 to apply to?

USING WITHOUTABOX WISELY

If you're one of the 125,000+ people who are members of Withoutabox, you know that there are over 2,000 festivals partnering with it. That's a lot of festivals to consider, especially if your target number of applications is 30. Rashaad Ernesto Green agrees, "Withoutabox is a tremendous resource for filmmakers. But Withoutabox will advertise all film festivals, so don't submit to everything. Go to the websites of the different festivals, research them a little bit. Which ones are hot, which ones are emerging? That's where you start, and then you investigate further. You go on the festival's websites — does it look cool, or does it look, you know, shabby? Look at the films that won last year. See if you can find them anywhere else... where else did they play?"

As for his personal approach targeting festivals, Green says, "First I start with the established ones because I would like my film to play in some of the bigger festivals. But if there's a small festival that won't charge me anything for applying, I'll definitely be giving my film to them because the more exposure the better. Now if it's a film festival I've never heard of, that charges me $50, chances are I'm not going to submit. It's a matter of balancing what's important to you and what will be most beneficial for you."

Here's a way to start thinking about which festivals to include in your initial target list of 30.

■ NEW YORK- OR LOS ANGELES-BASED FESTS

If your ultimate goal is to get industry attention, Atom executive Megan O'Neill recommends targeting festivals in New York or Los Angeles. "If you want to have the broadest number of industry people potentially see your film, you should probably focus on Los Angeles because that's where the industry is," O'Neill says.

Target hip mixed festivals (features and shorts) such as the Los Angeles Film Festival or Tribeca in New York. Once your film is accepted, employ a two-prong approach to get as many meetings as possible. First, notify any industry players you already know in that city that you are coming into town to attend the festival and would love to drop by their offices to give them copies of the film and tell them about your next project. On a second front, attend the fest and ruthlessly work every event, your goal being to meet additional people in the industry who can help advance your career.

■ HOME-COURT ADVANTAGE FESTS

While New York and Los Angeles might be tough nuts to crack, there is a place where you are pretty much guaranteed a grand hero's welcome. That place is your hometown. Always apply to festivals where you have some sort of local connection, e.g., you live, grew up, shot your film, or went to school there, etc. Although your work will be judged on its own merit, festivals do like to encourage natives. It doesn't hurt that they know you'll be able to pull in an audience of friends and family. You'll also merit press coverage way beyond what short filmmakers usually achieve. At home, you're a star with a solid fan base. Revel in it!

■ DON'T FORGET FOREIGN

With domestic festivals, there is usually an entry fee to apply, and writing too many of those $35 checks can quickly deplete your marketing fund. Foreign fests, on the other hand, have the benefit of no entry fees (usually). However, if your film gets in, it's a major pain to ship your material. You will become very familiar with the multiple forms needed to export your print or tape. To avoid paying any kind of duty costs, you'll learn the magic phrase: "For cultural purposes only — no commercial value." As your film jets off to France, Brazil, and Bermuda, you'll realize your short is having a better life than you are!

■ GENRE FESTS

It's easy to get lost in the shuffle of major festivals. Many short filmmakers have been disturbed to find their work showing in the middle of a Wednesday afternoon to a near empty theater. If

you want your film to get the audience it deserves, apply to the genre festivals. Not only will your film be eagerly embraced by programmers and audiences alike, you'll get sales offers from buyers who are looking for a certain type of film and figure the genre fests are where to find them. If your short is animated, target animation-only fests, such as Annecy Festival International Du Cinema D'animation in France (you're bound to get work out of showing there). If your short is comedic, the Just for Laughs Festival in Montreal should be top of your list. Fly yourself there and work the crowd, which will be filled with industry heavyweights and talent scouts. Try to meet an agent or manager while you're there.

If your film showcases a lesbian character, search out gay festivals such as the high profile and amazingly fun Outfest in Los Angeles. If it's kid-friendly, target venues such as the Chicago International Children's Film Festival. At the Fox Movie Channel, our very first short was directed by an Asian-American woman, featured an elderly character, and had a gay story line. That film was embraced by Asian festivals, women's festivals, old people festivals, and gay festivals across the world.

■ STUDENT-ORIENTED FESTS

Students, you need to approach every festival with a different eye. In the first place, there are festivals that are student only. This is probably the only time in your career you'll be able to play them, so take advantage while you can. Secondly, search out festivals that offer discounted entry fees for students. Thirdly, research those fests, big and small, that have student-only award categories. In addition to the glory of graduating from film school as an award-winning filmmaker, you'll discover that the prizes (cash or donations such as film stock) can really add up. If you're very successful, it's possible to finance a second short with your winnings.

■ FESTIVALS OFFERING BIG PRIZES OR CASH AWARDS

When you're on the fence as to whether to submit to a festival or not, check to see if there are interesting prizes or cash awards being offered. The Palm Springs International Festival of Short Films, for example, offered an Emerging Filmmaker Award in 2002 that netted filmmaker Alan Brown $15,000. For Brown, it was well worth entering that festival!

■ SHORTS-ONLY FESTS

You'll rarely find them talked about in festival roundups or guidebooks because they are beneath the radar of the feature filmmaker. But for us, shorts-only fests are major. Why? Because at mixed-length gatherings, it's the features that get the lion's share of attention. This is not the case at our own fests. "You feel like the festival is about you and your work," raves *The New Arrival* director Amy Talkington. "You get the best treatment. And you make real friends." The festivals are run by really great people who love shorts. You'll be treated like an honored guest and get into the A-list parties. You'll discover the panels are full of interesting information about the short-film world that you'll find incredibly helpful. With any luck, your film will be spotted by the many short-film acquisitions executives in attendance.

You might walk away with a licensing deal right then and there. You'll also qualify for more awards than at a mixed festival, including audience awards. You'll never regret going to a shorts-only gathering. The top five shorts-only festivals that you should definitely put on your list are:

1. Clermont-Ferrand Short Film Festival

Megan O'Neill calls it "the Cannes of short film." By submitting your film to the festival, your work is automatically placed in the festival's market, where buyers from all over the world come to scout. "Clermont-Ferrand's where your short is going to be sold," O'Neill explains. "If it's a suitable film for foreign television, that's your best shot." The festival itself is an experience. Located in an obscure town in the middle of France, the festival imports filmmakers from all over the world. You'll meet amazing film-makers, see incredible films, and have a great time. Go!

2. Aspen Shortsfest

Aspen Shortsfest is the Cadillac of American short-film fests. Not only does the festival show your film in the town's ritzy Opera House to a packed audience of swells, the folks who run the festival are truly the best in the business. And the festival actively encourages filmmakers to bond and enjoy themselves while in town. Many a filmmaker has made a lifelong friend at Aspen. Plus, if you attend, you — a poor, struggling filmmaker used to begging, borrowing, and stealing — will find yourself in the playground of the rich, downing complementary cocktails in Aspen's exclusive nightclubs. Don't you love the short-film world?!

3. Canadian Film Centre's Worldwide Short Film Festival in Toronto

A treasure to be found in the Great White North. "Canadian Film Centre's Worldwide is an excellent, very big festival," Big Film Shorts sales rep David Russell raves. "And the market is very good, too."

4. Palm Springs ShortFest

Another shorts-only festival taking place in the playground of the rich. This one offers very generous cash prizes. Additionally, short-film buyers and sales agents from all over the world come to check out the market. And since I organize the industry panels for the festival, I'll give them a plug. Every year the festival puts on master classes, workshops, panels, and one-on-one meetings with everyone who's anyone in the short-film world. Yes, it's killer hot in the dead of summer, but it's worth attending the fest.

5. L.A. Shorts Fest

The festival is based in Los Angeles, which means it has great value if you can use it as an excuse to come to Hollywood and make meetings. However, because it is Los Angeles, it is hard to get those hardworking VIPs to leave their offices and actually attend the screenings. Additionally, buyers don't target the festival since it doesn't have a market component. However, founder Robert Arentz has a strong commitment to programming hundreds of shorts, so your chances of getting in are better than at a smaller festival like Aspen.

■ THE ACADEMY QUALIFIERS

One way to qualify for Oscar consideration is to win the appropriate prize at a festival the Academy of Motion Picture Arts & Sciences recognizes. The list can change from year to year, so you should check the Academy website to see the qualifying festivals and events. You also can look at the Academy nod as endorsement that these festivals (or organizations) are legitimate and that winning a prize at them means something.

A WORLD VIEW

When I was doing short-film workshops in New Zealand, the following festivals were recommended to the native filmmakers by the organizers of the workshops. If you're looking to have a more international festival strategy, consider the following 30+ festivals recipe:

Australia: Flickerfest, Melbourne, Sydney
Belgium: Brussels International Festival of Fantastic Film
Canada: Canadian Film Centre's Worldwide Festival of Short
Films, Montreal
Denmark: Odense
Finland: Tampere
France: Annecy (animation), Cannes, Clermont-Ferrand
Germany: Berlin, Hamburg, Oberhausen
Ireland: Dublin International Film Festival
Italy: Venice
Japan: Hiroshima (animation)
Korea: PIFAN
Netherlands: Rotterdam
Spain: Bilboa, Sitges, Valladolid
Sweden: Goteborg (animation), Stockholm
Taiwan: Taipei Golden Horse
United Kingdom: Edinburgh, London
USA: Chicago, New York, Sundance, Telluride

Additionally, for a workshop I organized for the Palm Springs Shortfest, a Canadian expert in distribution put together this list of suggested festivals to make a "full and complete short-film festival strategy." I've eliminated those festivals duplicated from the New Zealand list and eliminated the Canadian fests:

Brazil: Sao Paulo Short Film Festival, Mostra Curta Cinema Rio
de Janeiro
China: Hong Kong
Czech Republic: Karlovy Vary

Germany: Inerfilm Berlin Short Film Festival, International Film Festival Mannheim-Heidelberg

Ireland: Cork

Italy: Milano, Torino

Korea: Pusan

Mexico: Expresion en Corto

New Zealand: New Zealand Film Festival

Spain: Cinema Jove, Huesca, Valladolid

Sweden: Uppsala

United Kingdom: Brief Encounters — Bristol International Short Film Festival

USA: AFI, Aspen Short Film Festival, Cinequest, Mill Valley, Palm Springs Short Film Festival, San Francisco, Seattle, SxSW — South by Southwest, Tribeca

A FEW OTHERS

"I've heard great things about the One-Reel in Seattle," lobbies David Russell of Big Film Shorts. "And the Crested Butte Reel Fest is wonderful — been there and the filmmakers are treated great." Tribeca, of course, is a NY hotspot. Filmmaker Amy Talkington throws in a good word for the Hamptons Film Festival and "Sedona — they bring you in and put you up." Sandrine Faucher Cassidy, Director of the Office of Festivals and Distribution for the USC School of Cinema-Television, lists off a bunch of foreign fests: "Flickerfest in Australia, Tampere in Finland, and Oberhausen." Cassidy also pushes the Savannah Film Festival, which is very good to all filmmakers. And Bill Plympton raves about the Mexican film festival called Expresion en Corto. British filmmaker Osbert Parker came to Los Angeles and walked away amazed by AFI's Kodak Connect — "by far the best thing about the festival."

RECAP

- Budget enough money to apply to at least 30 festivals.

- Good things can happen to you on the festival circuit, whether or not you get into Sundance. But being an official selection of the Sundance Film Festival can catapult your career.

- Every short filmmaker should apply to Clermont-Ferrand to be part of the market. It's the "Cannes" of short film.

- Target festivals offering cash-based awards. You can earn thousands of dollars on the festival circuit.

- Short-centric festivals will be your best festival-going experience. Enjoy them!

CHAPTER 19

WORKING THE FESTIVAL CIRCUIT

YOU CAN HAVE THE TIME OF YOUR LIFE ON THE FESTIVAL CIRCUIT IF YOU KNOW HOW TO WORK IT.

There are so many wonderful things about getting accepted by a festival. Perhaps the most fulfilling thing about being an "official selection" is the knowledge that professional programmers think your film is worthy of having strangers buy tickets to see it. Greg Ivan Smith explains, "It feels very validating after sitting in the editing booth for two years, thinking my film's good, but not knowing if anyone else does. As a first-time filmmaker, I'm calling myself a filmmaker, not knowing if anyone else is. So when I got that first acceptance letter, well, someone else thinks I'm a filmmaker, too! It's sad that we need that outside nod, but film is a public forum. I'm not making these films on my Citibank card just to show to my mother!"

After submitting 19 films to festivals all over the world, I've discovered several ways to make the festival application process go as smoothly as possible, so you can set yourself up for success.

■ USE WITHOUTABOX.

In the old days, you had to type out all the festival applications individually, but now Withoutabox makes applying so much easier. Filmmaker Heath Mensher is a satisfied customer, swearing "Withoutabox keeps you very organized."

■ LABEL YOUR DVD SCREENER WITH YOUR CONTACT INFORMATION.

Because your DVD definitely will be separated from its original container, make sure your film's name, your name, and contact information are on the actual DVD.

■ USE AN EMAIL ADDRESS YOU CHECK FREQUENTLY.

Most festivals notify you of acceptance via email or phone calls.

■ MAKE SURE YOUR FILM IS SUITABLE.

Too often, filmmakers waste money submitting to festivals that would never, in a million years, show their films. When I worked for Live Earth trying to get their catalogue of environmentally themed shorts into festivals in the United States, I beat my head against the wall trying to convince festivals, which had their own agendas (gay, Latino, etc.), that they should add in a green-themed screening. Save yourself such frustration. Carefully research what kinds of films each festival programs to make sure yours is a suitable candidate. Exhibition format is another thing to take into consideration. If a festival has restrictions regarding exhibition, don't think you can be the exception to the rule. Sharon Badal from the Tribeca Film Festival gives an example, "We only project on HD or 35mm. That's it. In our rules it says if you are accepted, you must provide one of these two formats."

■ KNOW THAT IT ISN'T A LEVEL PLAYING FIELD.

When asked what short filmmakers don't know about the festival world, L.A. Shorts Fest founder Robert Arentz shares, "This is just my opinion, but I think filmmakers think it's a level playing field for everyone. They don't know a lot of festivals invite filmmakers to be in their festivals and will waive entry fees. So if there are 100 programming slots for shorts at a festival, maybe half of those slots are already taken by films that the programmers have invited. When you're paying to enter these festivals, is it really a level playing field? Filmmakers have to make the decision whether or not the festival is worthy enough of the $40 or $50 entry fee. I assure them with us, it's a level playing field; your film absolutely gets looked at from beginning to end. I can't say that's always true with other festivals."

■ SUBMIT EARLY.

Not only are submission fees often cheaper if you submit early, festival screening committees can get burned out by the mountain of last-minute submissions. Better to be viewed by eager eyes rather than exhausted ones!

■ YOU CAN PUSH DEADLINES IF YOU CALL.

If you miss an entry deadline by a week or two, call the festival and ask if you can submit anyway. Because all-length festivals often program shorts last, sometimes they'll make an exception if you stress that yours is a very short film. It never hurts to ask.

■ FESTIVALS WILL SOMETIMES WAIVE ENTRY FEES.

If your film has won major awards, you'll get calls from festivals requesting you submit your film for their programming consideration. In this scenario, the programmers are reaching out to you and will waive the entry fees because they're making the request.

If you're the one calling, stress that what you really want is to screen at their festivals; unfortunately, you've already exceeded your budget for festival submissions, and you can't afford their fees. At worst, you might get them to discount fees. Your best angle, however, is if you've previously made a short that played that particular festival in past years. You then call, explaining you had such a great experience last time that you desperately want your new film to be considered; unfortunately, you're on a much stricter budget this year. See if they bite.

Rashaad Ernesto Green isn't shy about contacting programmers. "Address your email to that programmer," he says, giving an example of an approach, "Hi, I'm blah blah blah from NYU. I have a great little film about blah blah blah, and can you waive my festival fee because I'm poor." In his email, he'd also mention who's in the film and writes briefly about himself. Having just won an award, Green smiles, "Now I'll be leading with that. And I'll probably get more "yeses" then before."

■ SUBMIT THROUGH PROPER CHANNELS.

At any major festival, there's an entire system set up to log and route submissions. Giving your DVD personally to a programmer without filling out the festival's application form doesn't guarantee your short will be properly entered. Even if you're invited to submit by a programmer, you'll have to fill out an application. If you do have a personal in with programmers, email or call them to let them know your film has been submitted so you won't get lost in the shuffle.

■ PROVIDE A GREAT PHOTO.

Festivals need artwork for catalogue and press purposes almost immediately after locking programming. If the fest already has your photo, there's a very good chance your image will be used.

■ DON'T GIVE UP IF YOU DON'T GET IN TO THE FIRST FEW FESTIVALS YOU ENTER.

It's a matter of getting through the "noes" until you get the "yes." Persevere. Take inspiration from Douglas Horn's experience. "My short, *Trailer: The Movie!*, has enjoyed a very respectable run to date," states Horn. "It has been an official selection in 20 festivals, has received multiple distribution offers (which I'm currently deciding between) and has played in independent theaters before feature films (for pay, no less). Along the way, it garnered some very positive reviews. Not bad for a film that took six months to get its first festival acceptance!"

■ KEEP IN MIND THE IMPORTANCE OF PREMIERES.

I'll never forget the answer a veteran short filmmaker gave to a novice worried about turning down one smallish festival's invitation, in hopes of being in a more important festival's world premiere. The vet said you can stay pure waiting around for "the one," or you can get started having a good time right away. Yes, it's true some festivals prefer that they be your first, or that you haven't already given your film to one of their local competitors. If you have certain festivals that make you feel like you'll die if you don't get into them, keep your film unsullied until you get the official word from those festivals.

Greg Ivan Smith provides an example. "The Seattle Gay and Lesbian Film Festival said they wanted to show my film. So I contacted the Seattle International Film Festival to explain my situation and ask if I can't show in the city of Seattle before their festival. The SIFF programmer said, 'I can't guarantee we'll play it, but if you can postpone any other Seattle festivals, that would be great.' Don't be afraid to call if you're worried."

■ TRY TO CLUSTER FESTIVALS THAT YOU WANT TO TRAVEL TO.

Rashaad Ernesto Green is based in New York. He explains his rationale for which festivals he will fly to: "I strategize just in case I get into this festival, I'll also apply to all other festivals in the nearby area during this time. In one month, I made it into four festivals basically in the same Los Angeles area, so I just stayed out West the whole time and made the circuit. If it were only one festival, a mom and pop film festival, chances are I wouldn't fly out."

■ **HAVE THE PREVIOUS FESTIVAL SHIP YOUR EXHIBITION MASTER TO THE NEXT FESTIVAL FOR YOU.**

While most festivals will not pay to have your film master/ print shipped to them, they will pay to return your film after the screening. A good way to save shipping fees is to have the festival forward your screening master to your next scheduled festival. If you can keep the chain going, you'll never have to pay another shipping fee.

HOW TO SCORE A FREE TRIP TO A FILM FESTIVAL

Your film gets into the fun and funky South by Southwest Film Festival. Where would you rather be: in Austin watching audiences experience your film for the first time — or sitting at home watching *Barton Fink* on the Independent Film Channel for the fifth time? It's always better to be there. Unfortunately, most festivals do not cover travel and lodging for short filmmakers. Fortunately,  short filmmakers are used to begging for free stuff. Call the festival and ask to speak to the person in charge of arranging travel for filmmakers. One filmmaker I know talked a festival into putting her on a panel so her trip could be covered by the budget for panelists. Another offered to make airport runs and usher at screenings in exchange for volunteer lodging. If there's anything you have learned in your career as a short filmmaker, there's always an angle that can be worked.

HOW TO GET PRESS AT A FILM FESTIVAL

I always will be grateful for *indieWIRE* believing that short films are worthy of regular coverage. While the mainstream press tends to ignore short films at festivals, there are some reporters who will give you ink. Some short helmers do hire publicists to help them get publicity at festivals, but I truly believe this is a waste of time unless you are (a) very well funded (b) angling to get an Oscar (c) sure you have a very newsworthy angle or (d) a celebrity director who would naturally have a publicist anyway.

You can effectively be your own press agent. As soon as you get accepted to a festival, ask who the publicist for the festival is. At shorts-only festivals, that publicist will be glad to hear that you'll be attending the festival and will try to set you up with as many interviews as possible. At Palm Springs and Aspen, local coverage is amazing. Many a short filmmaker walks away from those fests with clippings.

HOW TO HANDLE Q & As AT YOUR SCREENING

Having been on both sides of the microphone at question and answer sessions after a short-film screening, I'm always amazed by those filmmakers who absolutely steal the spotlight from everyone else because they've got such great personality and wonderful answers to any question asked. Some of that can be attributed to natural charisma, but even the shyest filmmakers can shine if they take a moment to think ahead of time about how they want to present themselves at their screenings. During my short-film class, I give an assignment in which I require the filmmakers to script out what they'd say if they get a chance to introduce their films before screenings. Not that I'd ever suggest that filmmakers read from a script, but just writing it down once forces you to think about what you might say, extemporaneously, later.

When I asked Robert Arentz from the L.A. Shorts Fest how he'd recommend short filmmakers prep for Q & As, he replied, "Well everyone's personality is different and everyone's goal is different. Are you using that short to parlay it into a feature or do you have a big master plan? Definitely try to get the word out if you do have other projects — 'Hey if you like my short, I have a feature-length script,' or 'This could be developed into something more. I'm working on this.'"

Shane Smith from Sundance adds, "Be able to talk about your film. Number one, why you made this film. I can't believe the number of filmmakers who can't articulate their vision or their ideas or their passion. Q & A is all about selling your film and your vision. Not selling it in a crass way, but being able to talk about why you made the film the way you did. And if people have an issue with your film or a problem with the subject matter, you can explain the reasons behind the choices you made. Filmmakers, some of them are so shy — get over it! It's a business of relationships and selling yourself, for better or for worse. If you've got to take public speaking courses, do that. You're the package you're selling, so make it the best package that it can be. And no one can do that except you."

Smith adds, "If you can make an audience laugh — not get up there and be a comedian, but if you can tell a story or an anecdote that just endears audiences to you — they'll remember your film and remember you. As a moderator, I'm always asking "What was the most difficult part of making this film?" or 'What was best part of the experience for you?' I'm looking for some sort of story that opens up the world of this film for audiences and draws them in. Have little stories ready. Even if you've told them a million times, you haven't told them to this audience. It all helps to have you and your film stick in their minds."

One other trick is to have someone planted in the audience who can ask you a question you want to answer. Filmmaker Madeleine Olnek remembers, "When I was at Sundance, I was on a program with several other filmmakers, and our program showed several times. Every filmmaker had a shtick. A lot of foreign filmmakers had a thing they could talk about like 'In my country...' you know, working that angle. That 'In my country...' thing was very sexy. There was this other woman who would say 'Oh, thank you for asking,' every time someone asked 'Where did you find your actors?' Then I'm at the party, and the filmmaker introduces the

'Where did you get those actors?' person as her publicist! I realized she planted the audience! But that's fine. Get someone to ask a question that others are too shy to ask. People in the audience will go along with it, thinking 'Marvelous question.'"

HOW TO NETWORK AT FESTIVALS

If there's any message that I hope is coming through in this chapter, it's that you can't be shy when working the festivals. That doesn't mean be a pest. Every year at the Palm Springs Shortfest, there always seems to be one too-aggressive filmmaker who actively tries to land himself an insider position in every situation. His actions tend to rub people the wrong way, but he certainly gets attention.

NYU filmmaker Rashaad Ernesto Green told me while we were both at Palm Springs Shortfest, "I brought my film with me, and I'll talk to as many people as I can. But I'm not the kind of person who pushes too hard. Because everyone here is trying to do the same exact thing. If people see my film and like it, if it happens to win an award, then people will come to me. As far as me pushing it myself, I'll speak to people at the parties, I'll hand out my postcards, but I don't want to come off just like everybody else."

Shane Smith from the Sundance Film Festival says, "I hate to say it, but at a festival like Sundance, the main reason the industry is at Sundance is for the features. People are interested in the shorts, and they're interested in meeting you and talking to you. But don't drag it out, get in there quickly, tell 'em what you do, tell 'em what you know. Be cool. That's sort of my overarching advice: be cool."

MOST IMPORTANTLY: HAVE FUN

Madeleine Olnek cautions against putting too much pressure on yourself. "Once you enter a sort of nihilistic place, then it becomes really fun. But my first festivals — I was so scared, so nervous, that I couldn't even enjoy any of the events leading up to my screening — and my screening was the second-to-last day. Then my film ended up winning the Audience Award for best short. That was my first festival experience."

Animator Don Hertzfeldt emphasizes the enjoyment of seeing your film with an audience, "My latest movie took about two years of production in more or less solitary confinement, so I've been really eager to get out on the road with it and get that interaction again. You'll always have much bigger audiences when your movie later goes to DVD or TV, but you can't actually be there in people's living rooms to watch those connections happen, and that's probably one of the main reasons I think anyone makes movies."

Filmmaker Roy Unger still rhapsodizes about his time at the International Hamburg Short Film Festival. "They hosted these dinners every night," Unger smiles. "Totally comped. Filmmakers from around the world. Peter Greenaway was there. Jim Jarmusch. I met the Polish Brothers. People whom I would never have access to, just hanging out at dinner, eating, drinking, and talking film."

Greg Ivan Smith agrees, "The people at festivals are some of the nicest people you will meet. And the other filmmakers are some of the greatest people I've met in a long time. People are generally enthusiastic, so excited for you, that you're part of their experience."

Circuit vet David Birdsell also enjoyed his festival experiences. "See a lot of films while you're there," recommends Birdsell. "See what other people are doing. Meet other filmmakers. Get a sense that you're not alone out there. The thing that always inspires me about Clermont-Ferrand is seeing how much short filmmaking is going on all over the world right now, as we speak. How many different things are being tried. I wouldn't spend thousands of dollars traveling all over the world, because you don't generally go to a film festival and come back with some sort of film deal. But if you can go, it's great because you feel legitimized and encouraged."

RECAP

- Submit wisely, submit early.

- Whenever possible, attend any festival you get into.

- Introduce yourself to the festival's publicist so you can be a favored child.

- Make sure you use the Q & A session to your advantage.

- Have fun!

CHAPTER 20

iTUNES, CELL PHONES, AND BEYOND: HOW TO GET RICH OFF YOUR SHORT

SADLY, MOST SHORT FILMS DON'T EARN BACK ENOUGH MONEY TO BREAK EVEN.

If you made your short with the idea that you were going to sell it for big bucks and retire, I have bad news for you. While it's true a very lucky few can earn big bucks off their films, the majority of filmmakers dream of breaking even. While we all hope that iTunes sales, cell phone exhibition, and advertiser revenue-sharing websites will be our salvation, the reality is most short filmmakers operate at a loss. Especially when you add in the time personally invested.

How you're going to get rich is selling yourself — using your short to achieve a career that makes you a lot of money. The short is an investment. It's a demonstration of what you can do as a filmmaker. That's why shorts are often called "calling cards" — they represent you and your talents.

"How many people go into short films thinking they're going to be making a lot of money?" laughs short filmmaker and consultant John Halecky. "They're going into it for exposure, for the calling-card aspect, for getting something done, getting out there, getting their names known. And that's what they should be doing. A short can be a stepping stone for a bigger and better career in filmmaking."

You're not going to get rich, but you can recoup some cash — if your film has nothing that will prevent it from being copied, exhibited, distributed, and exploited in a commercial vein. Potential distributors will ask you if your film has all clearances and rights for commercial distribution. Do not lie about this. You're now entering a professional arena involving contracts, money changing hands, and potential lawsuits; you're expected to behave like a responsible professional studio as opposed to a flighty artist. What could happen if you lie? The offended parties could demand an injunction, stopping your film from being exploited. That's what happened with Todd Haynes and *Superstar*. Richard Carpenter didn't find the unlicensed use of his music and slanderous portrayal of his character very amusing. Consequently, you'll never find Haynes' film commercially distributed. Even worse, you could be required to pay damages. Of course, the resulting publicity can be a boost to your profile. But do you want to be known throughout the industry as the filmmaker that pissed off Richard Carpenter? The fact is, if you're attempting to make money off your short, your work does have value and you should be taken to task like anyone else making a commercial product.

"If you want your film to be sold — and I've never met a filmmaker who afterwards didn't want his or her film to be sold — do not use music you haven't paid for," reminds Atom's Megan O'Neill. Distributors also will ask if your project was produced under any guild or union agreements with any potential distribution issues. For example, if you signed a Screen Actors Guild contract stipulating you must pay all your actors their SAG fees in full the moment your film earns one penny, you might not be able to accept sales offers too small to cover your SAG bill.

SO HOW MUCH CAN YOU MAKE?

The good news is there are so many new ways for short films to make money. We'll explore each avenue in a minute, but let's cut to the chase and ask the experts exactly how much money a short film could potentially rake in.

Megan O'Neill of Atom: "It really depends on the film. There are filmmakers who have probably seen tens of thousands of dollars; and a rare few, who have done amazingly well, have seen maybe one hundred grand over time. I'm a little skeptical that people could see more than that — and definitely that is not the norm. Most filmmakers, I would say, over the length of their film distribution, would see thousands, maybe tens of thousands. In the low tens. If the film has done fairly well. And if it's more than five-minutes long. Because a lot of the television stations pay by the minute. That's the Catch 22. There are still a lot of places that are paying by the minute."

David Russell of Big Film Shorts: "What the average film gets is around $5,000, and that's selling to multiple markets worldwide. Such low numbers are not the film's fault or a reflection of its appeal. No one who buys shorts pays very much. In fact, there are even less buyers now."

Carol Crowe of Apollo Cinema: "Not every short out there is going to sell. Remember that. Every year there is going to be that handful that you will continually see on the festival circuit. And those are the ones that most of the buyers are interested in. Frankly, shorts are so hit or miss. I would say just to be safe, if you're lucky, an average film will earn five grand."

Fred Joubaud of Premium Films: "It depends on the length of the movie, it depends on which TV stations. The international average is 100 Euros a minute. I would say with the more generous TV stations, like Canal+, the license fee is around 500 Euros a minute. Good films, like *Tanghi Argentini*, we've sold it twice already, and there's already another TV station ready to buy it. If your short film sold to five or six TV stations, I'd say you could hope to get about 1000 Euros a minute. So if the film is five or six minutes, you can expect around 5,000 to 6,000 Euros."

The important thing to remember is you're not selling your film just for the money, but for the exposure. Filmmaker Roy Unger licensed his film to the Sci Fi Channel. The problem was the money wasn't great. "As I made the festival circuit, I was getting offers, it's just that none of the offers was good," Unger recalls. "The Sci Fi thing was an offer to get it on television. Everything else was an offer to stream it, or this or that. This Sci Fi thing was a crappy deal, but at the time it was a hot show for a filmmaker to get his or her stuff seen. So I made the deal with the help of a lawyer, whom I had look at the contract, and his fees ate up a third of what I made! But I had to protect myself; I didn't want to sign something giving Sci Fi Channel rights to exploit me. I got my film on air, and within days I had people calling me and I got meetings. More people saw my film on one night on cable television than ever saw it in all 34 film festivals around the world."

Of course, the Internet has the furthest reach of all. If you're goal is exposure, you really might be best uploading your short everywhere you can. "I think it benefits me more just to put my work online for free and let everyone watch it," animator Carson Mell told *indieWIRE*.

Jennifer Chen, who spent years distributing shorts in Canada, lists desirable qualities to increase salability. "The film should have salability on multiple platforms throughout the world. A universal message that could speak to a broad audience. Very short, definitely under 15 minutes, preferably under 10 minutes. Something genre. Or funny."

WHAT MIGHT STOP YOUR FILM FROM SELLING COMMERCIALLY

David Russell describes them: "If there's a lot of nudity or perfunctory nudity, that will kill a deal. Drug use. If there's excessive bad language, even if it fits the character, buyers shy away. If you're a documentary filmmaker, make sure you have releases for everything. Buyers are very scared of documentaries not having proper releases. To make a sale in Germany or German-speaking countries, you almost always have to have an M & E track. They're the toughest. I just sold two films to a British DVD company, and they absolutely need the music cue sheet. IFC always wanted to see actor releases, composer agreements (those are the two most essential things) — and of course, the copyright. If you have any logo or trademarks of clips, you have to have that permission in writing."

MARKETS TO EXPLOIT

Unlike features, which have a set flow of windows, shorts can be exploited in all markets at all times.

■ THEATRICAL

Festivals are where short films get theatrical exhibition, but short filmmakers don't make any money from that. On a rare occasion, you might find an individual theater or chain willing to pay to show a short film before a feature. But it's mostly packaged touring shows that do well theatrically. Magnolia has had great success with touring the Academy shorts. And animators Don Hertzfeldt (*Rejected*) and Mike Judge (*Beavis and Butt-Head, King of the Hill*) made inroads with an ambitious theatrical tour called *The Animation Show*, a collection of the world's best animated short films, personally programmed by Hertzfeldt and Judge. The guys said in their initial announcement, "As animation continues to be plagued as the single most misunderstood film medium, the animated short film is sadly undervalued and underexposed in American cinema, despite widespread appreciation throughout the rest of the world. With luck, popular animated shorts may see some manner of very limited theatrical play, but are all too often relegated to only being found in chopped-up form on television, or worse, are only exhibited on the Internet. Every year, *The Animation Show* promises to put animated short films into more theaters than any other animation festival in American history. We aim to finally give these filmmakers the wide exposure their work deserves and to share these short masterpieces on the big screen, where they belong."

■ NON-THEATRICAL

Non-theatrical opportunities include schools, colleges, libraries, military institutions, prisons, museums, churches, etc. Short docs, in particular, can earn good money licensed to these organizations. Filmmakers can ask for a rental fee for allowing their films to be shown in such markets or can ask for a percentage (35-50%) of ticket sales. If you attend the screening and participate in a question and answer session, you can also ask for a speaker's fee. The other advantage of attending such screenings is that you can sell your DVDs at the event, thus pocketing extra money via DVD sales.

■ TELEVISION — DOMESTIC AND FOREIGN

Licensing to television is where the bulk of your money will be made. In general, it's the long-established foreign television channels, such as France's Canal+, which will pay the biggest licensing fees (paying by the minute). In the U.S., independent-film-oriented cable stations and PBS still buy shorts, and in Canada, Movieola is devoted to showing shorts 24 hours a day. However, fewer and fewer channels are buying shorts. Fred Joubaud explains, "TV buyers said it was too expensive — not that the acquisition is expensive, but dealing with short films is expensive. Why? Because they have to make a contract for a five-minute short film. Then they have to deal with the programming, all the material required for delivery — in the end, at least three or four people may work on acquiring that short film. It's less expensive to buy an American TV show — one client, one delivery, one contract — and they're sure they're going to get the material on time. Dealing with short films was too expensive or time demanding."

■ VOD

Video-on-demand has resulted in more opportunity for cable channels and operators to show short films. However, on your own, you'll find it hard to make these sales, as the exhibitors are making acquisition deals with large-content aggregators rather than individual filmmakers.

■ AIRLINES

Another venue where the buyers prefer to deal with distributors rather than individuals. With seat-back viewing stations, more and more airlines are programming short films. Airlines are notoriously cautious about the type of material they show. Rules against drug use and excessive violence apply here. And any film featuring a plane crash is a definite no-go.

■ DVD

Because DVD is the perfect format for short-film compilations, new DVD series are constantly being launched. *Wholphin* out of San Francisco is one of the coolest. When asked what qualifies a short film for inclusion on *Wholphin*, co-founder Brent Hoff mused, "We're attempting to really carefully curate based only on what we think is amazing and nothing else at all. I think that's enough."

The good news is DVD companies are generally interested in dealing with individual filmmakers. Unfortunately, most of these commercial compilations do not generate any real money (don't expect to see huge royalties). What they do offer is exposure. If DVD producers approach you about putting your short on their compilation, there's no reason to grant them exclusive DVD rights. If it's exposure you're looking for, make nonexclusive deals with as many DVD companies as possible.

If you want to make and sell your own DVDs commercially, you may want to investigate Amazon's CreateSpace service. Similar to those services that offer individual book publishing on demand, CreateSpace makes it possible to sell the DVD of your short on *Amazon.com*, Amazon Video On Demand, and other channels, including your own Estore. Professional DVDs (full color DVD-Rs in full-color cases like "real" DVDs you'd find in Blockbuster) are produced upon receiving a customer's order. The service deals with getting a UPC barcode and number, fulfillment, and customer interaction. Filmmakers still control their own rights and earn a percentage of the retail price of each sale. For example, if you sold your DVD via Amazon, you would get 55% of whatever purchase price you set. Because CreateSpace is part of the Amazon family, your DVD title becomes eligible for listing on *IMDb.com*. Additionally, your film can be made available as a video download through Amazon Video On Demand. What's great about this service is it puts you in the same league as the big boys — your little movie is being sold on Amazon!

■ iTUNES

In June 2008, *Variety* reported that iTunes was delivering 50,000 movie downloads *a day*. Unfortunately, there aren't statistics to say how many of those are short films, but the Academy Award-winning comedy *West Bank Story* has racked up somewhere in the neighborhood of 50,000 sales *total*. When Wes Anderson's *Hotel Chevalier* was given away for free on iTunes, it was downloaded more than 500,000 times. But that's the exception to the rule — it was a heavily promoted free download of the week, had recognizable names involved and a director with a large following. Additionally, the goal in that case was not to make money but to promote the theatrical release of *The Darjeeling Unlimited*.

Nevertheless, short filmmakers should rightly be excited about the opportunity to be on iTunes. Filmmaker Douglas Horn emailed me suggesting I write about iTunes for *indieWIRE*, sharing his story: "The big news is that *Full Disclosure* just went for sale at the iTunes Store, and in less than a week, it rocketed up to the #1 short film on the site. I haven't seen much coverage on *IndieWIRE* about shorts going up for sale on iTunes, but to me, it's the biggest story in short films today because it puts shorts out to a worldwide audience in a delivery system that millions of people are actively using — and it's returning revenue to filmmakers. I actually had offers from several competing sites, but I didn't think that any of them had or would capture the market the way that iTunes would — they're just so far ahead of the curve. You know, I've said for a while now that I had to stop making shorts because there was no way to make a career at it, but now I might be proven wrong."

The problem with iTunes is they don't want to deal with individual short filmmakers, mostly because of the enormous amount of work needed to legally check and collect assets per film, not to mention the encoding and delivery. Hopefully this will change, but right now the way to get in is via a distribution company that already has a deal with iTunes, such as Shorts International.

Of course, iTunes isn't the only way to offer digital downloads for sale. Amazon, Movielink, Jaman, GreenCine, CinemaNow and others offer similar services. Certainly Amazon's ever-expanding reach (owning Withoutabox and IMDB) means it can position itself as the ultimate place to pay to download shorts. But in this scenario, you have to attract customers, whereas buyers are already coming to iTunes.

As for how much money a filmmaker can earn from iTunes, those figures aren't public. However, when the Sundance Film Festival short films were sold on iTunes, Netflix, and X-Box Live, the filmmakers were given a 57% net profit from each download.

Fred Joubaud, who represents several Academy-nominated shorts on iTunes, sighs, "I was very disappointed, I thought there'd be more money. I thought the number would be much stronger. I think there are two reasons the iTunes sales are not strong. One, I think people are not ready to pay for short films. Why would people pay to watch a short film? I would love for them to do that, don't get me wrong! But the problem is why should people pay to watch a short film when technically they can watch so many short films for free on the Internet? If you just want to watch a short film as a way to entertain yourself, you find good stuff on the Internet for free. So why would anyone buy a short film on iTunes? Unless you're really into the short-film market and you're looking for a specific title... The second reason is you really have to look for the short films on iTunes. You pretty much have to do a search by the title to find it."

■ INTERNET SITES

Distributor David Russell reports, "We get an offer a week from some new Internet site that wants free movies. There are few, and MiniMovies is one, actually paying cash. Others are offering some back-end of download fees or potential ad revenue. Filmmakers can ask for some sort of revenue share should the sites profit in anyway. None of the sites have a model of how they can profit. They have plans way down the road of being able to attract enough advertising to make their money back. Even now with the appearance of some pretty solid websites, you have no idea of what's going to happen. You just don't know. Right now if they're paying the filmmakers, they're paying out of pocket."

If your short is Internet-friendly, you'll get all sorts of offers to show it on various sites. "As a distributor, I say try to get some money out of it," counsels sales rep Carole Crowe. "But otherwise, you are getting exposure, which can translate into a dollar figure at some point." If the name of the game is exposure, why not say "yes"? One reason to hesitate: some television networks won't take your short if it has been on the Internet. Keeping in mind that the most lucrative market for shorts is television, why jeopardize this revenue stream by putting your film on the Internet without any financial gain?

If you want to make money via YouTube, you need to get into their Partners program. All you have to do is apply via their web-site. Once your film is vetted by the company (making sure you own everything contained within, i.e., no illegal music, etc.) and accepted to be part of the program, advertising will be added to your film's YouTube page. It could be a text ad, a banner ad, or an in-video ad (which has the highest rate of return). All three are performance-based models of advertising revenue sharing. The better the shorts do, the more money filmmakers can make. Films in YouTube's Screening Room are automatically part of the Partners program. Although YouTube won't release what kind of numbers they're talking about, if you have strong content that draws many eyeballs, there's no reason you can't do well.

As for shorts that are being made specifically for the Internet in hopes of attracting enough viewers to get advertising and make serious income, the magic number seems to be around 5 million viewers. The popular series *French Maid TV* racks up those kinds of numbers and makes money.

■ CELL PHONES

Good news that cell phones are the biggest distribution platform on Earth. The statistic thrown around is there are about a billion television households worldwide, also about one billion PCs with Internet, but there are about two-and-a-half billion cell phones. Cell phones are the largest platform on Earth by a factor of two! The bad news is the content applications are still very primitive. And the competition is already fierce. How is your little short film going to compete with sports updates or mini-episodes of *The Simpsons* or *Family Guy*?

Shane Smith says, "Mobile is emerging as a platform in the United States. It's already very well established in Asia and Europe. But remember mobile has its own constraints, too — running time being one of them. Mobile companies don't want anything that's over three minutes in length, they prefer under two minutes. And content is an issue, too, in terms of language, sexuality, violence, and that kind of stuff. The companies are a little weary about being too edgy."

HOW TO GENERATE OFFERS

Play the festival circuit. This is where sales reps and the buyers scout for material. If offers don't come to you via festival exposure, you can contact the buyers directly. Most television channels have a fairly quick evaluation process, usually 45 to 90 days. Most networks and Internet companies do keep records, so don't resubmit if you have officially been passed on. Seek other opportunities. Remember, it's just a matter of getting through the "noes" until you get a "yes."

HIRING A PRO

If offers come to you, you can either accept the deals and sell the film yourself, or you can sign with a sales rep or distributor who will broker deals for you. "It's all about the relationships," points out filmmaker Amy Talkington. "How are you going to track down and get someone from Canal+ on the phone? Ideally the rep has relationships with all the foreign television networks and venues you aren't even aware of, like airlines or Internet deals. Reps know what windows to do first so you don't mess up other possibilities. Also, it gives you that experience of working with an agent, a professional relationship similar to what you hope to have in the future."

Carol Crowe from Apollo Cinema adds, "The advantage of going with a film rep, distributor, or sales agent is that we can do the job while you've moved on to doing other things. You should be busy getting your feature going, not still working your short. Without a doubt, you can sell your film yourself. But it can be time consuming, and it can feel daunting looking at legal agreements. Some filmmakers want to show licensing agreements to an attorney. If you show it to an attorney, right there it's cheaper to go with a sales agent."

How do you get a sales agent? Like buyers, they cruise the festival circuit looking for hot films they think they can sell. Remember, they're not representing your career; they're representing a property which they'll exploit for both your profit and their profit. If no sales reps contact you, you can contact them. Doing a Google search will turn up a listing of potential short-film sales agents.

A filmmaker named Matt emailed me asking, "Is there one distribution company that you would recommend? Also, do you have any recommendations on a profit-sharing model versus a flat fee?" Truthfully, I'm the worst person to ask about recommending a distribution company because I am friends with many of them and couldn't pick one over the other. Better to ask other filmmakers who are clients. You should be able to tell from the distributor's website which other filmmakers they represent. Seek out films that look closest in nature to yours, then Google those filmmakers to ask them directly about their experiences. Additionally, when you're at festivals, ask other filmmakers if they've been approached by distributors and what they've heard/experienced. As for the percentage or flat fee, remember that the money you're talking about isn't boatloads of cash. Pick whichever matches your personal needs at the time.

Jennifer Chen, formerly of the Canadian distribution company Ouat Media, chimes in, "When you're looking for distribution, you want to take a look at the company's catalog, you want to get a flavor for the kind of work that they distribute — because buyers will know the flavors of their catalogs and will go to them for that kind of content. Secondly, as part of your due diligence, you always, always should try to find filmmakers who are already represented by that distribution company and talk to them. And you're going to want to ask how responsive the company is (if that matters to you), how often they pay (that will definitely matter to you), how they split out expenses — even though it's all spelled out in the agreement, you'll want to ask about all that. And then you can make an educated, informed decision."

Agreements with reps vary. Some offer an advance against future earnings. Some take a percentage of whatever deals they broker. When you sign with a sales rep, you will sign an agreement that will cover the following:

■ GRANT OF RIGHTS

You do not need to have the rep handle all rights. If you've already sold your film to certain markets on your own, those can be excluded from the agreement. Or you can split the film's rights to have a North American rep and a European rep.

■ DISTRIBUTOR'S CREDIT

Some sales agents who also act as distributors will insist their logo is placed on your film. This isn't necessarily a bad thing, but be aware that it is an issue that should be clarified.

■ COMMISSION

It can range anywhere from to 30% to 70% in some markets. While such large percentages may sound like a lot, sometimes the amounts being earned are less than $100. If your rep is covering costs out of his/her take, a sizable percentage isn't unreasonable.

■ EXPENSES

This is another element that varies. Are you being charged for phone calls, faxing, shipping, tape duplications, etc.? Make sure your agreement spells out what the agent/distributor can charge back against any monies generated by the film. See if there's any wiggle room. Because you're probably a better bargain hunter than they are, offer to provide screening DVDs, clones of your master, etc.

■ PAYMENT

Some reps will pay you as soon as they get a check in hand, others will report quarterly, semi-annually or even annually. Remember, a big part of the representative's job is getting money for you — but it does take time to get checks from the companies they license to.

■ LENGTH OF AGREEMENT
Make sure it's clear how long your deal will exist and how you can break the relationship if you aren't pleased with the results.

SELLING YOUR FILM YOURSELF

The first thing you need to know is that the word "sell" is misleading. You should never sell your film outright. Exhibitors pay you a fee to license your film for an agreed-upon period of time, for a specific medium and territory. For example, you might say you sold your film to the Sundance Channel, but the reality is the Sundance Channel licensed your film for two years, exclusive domestic television, for $1,500.

A producer with a hot NYU student film emailed me saying, "I'm looking for some advice on foreign distribution deals for short films. Specifically, I've been approached by German-speaking territory distributors and we're looking to negotiate foreign territories on our own (with the help of our lawyer) for lessons we can hopefully apply to future films. Unfortunately, our lawyer doesn't have the expertise on foreign distribution." My general advice regarding television sales is that reputable TV channels, especially European ones, have a standard deal contract for short films and they won't really cough up more money since they tend to have a fixed rate they pay per minute. If it's a short-term contract (i.e., not for several years, but several months for a limited run), you're pretty safe just signing the standard deal and you won't feel like you got ripped off. And if it's a company that you're not too sure of, I say don't make the deal in the first place.

When you make a deal, you will be asked to "represent and warrant" that you have the exclusive right to use and grant rights to everything in your film and, therefore, hold the licensing company harmless of any and all negligence in connection with your film. And because television channels will make payments to the composer's organization (BMI, ASCAP, SESAC), a music cue sheet will be required.

When the deal is finalized, you will be required to deliver a master. This is not your real master, but a clone of it that you will give to the company for the duration of their licensing. Although HD will certainly be the norm soon, currently the most preferred format for delivery is DigiBeta.

Many cable channels will also ask for a standard set of deliverables. Features must have everything, but it's perfectly acceptable for you to say, "It's just a short film, I don't have that material." For example, you may be asked to deliver:

■ POSTERS

Try to substitute your postcard.

■ TRAILER

Inquire if they really need this for a film as short as yours.

■ A CLOSED-CAPTIONED VERSION

Offer up your dialogue list instead. If they insist, ask for a bigger licensing fee to cover the cost of making a closed-caption version.

■ M & E (MUSIC AND EFFECTS) TRACK

This is a dialogue-less version of your film for foreign television. If you didn't make a textless/split audio version, offer up your dialogue list for subtitled translation.

■ E & O (ERRORS AND OMISSIONS) INSURANCE

Most short films don't have E & O insurance, which is very expensive. Luckily, the cable or DVD companies requiring E & O usually offer a bigger licensing fee to cover the policy coverage cost. If this isn't the case, offer to sign whatever legal forms the acquiring company wants you to sign to indemnify them against any possible errors and omissions.

DEALING WITH CONTRACTS

Don't be intimidated by the paperwork. Most acquisition deals are very straightforward. The basic elements in a licensing contract will generally include:

■ DESCRIPTION OF THE CONTENT, INCLUDING RUNNING TIME

Do not lie about your running time when it comes to licensing. Your running time must be exact, in minutes and seconds. Some television channels or DVD companies pay by the minute.

■ THE TERRITORY COVERED BY THE AGREEMENT

It can be just a specific area (U.S. and Canada, for example) or it could be the world.

■ TERM

The contract should spell out exactly when the agreement begins and when it terminates. It could be for a limited window (a few months or a few years) or in perpetuity. In general, you should be wary of long contracts.

■ RIGHTS GRANTED

Is it exclusive (meaning you can't license it elsewhere) or non-exclusive? What media does it cover? Some TV channels, for example, are now asking for Internet rights, as well.

■ DELIVERY INFORMATION

Exactly when and how you should deliver your master and other required materials should be spelled out.

■ LICENSOR WARRANTIES

This is where you must make your guarantees that everything is on the up and up. It usually includes statements that you are the sole owner of the copyright, there is no agreement with someone else that will interfere with the rights you granted, the content is free and clear of any encumbrances, and that you will make all necessary talent, production, royalty, union, and other such payments. You are usually required to indemnify the licensing company against any claims or lawsuits that might develop.

■ PAYMENT SCHEDULE

Some licensing deals are royalty-oriented. Other companies will pay you part of the licensing fee upon signing the contract and the rest when your short first airs or is first put in stores (in the case of DVDs). Ideally, you'd want 100% of the license fee payable upon receipt and technical acceptance of the delivery materials.

THINGS TO WATCH OUT FOR

When reviewing contracts, keep an eye out for the following issues:

■ IF THE LICENSOR FINDS THE MATERIAL DEFECTIVE, INCOMPLETE, OR UNACCEPTABLE

For example, what happens if your master is rejected for not being of acceptable broadcast quality? It might not be financially worth your while to bring your material up to acceptable standards. Look for an out-clause, making the contract null and void if this happens.

■ EDITING RIGHTS

Filmmakers usually freak out about this. But often editing means a TV network will squeeze your film's end credits or run them at the end of a compilation program of short films. Rarely are shorts edited for content.

■ ASSIGNMENT OF GRANTED RIGHTS TO OTHERS

When companies license shorts, the films become company assets that can be traded, sold, or "assigned" to other companies as long as the license period lasts. You may sign up with one DVD company, only to find they've gone out of business and sold

262

to someone else. You can ask to have this clause stricken from the contract, but most companies won't go for it. If nothing else, ask for the agreement to become null and void if the company declares bankruptcy. Many short films have been tied up in long contracts with companies that have gone bust.

■ PAYMENT PROCEDURES

Check to see if you need to send an invoice to get paid. If so, make sure you keep your eye on the calendar and submit invoices promptly. An invoice can be a simple memo from you to the company requesting payment. Make sure you include an invoice number at the top of the memo (corporations are used to dealing with invoice numbers).

THREE ESSENTIAL NEGOTIATING TERMS

You just want to make money, not be a lawyer. Don't be intimidated by the process. You can survive contract negotiations by knowing three magic words.

1
"FEE"

You don't pay the licensing fee. They do. Unfortunately, a lot of the fees you will be offered, especially for Internet or DVD compilations, will be "gratis." Always insist on some sort of nominal fee — if only to cover costs of making a master and shipping it to them.

2
"NONEXCLUSIVE"

Nonexclusive means you can license your film again and again in the same market — no one can have the exclusive right to it. "Be aware once you sign your first nonexclusive agreement for that right, you can never go back and do an exclusive anywhere," cautions sales agent and distributor David Russell of Big Film Shorts. "This can be a problem for some broadcasters. Once you've gone to the broadcasters who are exclusive, then you're free to do all the nonexclusives. All PBS stations are nonexclusive, for example. So start with broadcasters that are exclusive. Simultaneously, you can do DVD, airlines, all the other markets because they don't conflict and there isn't the order of windows like there is with features."

3
"NO"

"Don't be afraid to say 'no,'" film sales agent Carol Crowe counsels filmmakers. "That's the key thing in shorts. Everyone's always afraid when they get an offer — 'I better do it, I better do it.' But it's okay to say 'no.' It's okay to walk away. Everyone wants your films for free, whether it's the Internet or whatever. I just don't think you should give something for free. You worked so hard and all your money's in there. My big thing I say to every filmmaker is: You are worth your wage!"

MORE MONEY

Who really knows what tomorrow's technological innovations will be and what new licensing opportunities will develop? As a studio, you must consider your short an asset to be continually exploited. Spread the distribution of your film as wide as possible and embrace every opportunity that comes your way. Take a page from Mark Osborne's *More* playbook. "*More* keeps selling," exclaims sales agent Carol Crowe. "He keeps breathing more and more life in it." Just when it seemed as if every possible venue for *More* had been exploited, Osborne recut it and got it played as a music video on MTV2. When YouTube launched its Screening Room, *More* was there. When everyone is watching shorts on cell phones, *More* will undoubtedly be a favorite on cells, too.

A FINAL WORD ABOUT SELLING YOUR FILM

Shane Smith reminds us, "It's a rare film that crosses over and works equally well on all platforms. So don't be disheartened if your film works well in one medium but doesn't work as well in another medium. It's only natural. And really, you shouldn't be trying to make a film that pleases all audiences on every platform every time. You should be making the film that you want to make."

RECAP

- While an extremely successful short film might generate tens of thousands in licensing fees over a period of years, most shorts are lucky to score $5,000 total.

- Always read contracts carefully.

- Try for nonexclusive deals.

- Don't be afraid to say "no."

- New markets will always open up, extending the life of your film.

CHAPTER 21

PARLAYING YOUR LITTLE FILM INTO A BIG CAREER

ALWAYS HAVE SOMETHING
YOU WANT TO DO NEXT.

ere's the dream version: An important agent, an indie film maven, a Hollywood studio exec, a high-profile ad guy, a music video production company owner — you fill in the blank — catch your short film at a festival (or a screening) and instantly realize they must give you loads of money to make fabulous things for them. Or you put up on YouTube a comedy short that you and your buddies filmed in your backyard over the weekend. Suddenly Jimmy Kimmel's bookers are asking you to come out to Hollywood to be on his show. In reality, this does happen. Short filmmakers pay off their credit card debt with the obscene fees they earned shooting Budweiser or Burger King commercials. NYU graduates turn their thesis shorts into features shown in mall multiplexes across America (in Peter Sollett's case, it was expanding the half-hour *Five Feet High and Rising* into the feature-length *Raising Victor Vargas* and then following up by making the heavily promoted mainstream hit *Nick and Norah's Infinite Playlist*). Judd Apatow signs 18-year-old Bo Burnham to make a major motion picture based on his YouTube pieces. "It's not that that isn't going to happen," sighs short-film distributor David Russell, "it just doesn't happen all the time."

When you step out beyond the short-film world, you'll discover that potential employers aren't interested in your short as a piece of valuable property. Their interest lies in you — and what you can do for them. To make the next step, short filmmakers must have skills and/or future projects that agents, indie film mavens, Hollywood studio execs, high-profile ad guys, music video production company owners, Judd Apatow — you fill in the blank — will find interesting and, most importantly, potentially profitable.

A filmmaker named Ray emailed me wondering, "How does one approach the big agencies correctly? I know they all have No Unsolicited Material Policies so how can you get their attention?" The trick is to have the agents come to you — via your exposure in festivals (or online). If you have specific agents you are interested in, you send them postcards letting them know your short is playing at a festival in Los Angeles and offer to send them a copy of the film if they can't attend. Additionally, you have to hope that agents you don't know are attending the festival trolling for new talent or supporting their current clients by going to their screenings. Then you network like mad at the event trying to get someone to introduce you to the agents.

You can also ask the people who program the festival (or handle the Q & A at your screening) if they know any agents whom they could recommend you to. You also ask all filmmakers you meet at the festivals if they have agents and if they could recommend you to their agents, etc. Also, don't forget about managers. Many producer/managers are more interested in new filmmakers than the major agencies are.

How can you impress these future employers? "Some filmmakers fall into the trap of making shorts that look exactly, structurally, like episodic television comedy," remarks festival programming veteran Jennifer Stark. "Even though, in theory, that shows that you can handle that type of directing assignment, that's not going to sell you to Hollywood. What sells filmmakers is presenting something completely unique that catches people's attention. It's hard because on one hand you're creating a calling card to demonstrate your technique. But on the other hand, the director whose talent is going to spark interest is somebody who is doing something different."

Megan O'Neill of Atom pinpoints a director who was able to parlay her short into a very successful directing career. "I think a really good example is Kim Peirce, who went on to direct *Boys Don't Cry*," says O'Neill. "Years ago she made a terrific short film in which she had two Frank Sinatra songs. The songs fit the film perfectly. Just exquisite. I called her saying, 'Would you ever consider changing that music to sell the film?' She said, 'No, I really wouldn't. I don't want to sell it. I just did it because this was the story I wanted to tell.' I thought, 'Good for you!' Her film was so good that you knew she was going to make it. You knew she was going to get a shot because it was original, it was personal, it had a vision, and it didn't really matter if it sold or not. I think that Kim Peirce made it because she had that vision, and she knew what she wanted to accomplish."

Consultant Thomas Harris agrees. "If you can create a compelling character — an all-out original three-dimensional human being — or you can capture an emotional honesty on screen in a short-film capacity, you will turn heads really fast," Harris swears. "I firmly believe if you do that, you'll find doors opening to you. It may not be a deal at Paramount or Universal. But it might very well be somebody who can lead you to some financing for your feature, or maybe for your next short, or whatever it is you want to do." Harris adds, "The best way to have good fortune is to have a short that is really well liked on the festival circuit, and at the same time that that's happening, have a feature film script underneath your arm ready to go."

It's also important to keep your eyes focused on what's important to you. When I emailed the director of *West Bank Story* asking if he'd do a special master class showing his film and be on the jury at the Palm Springs Shortfest, he emailed back explaining "Normally I would be interested but unfortunately I am just too busy at this time and am having to take a break from showing the film in order to get my next projects off the ground. Thank you so much for thinking of me and so sorry to have to decline." Remember, all those times you heard "no" on your way to getting a "yes?" Now you're in a position where you have to be the one saying "no."

Lexi Alexander, who found herself being wined and dined after her short *Johnny Flynton* was nominated for an Oscar, played it smart. "I have met with pretty much every executive in town," she explains. "There have been several scripts offered to me to direct, but I have been holding off to set up my own script. It now has found a home, and I am excited to make my feature debut with a subject that is dear to my heart."

USING YOUR SHORT TO LAND YOUR DREAM JOB

"A lot of filmmakers think once you start the festival circuit, everything's going to come to you," observes long-time sales agent David Russell. "The thing filmmakers need to know is once you've made your short, that truly is just the beginning. It's up to you to get to New York or Hollywood. It's up to you to get the meetings. You can't stay out of the loop, just hoping that having made a film is enough to change your life. You need to use your short as a tool for getting your career kickstarted. And no one can do that better than you. I tell filmmakers, 'I don't represent your career, I represent your film. If you want a career, you better get here and start it. And a short film can help it.'"

So what kind of career do you want to kickstart?

■ FEATURE FILM DIRECTOR/SCREENWRITER

When asked if a filmmaker should spend money making a really slick-looking short or skip the short and go straight to making a no-budget feature as a calling card to get Hollywood's attention, no-budget filmmaking guru Mark Stolaroff replies, "There is one school of thinking that if you ultimately want to make a Hollywood movie, make something slick — a 30-second commercial or a two-minute music video or a 10-minute short. However, if you're a filmmaker like a Chris Nolan, if you want to make big Hollywood movies (which is always what he has wanted to do, he never wanted to make low-budget films), was it better for him to make his feature *Following* for $12,000 and eventually get *Batman Begins,* or would he have been better off making commercials, music videos, or short films? Obviously he did it the no-budget way, and it worked. For career launching, it certainly has worked both ways."

If you're a documentary filmmaker, it's important to have feature projects and proposals ready to go. As you meet people during the festival circuit, seek out information about funding opportunities.

For animators anxious to get into features, you'll find Dream-Works, Pixar, and the CGI companies cruising the student showcases and festivals, snapping up new talent. You might not get to direct your own feature right away, but you'll definitely find work.

If your goal is moving into features, have projects ready to go. If someone shows interest in you or your film, that's your in. Don't blow it by not following up. It's up to you to drive the relationship forward. Always ask for a business card from anyone who compliments your film. I've seen Hollywood bigwigs plug filmmakers' phone numbers in their cells upon ending a meeting. That's how you know someone is serious about you. And even if it's not clear how that person can help you, you never know where that connection might lead. Networking is everything.

When you attend festivals, ruthlessly work the crowd. Meet and talk to anyone associated with feature films. Ask other directors you encounter for advice. See if you can get them to introduce you to their agents or their producers. Referrals are invaluable. "When you get that friendly 'in,'" stresses director Mat Fuller, "it's like the difference between going to a job interview that your buddy hooked you up with and one where you don't know anybody."

Of course, getting meetings is much easier if you have an agent. If you're lucky enough to have a hot film, agents and managers will seek you out. "My agent came through a screening my school did in Los Angeles," reveals Columbia grad Amy Talkington. "An agent from UTA came and said, 'I think this new agent here would really like your work.' I had interest from three or four agents, but I wanted to wait until I had a feature script because I wanted to make sure I was on the same page completely with someone."

Making sure you and your new "team" have the same game plan is crucial. "When I won at Sundance, lots of agents and managers suddenly wanted to talk to me, wanted to know what I wanted to do next," remembers *More* director Mark Osborne. "That same weekend was when I found out my film was short listed for the Academy Award. It wasn't until two weeks later that we knew we were nominated. That period of time was insane. Once the nomination came through, that was a whole other realm of calls from agents and managers. I knew nothing about the industry. The world of agents and managers and going to the next level was something that I wasn't really prepared for and didn't know anything about. It's funny because I definitely had my foot in the door, but I didn't have my next project figured out. I had a live-action project that my brother and I had been developing for years, sort of our pet project. But that was a difficult step to take because I had a lot of heat as an animation director. If I had jumped right from there to music videos, I probably would have had an easier time. But what I did was get independent money and make the live-action feature. I ended up signing with ICM, which turned out to be a mistake. ICM just wanted to say they had another Academy-nominated guy. I think they just wanted to rep me, just in case I won. And when I didn't win, it was like 'Oh, well....' They're okay guys. They're all just trying to make a buck.

They didn't know what to do with me. What was problematic was I wasn't meeting people because of the work; I was meeting people because of the accolades. It took me a while to figure that out. You know, I always felt that I needed an agent or manager to get somewhere. And when I just went ahead and made my film, they all wanted to talk to me. I still don't understand —there's no magic solution. I don't have an agent or a manager now. And I got my own job at DreamWorks without an agent or manager. I got my own job just for doing work. I see having an agent or manager as relatively unimportant. It's the work that matters. If you feel like you need somebody to help you find the right projects or whatever, then that's something to look into. But find somebody you connect with. And remember — all they care about is the money."

■ TV WRITER/DIRECTOR

If you want to be hired on to an existing show, you'll want to get an agent who can send you out on meetings. If you want to pitch a new show, hook up with an established production company. Karl Hirsch got an option deal with Broadway Video to develop his short, *Media Whore*, into a TV show. "I happened to meet a marketing guy who works for Broadway Video," recalls Hirsch. "We were just sort of talking. He said, 'What else is going on?' I told him that I had just done a film, and I gave him the *Media Whore* postcard. And he said, 'Wow, this looks really good. I'd love to see it.' Then I added, 'We have this whole TV show pitch based on the film.' With Broadway, we pitched the show to Fox, E! Entertainment, and Comedy Central. So even though nothing happened, I got to meet all these network people. And it wasn't like I met them saying, 'Can I please work in your mailroom?' It was more like 'Hey, I'm a legitimate producer!'"

Another great example is Steve Dildarian, whose crudely animated short *Angry Unpaid Hooker* became a de facto pilot for an HBO series called *The Life & Times of Tim*. Like so many of these stories where a short filmmaker scores a TV deal, Dildarian wasn't exactly a nobody from nowhere, and his success didn't happen without major Hollywood assistance. Dildarian made his living as an ad guy, involved in several Super Bowl ad campaigns. Previous to making the *Angry Unpaid Hooker* short, he had written and sold sitcom pilots to networks (of course, none of them got made). *Angry Unpaid Hooker* got into the now-defunct U.S. Comedy Arts Festival, where it walked away with the Best Animated Short garland. It was this launch pad that attracted the interest of major Hollywood player Jimmy Miller, a manager/producer who reps Judd Apatow. The rest of the story is typical Hollywood machinations. But before we get too cynical, it's important to note that Dildarian's short is legitimately wonderful. I can tell you it also played the Palm Springs Shortfest that same year as the U.S. Comedy Fest, and everyone at the PS festival office adored that short and highly recommended it to anyone who asked what was good at the festival that year.

Of course television deals are being offered left, right and center to filmmakers who make a big splash on the Internet. David Lehre made the Web sensation *MySpace: The Movie*, which the filmmaker proudly points out, has had over 30 million hits. As a result, Lehre got a deal to make a $300,000 late-night pilot for Fox. Of course, middlemen helped Hollywood connect with the Web star. Lehre's show is executive produced by his manager, Scott Vener of The Schiff Company, whose other clients include such nobodies as Eminem and Justin Timberlake.

■ MUSIC VIDEO DIRECTOR

If you're interested in being a music video helmer, make a visually interesting short with a strong MTV sensibility. "I've shown shorts to people who have ended up hiring those filmmakers to make videos at Sub Pop Records for $10,000," proclaims formerly Seattle-based short-film exhibitor Joel S. Bachar. "So those opportunities do exist." You'd also be wise to make a few music videos on spec to demonstrate your talent to future employers.

■ COMMERCIAL DIRECTOR

Ad execs frequently attend festivals trolling for new creative talent. Short filmmakers who aspire to enter the world of commercials soon discover that in order to get work they need a reel. To build a reel, you can either do spec commercials or recut your short into a spec. "I didn't want to bastardize my film," explains *Requiem* director Roy Unger. "But I talked to commercial agencies who said, 'The film's great, but you should figure out a way to make it into a commercial for Playstation or a futuristic high-tech product.' If you want to do commercials, you've got to have commercials — that's the bottom line. They don't really want to see anything else. The same thing for the music videos. They want to see music videos on your reel."

■ WEBSERIES CREATORS

Nothing is stopping you from making webseries on your own. But if your dream is to be paid to make pieces for the Web, take heart that more and more new media companies are being formed to produce such material, and they're eager to find new talent. Hollywood is hot on the action. The United Talent Agency started a division called UTA Online to sign Internet artists and develop a sustainable business online in which content developers can make a living. More and more will follow the lead of Peter Safran, who ditched his job as a talent manager to form the Safran Digital Group to finance, produce, and distribute Web-oriented entertainment.

MEETING WITH HOLLYWOOD SUITS

One question that comes up with surprising frequency when I talk to aspiring Hollywood sell-outs is how short filmmakers should handle themselves once the door is open and they start taking meetings. Obviously your work speaks for itself, but how you present yourself in a room does come into play. Remember you're a talented filmmaker who is going to go far, people are lucky to be working with you. Dress and act accordingly. You'll be fine.

You may find yourself going to meeting after meeting yet feeling like nothing's getting accomplished, despite leaving the room feeling like you're the King of the World. The problem is in Hollywood everyone wants to meet you to say they've met you, but they don't necessarily need to hire you. That's why it's important you have something you want to peddle to them. If they're not interested in what you're selling, there will always be another meeting with someone else who might be. Remember it's just a matter of getting through the "noes" until you find the "yes."

IF AT FIRST YOU DON'T SUCCEED...

If you can't parlay your first film into the career you want, make another short. Many filmmakers find they've laid the groundwork with their first shorts, but industry success came with their second films. If you have the time and money to make another short, and you think you'll get something out of it, do it. You'll discover both making and marketing a short are much easier the second time around. "If you can find a way to make a film within the resources that you can manage, you should always be making something," filmmaker David Birdsell reminds us.

MAKING IT BIG IN SHORTS

By taking an idea for a short film and making it a reality, you've discovered something very important: You can make things happen. Once you understand that your dreams and ambitions are nothing but a series of ideas that you need to turn into reality, you'll recognize that you already have the skills necessary to "produce" your idealized future. Dream of getting into Sundance? Fill out the entry form. Want to win an Academy Award? Qualify for a nomination. If you don't get into Sundance or win an Oscar with your first short, you might succeed with your second. Or third. It's just a matter of getting through the "noes" until you get a "yes." Want an agent? Think organically. Look around. Whom do you know who has an agent already? Ask them to refer you. Why should their agents want to represent you? Because you're a talented filmmaker who is going to go far. Be an egoist. You can make anything you want happen. Nothing is harder than making a short film that you can be proud of. Everything else is a cakewalk.

TWO FINAL TIPS FOR SUREFIRE SUCCESS

Filmmaker Mark Osborne: "Make shorts that are true to your voice, to what makes you special as a filmmaker. That's your best chance of getting noticed, that's your best chance of getting an audience, that's your best chance of being unique. When I was teaching at Cal Arts, that's what I'd always say. Don't worry about getting a job. Don't worry what anyone else is doing. Don't worry about competing. Just figure out what's special about you and follow through on that."

Filmmaker Eileen O'Meara: "Do exactly what you want to do. Follow your vision. And enjoy the process. Because you never know what's going to happen. So you might as well enjoy it."

RECAP

• Set yourself up for success.

• Make a short that best represents you and what you can do.

• Always have at least a few projects that you want to do next.

• You're a talented filmmaker who is going to go far. People are lucky to get to meet you and help you achieve your dreams. Let them.

• You're a short filmmaker. You can have the skills to make any dream come true. What are you waiting for? Make it happen.

PHOTO AND
ILLUSTRATION
CREDITS

All photos by the author, except where noted.

vii, Demonstrating an iPhone.

viii, Demonstrating a directorial pose.

ix, Demonstrating a mini-DV camera.

ix, On the set of *A Fine Day for Flying*. Director: Russell DeGrazier. Photographer: Sylvia Abumuhor.

3, Demonstrating the Cannon Zoom 250 Super-8 camera.

7, Publicity still from *Hotel Chevalier*. Director: Wes Anderson. Courtesy of Fox Searchlight Pictures.

9, Publicity still from *Deveria*. Director: Mat Fuller. Courtesy of Mat Fuller, *www.americanphil.com*. Photographer: Mike Witherspoon.

15, Publicity still from *Peel*. Director: Jane Campion. Courtesy of Women Make Movies.

24, Publicity still from *More*. Director: Mark Osborne. Courtesy of Mark Osborne, *www.happyproduct.com*.

27, *Hardware Wars* DVD cover. Courtesy of Michael Wiese.

31, Demonstrating Kodak's Stop By Shoot Film workshop.

37, Demonstrating a vintage Yashica 25 Super-8.

41, Publicity still from *Rejected*. Director: Don Hertzfeldt. Available on DVD via *www.bitterfilms.com*. Courtesy of Don Hertzfeldt.

47, Publicity still from *Bad Animals*. Director: David Birdsell. Photographer: Mark Skoner.

53, Publicity still from *Bad Animals*. Photographer: Mark Skoner.

64, Scouting photo. Photographer: David Birdsell.

69, Demonstrating YouTube.

78, Demonstrating the Internet.

81, Demonstrating a tripod.

88, Scouting locations.

93, Demonstrating the Ultravision 35mm camera on the set of *Angry Boy.* Directors: Josh Gordon and Will Speck. Photographer: Suzanne Hanover.

98, Demonstrating a mini-DV cam.

105, Five Puppies on the Run storyboard by Lauren Beaumont, age eight. Courtesy of Bear Fisher.

113, I'm on Fire storyboard by Ryan Rowe.

117, On the set of *Bad Animals.* Photographer: Mark Skoner.

119, Publicity still from *Phil Touches Flo.* Director: David Birdsell. Photographer: Suzanne Hanover.

126, On the set of *Bad Animals.* Photographer: Mark Skoner.

129, On the set of *Birthday.* Director: Greg Brooker. Photographer: Sylvia Abumuhor.

136, Publicity still from *The Back Room.* Director: Greg Ivan Smith. Photographer: Eric Hauser.

143, On the set of *Hope Street.* Director: Alex Metcalf. Photographer: Suzanne Hanover.

147, On the set of *Beeker's Crossing.* Director: Robbie Consing. Photographer: Sylvia Abumuhor.

150, On the set of *H@.* Director: Jason Reitman. Photographer: Sylvia Abumuhor.

151, Publicity still from *One Hand Left.* Director: Corky Quakenbush. Photographer: Suzanne Hanover.

155, On the set of *Sidewalkers.* Director: Tara Veneruso. Photographer: Lance Mungia.

159, On the set of the *Beeker's Crossing.* Photographer: Suzanne Hanover.

167, Demonstrating editing.

173, Demonstrating sound mixing.

181, Demonstrating live music. Photographer: Craig Adelman.

188, Demonstrating composing.

193, Promotion at Palm Springs Shortfest.

199, Promotional T-Shirt. Available at *www.arigoldfilms.com.*

201, Demonstrating a short-film Oscar statue.

205, Requiem man. Director: Roy Unger. Courtesy of Roy Unger.

214, Media Whore postcard. Director: Karl T Hirsch. Courtesy of Aglet Productions. Photographer: Ramon Estrada.

219, At the Sundance Film Festival. Photographer: Noah Edelson.

226, At the MOCA auditorium.

233, At the Focus on Female Directors screening.

238, At Palm Springs Shortfest.

245, Demonstrating the iPhone.

249, At the Focus on Female Directors screening. Photographer: Andrea Richards.

267, Going Hollywood.

276, Going Sundance. Photographer: Bear Fisher.

[Author photo] Photographer: Carol Sheridan.

ACKNOWLEDGMENTS

The author wishes to thank (in alphabetical order):

Sylvia Abumuhor, Kevin Ackerman, Derth Adams, Molly-Dodd Wheeler Adams, Craig Adelman, Howard Adelman, Nancy Adelman, Lexi Alexander, Robin Alper, Eileen Arandiga, Dominique Arcadio, Robert Arentz, Elena Arroy, Jamie Babbit, Joel S. Bachar, Sharon Badal, Carin Baer, Aparna Bakhle, Harriet Baron, Shanin Michelle Beard, Lauren Beaumont, Spencer Beglarian, Nina Berry, Sue Biely, David Birdsell, Scott Boettle, Mark Borchardt, Mark Steven Bosko, Jess Bowers, Melissa Brantley, Greg Brooker, Brian Brooks, Kimberley Browning, Maria Burton, Ursula Burton, Andrew Busti, Patrice Callahan, Colin Campbell, Jane Campion, Steve Carcano, Robert Carrasco, Matt Cartsonis, Susan Cartsonis, Sandrine Faucher Cassidy, Jennifer Chen, Michele Chong, Curtis Choy, William Clark, Lilli Cloud, Robert Cobb, Peet Cocke, Becky Cole, Keiann Collins, Robbie Consing, Charles Cook, John Cooper, Jan Cox, Jeff Cox, Andrew Crane, Carol Crowe, Carmen Cuba, Natasha Cuba, Lisa Daniels, Bob Davis, Russell DeGrazier, Maria de la Torre, Sebastian del Castillo, Greg Dellerson, Jim Denault, Matt Dentler, Jennifer Derwingson, Balinda DeSantis, John Dickson, Chip Diggins, Leslie Dinaberg, Dan Dubiecki, Scott Dwyer, Guy Dyas, Stephen Earley, Christine Ecklund, Noah Edelson, George Eldred, Martin Etchart, Chris Fahland, Victor Fannuchi, Tai Fauci, Debbie Felton, Bear Fisher, Kathleen French, Brenda Friend, Mat Fuller, Glenn Gaylord, Natalie Gildea, Terry Gilliam, Ari Gold, Jelani Gould-Bailey, Josh Gordon, Linda Gordon, Bennett Graebner, Rashaad Ernesto Green, Trevor Groth, Kevin Haasarud, Shana Hagan, John Halecky, Bryan Hale, Billy Hall, Ric Halpern, Suzanne Hanover, Thomas Ethan Harris, Gavin Harvey, Eric Hauser, Jim Healy, Carol Heikkinen, Eleo Hensleigh, Eugene Hernandez, Don Hertzfeldt, Karl Hirsch, Douglas Horn, Jordan Horowitz, Mike Horowitz, Anne Hubbell, Michelle Hung, Doug "Disco" Hylton,

Larry Hymes, Peter Ignacio, James Israel, Eugenia Ives, Andre Jacquemetton, Maria Jacquemetton, Deb Jarnes, Liz Jereski, Allan Johnson, Fred Joubaud, Sara Juarez, Amy Jurist, Caroline Kaplan, Howard Karesh, Nancy Keystone, David King, Samuel Kivi, Cathy Kline, Zak Klobucher, Gayle Knutson, David Koff, Tony Kountz, George Langworthy, Ellie Lee, Ken Lee, Sunny Lee, John Lehr, Gail Lerner, Rhea Lewis-Woodson, Kyle Heath Leppert, Suzanne Lezotte, Lorraine LoBianco, Todd Longwell, Justin Lowe, Darryl Macdonald, Beth Macheleny, Bob Mandel, Holly Mandel, Karen Mann, Chris Marker, Carol May, Brian McConnell, Brian McDonald, William McDonald, Francine McDougall, Genevieve McGillicuddy, Kathleen McInnis, Jim Melvin, Heath Mensher, Andrew Mersmann, Alex Metcalf, Joel Metzger, KJ Middlebrooks, Clinton Miguel, Loren Miller, Melanie Miller, Dean Minerd, William Mochon, Matthew Modine, Ron Modro, Tony Molina, Amber Montervino, William Morosi, Frank Morris, Robert Morris, Meg Moynihan, Andrew Mudge, Lance Mungia, Roberta Marie Munroe, Brent Muscay, Jessie Nagel, Jamie Neese, Marni Nelko, Sandra Neufeldt, Steven Nily, Matt Nix, Austin Olah, Susan O'Leary, Kimberly Olivo, Madeleine Olnek, Colleen O'Mara, Eileen O'Meara, Megan O'Neill, Linda Olszewski, Mark Osborne, Lynn Padilla, Raena Padilla, Lumi Padilla-Adelman, Greg Pak, Nicholas Panoutsopoulos, Peter Paras, Osbert Parker, Jeff Payne, David Pearlman, Christopher Pearson, Bob Pederson, Laura Phillips, Stacey Pianko, Tracy Nan Pion, Bill Plympton, Michael Price, Cynthia Pusheck, Greg Pyros, Corky Quakenbush, Linda Quakenbush, Doris Quon, Leslie Rabb, Abu Rasheduzzaman, Orly Ravid, Robert Redford, Allison Reeds, Jason Reitman, Kenny Rhodes, Andrea Richards, Phillippa Rick, Michael Rivkin, David Rooney, Salena Roper, Billy Rose, Anne Rosellini, Andrew Rosen, Douglas Ross, Wendy Rothman, Ryan Rowe, Dave Rudd, David Russell, Edward Saile, Ralph Sall, Mika Salmi, Vikki Sanchez, Christina Sasse, Gregory Schaefer, Michael Schlitt, Marliese Schneider, Mike Schwab, B.J. Schwartz, Mara Schwartz, Rick Scott, Kimberly Sharp, Linda Sheetz, Carol

Sheridan, Katie Shiban, Ricardo Nobuo Shima, Tricia Stewart Shiu, Lesley Marlene Siegel, Jason Simon, Kelly Simpson, Monika Skerbelis, Mark Skoner, Paul Skorich, Leslie Kollins Small, Alex Smith, Andrew Smith, Cat Chapman Smith, Greg Ivan Smith, Roger Smith, Shane Smith, Mark Sonenberg, Will Speck, Sarah Stanley, Jennifer Stark, John Starr, Eric Steelberg, Jonathon Sterns, Greg Stewart, Mark Stolaroff, Hebe Tabachnik, Amy Talkington, Mary Ann Terry, John Teska, Jacques Thelemaque, Laura Thielen, Arayna Thomas, Betsy Thomas, Beth Hall Thrasher, Gabe Torres, Colby Tseng, Antti Ukkola, Roy Unger, Peggy Van Norman, Amanda Veith, Tara Veneruso, Pat Verducci, Nacho Vigalondo, Morrie Warshawski, Andrew Weiner, Nate Weinstein, Richard Weiss, Chris Wells, Craig Wells, Jakob White, Jason White, Michael Wiese, Bergen Williams, Doug Williams, Rob Williams, Ted Williams, Holly Willis, Chad Wilson, Steve Wilson, Wendy Wilson, Alison Winward, Mike Witherspoon, Women Make Movies, Mark Wynns, Jamie Wynns, Kathie Fong Yoneda, Shaun Young, Jessica Yu, and Kim Yutani.

ABOUT
THE
AUTHOR

Kim Adelman is the short-film correspondent for the acclaimed independent film news service *indieWIRE*. She also teaches *Making and Marketing the Short Film* and *Low-Budget Filmmaking* at UCLA Extension and leads filmmaking workshops across the United States, Canada, and New Zealand. Since 2000, Adelman has organized and moderated the educational industry panels, master classes, and workshops at Palm Springs Shortfest.

Additionally, Adelman co-programs the American Cinematheque's high-profile Focus on Female Directors screening series and is the author of *The Ultimate Guide to Chick Flicks*. She previously produced *Short* and *International Release*, the acclaimed short-film compilations issued on DVD by Warner Home Video.

Ms. Adelman began her short-film career by launching the Fox Movie Channel's short-film program in 1996. The 19 short films she produced for Fox won 30+ awards and played over 150 film festivals worldwide, including the Sundance Film Festival, four years in a row.

Kim Adelman can be reached at *www.kimadelman.com*

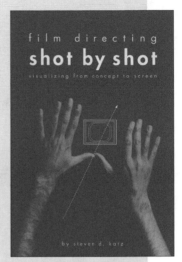

THE WRITER'S JOURNEY
3RD EDITION

MYTHIC STRUCTURE FOR WRITERS

CHRISTOPHER VOGLER

BEST SELLER
OVER 170,000 COPIES SOLD!

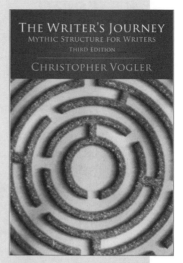

See why this book has become an international best seller and a true classic. *The Writer's Journey* explores the powerful relationship between mythology and storytelling in a clear, concise style that's made it required reading for movie executives, screenwriters, playwrights, scholars, and fans of pop culture all over the world.

Both fiction and nonfiction writers will discover a set of useful myth-inspired storytelling paradigms (i.e., "The Hero's Journey") and step-by-step guidelines to plot and character development. Based on the work of Joseph Campbell, *The Writer's Journey* is a must for all writers interested in further developing their craft.

The updated and revised third edition provides new insights and observations from Vogler's ongoing work on mythology's influence on stories, movies, and man himself.

"This book is like having the smartest person in the story meeting come home with you and whisper what to do in your ear as you write a screenplay. Insight for insight, step for step, Chris Vogler takes us through the process of connecting theme to story and making a script come alive."
> – Lynda Obst, Producer, *Sleepless in Seattle, How to Lose a Guy in 10 Days;* Author, *Hello, He Lied*

"This is a book about the stories we write, and perhaps more importantly, the stories we live. It is the most influential work I have yet encountered on the art, nature, and the very purpose of storytelling."
> – Bruce Joel Rubin, Screenwriter, *Stuart Little 2, Deep Impact, Ghost, Jacob's Ladder*

CHRISTOPHER VOGLER is a veteran story consultant for major Hollywood film companies and a respected teacher of filmmakers and writers around the globe. He has influenced the stories of movies from *The Lion King* to *Fight Club* to *The Thin Red Line* and most recently wrote the first installment of *Ravenskull*, a Japanese-style manga or graphic novel. He is the executive producer of the feature film *P.S. Your Cat is Dead* and writer of the animated feature *Jester Till*.

$26.95 · 300 PAGES · ORDER NUMBER 76RLS · ISBN: 193290736x